BUCKNELL REVIEW

"Turning the Century": Feminist Theory in the 1990s

STATEMENT OF POLICY

BUCKNELL REVIEW is a scholarly interdisciplinary journal. Each issue is devoted to a major theme or movement in the humanities or sciences, or to two or three closely related topics. The editors invite heterodox, orthodox, and speculative ideas and welcome manuscripts from any enterprising scholar in the humanities and sciences.

This journal is a member of the Conference of Editors of Learned Journals

BUCKNELL REVIEW
A Scholarly Journal of Letters, Arts, and Sciences

Editor
PAULINE FLETCHER

Associate Editor
DOROTHY L. BAUMWOLL

Assistant Editor
STEVEN W. STYERS

Contributors should send manuscripts with a self-addressed stamped envelope to the Editor, Bucknell University, Lewisburg, Pennsylvania, 17837.

"Turning the Century": Feminist Theory in the 1990s

Edited by
GLYNIS CARR

Lewisburg
Bucknell University Press
London and Toronto: Associated University Presses

© 1992 by Associated University Presses, Inc.

Associated University Presses
440 Forsgate Drive
Cranbury, NJ 08512

Associated University Presses
25 Sicilian Avenue
London WC1A 2QH, England

Associated University Presses
P.O. Box 39, Clarkson Pstl. Stn.
Mississauga, Ontario,
L5J 3X9 Canada

The paper used in this publication meets the
requirements of the American National Standard for
Permanence of Paper for Printed Library Materials Z39.48-1984.

(Volume XXXVI, Number 2)

ISSN 0007-2869
LC 55-58217
ISBN 0-8387-5241-1

PRINTED IN THE UNITED STATES OF AMERICA

Contents

Recent Issues of BUCKNELL REVIEW

The Arts, Society, Literature
Text, Interpretation, Theory
Perspective: Art, Literature, Participation
Self, Sign, and Symbol
Criticism, History, and Intertextuality
New Interpretations of American Literature
The Senses of Stanley Cavell
John Cage at Seventy-Five
Comedias del Siglo de Oro and Shakespeare
Mappings of the Biblical Terrain: The Bible as Text
The Philosophy of John William Miller
Culture and Education in Victorian England
Classics and Cinema
Reconfiguring the Renaissance: Essays in Critical Materialism
Wordsworth in Context

Notes on Contributors

GLYNIS CARR is an assistant professor of English at Bucknell University. She has published articles on Zora Neale Hurston, Virginia Woolf, Fannie Hurst, Caribbean women writers, women's personal experience narratives, and the impact of the canon debates on courses in literary critical theory. She is currently working on a book about interracial friendship in U.S. women's fiction.

MARY DEVEREAUX is an associate professor of philosophy at Bucknell University. She writes on aesthetics, feminist theory, and film. Her current project is on art and censorship.

TERESA L. EBERT teaches postmodern critical theory and feminism at the State University of New York at Albany. She has written a book on postmodern materialist feminism entitled *Patriarchal Narratives*. Her articles have appeared in such journals as *Cultural Critique, Rethinking Marxism,* and *Comparative Literature Studies*.

DIANE P. FREEDMAN is a visiting assistant professor of English at Skidmore College. She is the author of *An Alchemy of Genres: Cross-Genre Writing by American Feminist Poet-Critics* (1992) and editor, with Olivia Frey and Frances Zauhar, of *The Intimate Critique: Autobiographical Literary Criticism* (forthcoming).

CARLA KAPLAN is assistant professor of English at Yale University, where she teaches courses in American literature and feminist theory. She is completing a book entitled *The Erotics of Talk: Women's Writing and Feminist Paradigms*. Her study of black and white women's writing of the American 1920s is in progress.

LAURIE LANGBAUER teaches critical theory and the novel at Swarthmore College. Her book *Women and Romance: The Consolations of Gender in the English Novel* was published in 1990. She is working on a study of the category of the everyday in late nineteenth-century fiction and current theory.

NELLIE Y. MCKAY teaches American and Afro-American literature at the University of Wisconsin, Madison. Her publications include *Jean Toomer, Artist: A Study of His Literary Life and Work* (1984) and an edited collection, *Critical Essays on Toni Morrison* (1988). She has also published many articles on black American literature and on issues of race, class, and gender.

ANURADHA DINGWANEY NEEDHAM teaches Anglophone literatures of the Third World at Oberlin College. She has published essays on British Romanticism, Salman Rushdie, and feminist pedagogy. Currently, she is co-editing a collection of essays on cultural translation entitled *Between Languages and Cultures: Translation and Cross-Cultural Texts.*

DAPHNE PATAI is a professor of women's studies and of Portuguese at the University of Massachusetts at Amherst. In addition to many articles, she has written three books: *Myth and Ideology in Contemporary Brazilian Fiction* (1983); *The Orwell Mystique: A Study in Male Ideology* (1984); and *Brazilian Women Speak: Contemporary Life Stories* (1988).

SUSAN RITCHIE, AMY SHUMAN, and SALLY MECKLING began working on their collectively authored paper as they team taught a course, Folklore and Sexual Politics, for the English department of The Ohio State University. They are currently researching, respectively, the institutional history of poststructuralism, the relationship between technology and the aesthetic in an Italian artists' community, and star biographies. Among them, they edit the *Journal of American Folklore* book review section and publish on a variety of topics in cultural studies.

ROBYN WIEGMAN is an assistant professor of English at Syracuse University. She recently completed a manuscript on race and gender in United States culture. Her work has appeared in *Cultural Critique, American Literary History, Criticism,* and the anthology *Unspeakable Images.*

Introduction: "Turning the Century"

I like to think about Bernice Johnson Reagon's presentation at the West Coast Women's Music Festival in 1981, a speech that was reworked for inclusion in Barbara Smith's *Home Girls* a few years later. Subtitled "Turning the Century,"[1] Reagon's talk was about the difference between feeling *at home* in feminism, between having "a space that is 'yours only'—just for the people you want to be there" (357) and crossing what she called "first people boundaries" to make a revolution—that is, *"really* doing coalition work" (356), the crucial work for feminists as we look forward to the twenty-first century.

Now some people would say that the gaps—racial, cultural, political, and discursive—between Bernice Johnson Reagon and most academic feminists in the 1990s are absolutely unbridgeable.[2] Which may well be true. But those very gaps also signify not the irrelevance to academic feminists of Reagon and the variety of street-wise black feminism she represents (or vice versa), but compelling reasons to attend closely to her analysis. In "Turning the Century," Reagon asks feminists (including academic feminists) to examine three major issues: the tensions between separatism and coalition building (both of which, she holds, are politically necessary), the dangers of "mono-issue" critical perspectives and agendas for activism, and the destructiveness to feminist communities of forgetting "the principles that are the basis of [our] practice" (361). Today, more than a decade later, these issues are still important and far from being resolved.

This volume of feminist theory continues the debates of the early 1980s, formative years for academic feminism in the U.S. because a critical mass of feminist scholars were promoted or granted tenure, Black, Chicana, and other "Third" World feminists solidified a separate power base, multicultural feminist organizations such as the National Women's Studies Association came of age, and French feminist works were published in English translation for the first time. The traditional concerns of feminism—how to analyze women's oppression and act politically to end it—were moved to a new level of complexity as an understanding of women's differences became practically and theoretically more urgent and feminists were empowered in startling

11

and unprecedented ways. The writers represented here do not all speak in the same voice, but they do all address the issues of difference—how to think about it and how to build an effective feminist movement around it—so eloquently articulated by Bernice Johnson Reagon in 1981.

In "A Troubled Peace," Nellie McKay updates an article she wrote the same year Reagon gave her speech on coalition politics.[3] Here, McKay describes the experiences of her generation of black women scholars, women who pursued their "intention to survive" in white academia. Examining the politics of black women's location in the profession, McKay makes plain that the white academy as "home" has offered neither safety, refuge, nor comfort for black women scholars. Instead, they have been metaphorically and actually marginalized. McKay analyzes certain psychopathologies of racism and sexism in everyday academic life,[4] dis/eases embodied in institutional structures and dramatized in social practices. McKay's conclusion is admittedly pessimistic: she sees no evidence of the activist commitments necessary to mitigate her generation's "grave disappointments, unfulfilled dreams, and deep frustrations." Moreover, like Hazel Carby, McKay is alarmed that the present generation of black feminist scholars is not being reproduced.[5] What consequences, she asks, will this have for the gains made by black feminists in the 1980s?

Anuradha Dingwaney Needham takes up a similar problem: the containment of "Third" world texts in "First" world contexts. Needham examines "some very real difficulties in crossing boundaries when the objects of one's analyses are works from other cultures." Moving outward from problems of interpretation to problems of institutional reform, such as curriculum revision, Needham argues that we attend to "the power the 'First' world wields materially and discursively over the 'Third'." In the process, she criticizes certain institutional and disciplinary practices that both stem from and lead to a superficial vision of multicultural education—practices such as "tacking on" courses in "Third" world literature "to an already existing curriculum with its own agendas with which [such] courses may be at odds." The pitfalls can be avoided, she claims; existing power relations need not be duplicated as we expand our sense of "English literature."

Robyn Wiegman's essay concerns problems of moving beyond "mono-issue" analyses. Specifically, she asks how white feminists can integrate analyses of gender with analyses of race and other oppressions, thereby overcoming the historical limitations of white feminism as a movement focused exclusively on gender.

Wiegman juxtaposes Harriet Beecher Stowe's *Uncle Tom's Cabin,* an important and paradigmatic nineteenth-century feminist text, and essays by Teresa de Lauretis, revealing how contemporary white feminist discourse repeats the nineteenth-century mistake of "making race speak gender." Wiegman demonstrates, in other words, "[white] feminism's consistent failure . . . to negotiate the significance of race within its own epistemological and political categories." The solution she prescribes is that feminist theorists "relinquish [the] epistemological tie to sexual difference," an act that would necessarily "expan[d] feminist theory's gaze to include questions not only of masculine differences but also of disparities that traverse the sacrosanct division of gender, those in which women maintain power over various groups of men."

White feminists who write about racism often employ what Carla Kaplan, in the next essay, calls a "language of crisis." Such theorists join feminist postmodernists, and others who focus their work on the differences among women, in the shared project of questioning whether and how feminism can construct a viable subject. But Kaplan asks feminists to consider the possibility that "this language of crisis does not so much *represent* the current state of feminism as *construct* it in particular—and particularly disadvantageous—ways." Kaplan is of course not the first theorist to claim that we need not fear crisis and conflict as inevitably destructive. To my knowledge, however, she *is* the first to suggest that the fear of conflict is racially coded, that the feminism now in crisis is a white and privileged one made up of women who long nostalgically "for an imagined utopian moment of female solidarity and mutual support." Kaplan argues for a reformulation of the feminist subject that is "sensitive both to poststructural insights and to the challenges posed by the complexities of political work." She ends where this introduction begins, citing Reagon's appreciation of crisis. Although we may never learn to like it, crisis is good, Reagon says, because it forces you to "go beyond yourself" where "you can do wonderful things" (368).

As Kaplan implies, the debates among black and white women about the adequacy of various theories to understand differences among women are linked to debates about the emerging cultural practices (including practices of representation) we call "postmodernism." As Teresa Ebert has claimed elsewhere, "Postmodernism has become an unavoidable issue for feminists—activists and theorists alike," because, like black feminism, postmodernism "calls into question and overturns the basic practices and concepts grounding feminism" historically.[6] In her essay

here, Ebert retheorizes the political economy of mimesis in patriarchy, thereby rearticulating an important dispute between two
factions of academic feminists in the 1980s: Continental
poststructuralists (whom Ebert calls "textual feminists") and Af-
rican- and Anglo-American cultural feminists ("gynocritics"). She
then proposes a materialist feminist theory of representation.
Ebert resituates the poststructural critique of representation in
order to foreclose its neoconservative, apolitical potential—its
power, for example, to "mystif[y] political conflict as textual difference and abolish . . . social transformation in an endless play of
floating signifiers and textual gaps." She engages in a rigorous
critique of the uses of mimesis and its political and ideological
effects. Finally, Ebert draws attention to "the countersymbolic,"
"the forbidden contrary to the patriarchal symbolic, the utopian
way of organizing reality otherwise than according to the phallic
signifier." The countersymbolic, she claims, is "the fundamental
threat that patriarchy has to exclude and render unknowable,
unspeakable, and unrepresentable," whose terms it is imperative
that feminism articulate.

Laurie Langbauer's work represents the new interest among
feminists in "cultural studies" (which term simply indicates the
synthesis of feminism and Marxism practiced, for example, by
Hazel Carby and other critics associated with the Centre for
Cultural Studies at the University of Birmingham).[7] Like Ebert,
Langbauer is concerned with the concept of "the everyday" in
cultural studies, specifically with how theorists use it to "homoge-
nize" culture, a tendency Langbauer finds "at odds with the very
multiculturalism [that cultural studies] wishes to foster." Langbauer claims that "the everyday," being itself "shaky and unstable
ground," cannot ground (i.e., anchor or provide a stable reference for) theories of culture. Instead, she argues, theorists must
work toward an unreachable goal: "a [critical] practice that . . .
highlight[s] the ways it too keeps sacrificing the difficulties and
evasiveness of difference in favor of consistency and pattern."

Daphne Patai's essay "The View from Elsewhere" is also about
the everyday, or as she puts it, "the obvious." Patai begins by
reassessing the influence of Myra Jehlen's "Archimedes and the
Paradox of Feminist Criticism," claiming that Jehlen's prescription
for a radically comparativist feminist criticism of function as a
necessary Archimedean fulcrum overlooked (and devalued) an
important body of women's utopian fiction that could serve the
same purpose. Through close readings of some of these female
utopias, Patai questions the "obviousness of the concept of 'dif-

ference' between women and men." She then interrupts current debates to point out—another obvious fact—that *"the powerful group need never engage in this kind of discussion."* This suggests to her that "as long as [we] continue to engage in our habitual discussions of . . . difference—whether attempting to locate it, define (or redefine) it, apologize for it, or valorize it, [we are] replicating the very structures [we] set out to contest." Such an intellectual climate makes movement (in either sense of the word) impossible.

Patai's work reveals a healthy skepticism toward certain intra-mural debates of the 1980s, debates about the relationships between theory and practice, the question of which theories are best suited to set an agenda for feminist activism, and whether certain theories are politically useful for feminism at all. Most feminists agree with Sarah Franklin and Jackie Stacey that "in continuing [political] resistance, it is vital for us to have clear arguments and theories . . . with which to enter public debates and participate within . . . current struggle[s]."[8] But to the extent that critical theory was seen as an end in itself, a vehicle of "careerism," or a means by which to create a new female elite, the production of "theory" was understood as a retreat from, or even a hindrance to, feminist politics. To my mind, these conflicts of the 1980s were unproductive, perhaps because they posed the problem(s) in either/or terms—terms implying, that is, a single correct theory of feminism. It seems to me that what Eve Sedgwick claims to be true of the struggle against homophobia is also true of feminism—generally:

> the theorized prescription for a practical politics . . . is for a multi-pronged movement whose idealist and materialist impulses, whose minority-model and universalist-model strategies, and for that matter whose gender-separatist and gender-integrative analyses would likewise proceed in parallel without any high premium placed on ideological rationalization between them.[9]

Poststructural theory, Sedgwick claims, prescribes a movement of diverse, even contradictory, practices of naming, analyzing, and resisting the situation of oppression. The following two essays model that diversity.

In "Inappropriate Fertility," Susan Ritchie, Amy Shuman, and Sally Meckling examine "teenage pregnancy" as "a contemporary, locally situated category, not a biological fact." Suggesting that the politics of poststructuralism center around "exposing 'natural' categories as social constructions," they demonstrate that, even after one exposes the complex interests with which any such construction are invested, the political dynamics of oppression remain. Thus, Ritchie et al. cast doubt on the adequacy of poststructural paradigms to meet the needs of feminist activists. Although their work does not suggest an alternative to the oppositional practices that inform current struggles around teenage pregnancy, practices that might be condemned by poststructuralist theorists as "essentialist," they do make a case against the "emptied out subject" of male-authored poststructural theories. In the essay that follows, Mary Devereaux moves beyond critique to find grounds on which to recommend a political practice.

Devereaux's starting point is the "widespread, although not unprecedented, attack on the arts" exemplified by recent obscenity trials and disputes over funding between artists and government agents. Because the art community's preferred defense against censorship is to claim aesthetic autonomy and because feminist theories of art have been used to undermine this defense, Devereaux is "concerned to explore the political implications of the feminist recommendation that we abandon autonomy for a more politicized conception of art." She claims that "as feminists, we have an interest in carving out a protected space for art." Art deserves this space, she says, "not because it is inherently emancipatory (it is not) nor because its good consequences always outweigh its harms (they do not), but because as a practice art *can* function in an emancipatory way" (emphasis mine). According to Devereaux, it is precisely this possibility that feminist activists can and should protect.

Another question that vexed the 1980s was that of the language used by academic feminists. Articulated as a conflict about whether the feminist discourse produced by academicians should be "accessible" to nonspecialists, language (or rather, the use of theoretical "jargon") became a focal point in a number of feminist debates.[10] In the final essay here, Diane Freedman reopens this question in a way that implicitly deconstructs the old positions and oppositions of the eighties. Her essay, "The Creatively Critical Voice," disarranges former divisions, making "strange bedfellows" of cultural feminists, textual feminists, and male postmodernists alike on the basis that they all "create prose pulsing with personality—or multiple personalities" (in the absence of a unified subject). The result is a winning synthesis of Continental and cultural feminist concerns about language that encourages us seriously (or playfully, as Freedman demonstrates is also possible) to refocus some neglected common problems. Freedman draws attention to certain discrepancies between our professional practice and the imperatives of our critical theories, revealing how we sometimes exercise our authority in a way that squelches the creativity of ourselves and our students, reproduces oppressive cultural configurations, and undermines the antiauthoritarianism that impels and enlivens our theories. Blurring genres and taking other sorts of verbal risks, Freedman models an alternative to the unwitting reproduction of a critical practice that is adversarial, competitive, and lifeless.

No single volume could ever completely represent all the lines of inquiry now being carried out under the rubric of "feminist theory," for, as Annette Kolodny has claimed, feminist work "sustain[s] the widest possible variety of practices [and remains] polyvocal, multitheoretical, and impossible to simplify or contain."[11] In gathering together the essays presented in this issue of the *Bucknell Review* I have tried to respect this hard-won and valuable diversity of feminist voices: no feminist "party line" or standard of "political correctness" is here imposed on all. Still, my own biases and interests are evident. Psychoanalysis and deconstruction are less well represented, for example, than materialist feminism and cultural studies, and there is decidedly a bias in favor of things activist. The essays all concern, in one way or another, boundaries and their crossings—racial and other constructions of difference among women, conflicts between postmodern and more traditional theories of feminisms, contradictions between theories and practices. But not all the boundaries theorized here are crossed; nor would all the contributors agree that they can or should be.

GLYNIS CARR

Notes

1. Bernice Johnson Reagon, "Coalition Politics: Turning the Century," *Home Girls: A Black Feminist Anthology*, ed. Barbara Smith (New York: Kitchen Table: Women of Color Press, 1983), 356–68. All page references cited parenthetically in my Introduction are to this essay.

2. See, for example, Gloria Anzaldúa, ed., *Making Face, Making Soul Haciendo Caras: Creative and Critical Perspectives by Women of Color* (San Francisco: Aunt Lute Press, 1990).

3. In many ways, McKay's essay can be read as a response to Annette Kolodny's keynote address to the MLA in 1988 in New Orleans entitled "Dancing between Left and Right:

Feminism and the Academic Minefield in the 1980s." In that speech, Kolodny appealed for "multi- and inter-generational dialogue about ourselves and our histories [in order to dismantle] the minefield laid in the eighties" for feminist scholars. But while black women may read the "we" of Kolodny's feminism as ambiguous, McKay makes clear that her own collective subject is black women of a certain generation, who "had gone to white graduate schools between the late 1960s and early 1970s and were the first as a group (by race and sex) to find employment in predominantly white colleges and universities."

4. The phrase is Lenora Fulani's. See her anthology, *The Psychopathology of Everyday Racism and Sexism* (Binghamton, N.Y.: Harrington Park Press, 1988).

5. Hazel Carby's remarks to this effect were made after her public lecture, "The Politics of Fiction, Anthropology, and the Folk: Zora Neale Hurston," Bucknell University, Lewisburg, Pennsylvania, 11 September 1990.

6. Teresa L. Ebert, "Postmodernism's Infinite Variety," *Women's Review of Books* 8, no. 4 (January 1991): 24–25.

7. The 1990 Annual Convention of the Modern Language Association reflects well this shift of interest. Listed in the program were very few panels on deconstruction and Lacanian psychoanalysis, two schools which dominated feminist theory in the late eighties. It is not the case, however, that these theoretical approaches have been outmoded; rather, the insights they yield have been absorbed in an increasingly synthetic feminist theory which now is refocusing on other problems.

8. Sarah Franklin and Jackie Stacey, "Dyke-tactics for Difficult Times," *Out the Other Side: Contemporary Lesbian Writing,* ed. Christian McEwen and Sue O'Sullivan (Freedom, Calif.: Crossing Press, 1989), 221.

9. Eve Kosofsky Sedgwick, *Epistemology of the Closet* (Berkeley: University of California Press, 1990), 13.

10. For a particularly scathing denunciation of poststructural language as not only oppressive, but ugly, see Barbara Christian, "The Race for Theory," *Feminist Studies* 14, no. 1 (Spring 1988):67–79. The opposite side is well represented by Toril Moi's influential *Sexual/Textual Politics* (New York: Methuen, 1985). The debate over Moi's book crystalized the then-emergent factions.

11. "Dancing between Left and Right."

BUCKNELL REVIEW

"Turning the Century": Feminist Theory in the 1990s

A Troubled Peace: Black Women in the Halls of the White Academy

Nellie Y. McKay

University of Wisconsin, Madison

ALMOST a decade ago, in the early 1980s, I read a short paper at an MLA convention, a personal piece entitled "Black Woman Professor—White University" that was later published in a feminist journal. That essay has since been reprinted in two volumes, one on women in academia and the other on feminist resistance.[1] Although I make no claims for the objectivity of the views expressed in the piece, I wrote it to address some of the difficulties and discomforts I felt other black women and I were experiencing at that time in our new roles as college and university professors in predominantly white institutions of higher education. The conclusion to that essay reads:

> To be a black woman professor in a white university is difficult and challenging, but it is exciting and rewarding, and black women professors like it here. We aim to stay!

At the time, I did not ask: at what price?

There were a number of black women at the session when the paper was read, and they confirmed my suspicions. On one hand, I spoke largely out of my own experiences; on the other, I was part of a generation (not necessarily of similar age, but one that shared like academic experiences) of black women in my situation then. Most of us had gone to white graduate schools between the late 1960s and early 1970s and were the first as a group (by race and sex) to find employment in predominantly white colleges and universities. My language was sufficiently transparent to make clear the premises of the text: as a rule, black women did not feel welcome or appreciated in their new positions, but having broken the barriers of this stronghold of sex prejudice, they planned no retreat from gains hard won.

In fact, feeling unwelcome and unappreciated in the academic spaces they occupied was not a new sensation for these women.

21

Putting aside the previous history of racism in America, as recently as in their graduate school experiences most had lived
intimately with extreme alienation and repeated unpleasant encounters with white cohorts and white male professors (most of us
met very few white women professors during those years). The
difference was that in graduate school, although our numbers
were small, the presence of black peers among these predominantly white student bodies offered us a degree of emotional
support. In our job situations, there were few if any black colleagues, especially black women.

The exception to this individual racial isolation in the workplace
of white academia occurred when a black faculty member was part
of a Black Studies program, the cause that brought the largest
number of black faculty into a new space for them. Then, the
danger was group isolation, for chances were that all black faculty
in his/her institution were located in Black Studies, as though
black scholars had not received the same training as their white
peers in history and literature and sociology, etc. But this did not
matter. In breaking down the barriers that had relegated even the
W. E. B. DuBoises, Alain Lockes, and other great black lights of an
earlier era to the historically black colleges, these scholars made a
crucial discovery. They learned, first hand, that the gains of the
civil rights movement did not constitute a reform of racial attitudes toward black people. Few white institutions were interested in them other than for the calm they could bring to troubled
campuses by way of Black Studies classes to satisfy the demands of
obstreperous black undergraduates. Only a small number held
appointments in Black Studies *and* their disciplinary departments
as well. An even smaller number were hired solely in their
disciplines.

Nevertheless, this segregation had advantages for the new
field's development other than bringing black scholars from different disciplines together in intense situations. Among these,
faculty could concentrate on learning for themselves what had
been left out of their graduate education, and they could focus
exclusively on the needs of a new interdisciplinary curriculum.
This was helpful. It eliminated the possibilities of faculty feeling
split loyalties to other departments and lessened racial confronta-
tions within departmental work space. Black scholars who especially favored this isolation defended its merits by denouncing
racism within the discipline departments.

But, in spite of the benefits, some Black Studies scholars were
ambivalent about their positions outside of their home disciplines.

They questioned the effects of the separation on the new field for the long term, on their personal intellectual growth, and on cross-racial relations with other faculty with whom they shared interests. Those in this situation would have preferred the dual-appointment model, like Yale's and a few other institutions, which followed the patterns of African Studies and American Studies. All, however, agreed strongly, and correctly, that having been excluded from the academic curriculum until then, Black Studies absolutely required its own space to develop its own academic and political agendas and to carry out the intensive re-education that students and faculty needed in order to recuperate the intellectual dimensions of the black experience. In like manner, regardless of where black faculty were positioned within the structures of their institutions in their relationships to dominant traditional educational programs, Black Studies faculty rejected ideas of token status in the academy and its oppositional alienation from the center of the authority of the black intellectual tradition.

In my own attraction to the field, the turn to Afro-American literature was embedded in the politics of my own struggle against the disempowerment of people of African descent within the Western body politic. Personally, I endorsed a separate interdisciplinary space for Black Studies but favored a structure that insured black intellectual interaction with the community at large. A segregated Black Studies, I believed, would operate only within the boundaries of its own marginality and increase the difficulties of making significant educational and political changes within the systems of power in the academy. Such changes, I felt, would come only through the engagement between those located at the boundaries of the exclusive accepted knowledge we opposed and those at its center.[2] I understood Black Studies and my place in the white academy as a complex interweaving of political and educational issues. Like many of my colleagues, I was caught up in the fervor of reform. I wanted Black Studies to grow and develop into a force on college and university campuses across the country, but I was also concerned that our scholarship and teaching permeate the disciplines in the Arts and Sciences curriculum and thus completely transform them. The ideal goal was to reform conventional American education from its outside as well as its inside. Options on strategies to this end differ as widely today as they did then, but in the late 1960s and 1970s, for many black scholars, there was no choice: Black Studies programs were the only spaces available to them in white colleges and universities.

Nor, in the academic ghetto of Black Studies did the militant political rhetoric that so dramatically challenged racism build bridges between the new field and its discipline departments. Furthermore, in response to the unsettling presence of the revolutionary-minded inhabitants of this ghetto, white faculty threatened by curricular changes and the loss of the hegemony of Eurocentric-based knowledge defended the sovereignty of Western tradition on the basis that Black Studies was scholarly unsound and its fledgling faculty intellectually inferior to the rest of their campus colleagues. Obviously, this racist defense of the status quo increased hostilities between the opposing sides. Only many years later, with the emergence of more politically moderate black scholars as spokespeople for the field, with records of "acceptable" scholarship behind them, did large numbers of white faculty begin to acknowledge the merits of Black Studies. The forthcoming *Norton Anthology of Afro-American Literature,* the white literary establishment's final endorsement of this field, will mark one of the single most significant events in the history of Black Studies.[3]

But back in the 1970s and early 1980s, amidst conflicting ideologies and their struggles against black male sexism in Black Studies programs on a day-to-day basis, black women faced unnerving worlds. Still, having beaten the odds and successfully completed their graduate education, implicit in these black women's decision to face the challenges of climbing the professorial ladder was the idea that, under the circumstances, the best revenge was to survive and succeed. Struggle was a way of life for them. They followed in the footsteps of generations of black foreparents who had carried out similar resolves and sometimes succeeded under far more difficult circumstances and for much less in tangible rewards.

Today, the reality of Black Studies is different from that of its early days. In a combination of economic downturns and a lack of commitment on the part of white faculty and administrations in some institutions, many programs did not survive the 1970s. Among those that did, however, several are now flourishing and with two decades of excellent scholarship in the field its proponents have gained academic respectability even from originally resistant white faculty and administrators. Scholars, black and white, now contribute to research that is some of the most exciting in almost every discipline within its purvue. In addition, a much larger number of Black Studies scholars now hold appointments in the field and in their discipline departments, ending the academic isolation that many were ambivalent toward in the 1960s and 1970s. Among black scholars, the most productive and highly sought after, in history, literature, and sociology in particular, have made their names through the study of the black experience. The contributions of black women to this new status of Black Studies is indisputable.

Historically, education is familiar ground for black women since, professionally, it was always one of the few respectable professions open to the group. In terms of the power of decision making, however, until recently they occupied only secondary roles within its parameters. In the nineteenth century, middle-class black women were school teachers among free blacks before and after emancipation and few obtained positions above employment in black elementary and secondary schools. Still, today black women in education and all black people point with pride to a long list of distinguished black women educators from earlier times, women like Fanny Coppin, Lucy Moten, Frances Watkins Harper, Margaret Washington, Mary Church Terrell, and Anna Julia Cooper, to name some of the most well known. Without the efforts of these women between the 1850s and the early part of this century their race would never have produced the women and men who held high the torch of freedom and literacy for black people from the mid-nineteenth century through the 1950s and beyond. For although on all levels, until our time, racism remanded black women and men to historically black schools, and black male sexism consigned the handful of black women in the historically black colleges to activities associated with the female arts—home economics, for instance, or to other specific duties closely linked to the interests of women students—these women provided the shoulders on which today's black women educators stand. They are our most revered role models.

In 1983 when "Black Woman Professor—White University" first appeared in print I was still an untenured professor, five years into my first job after graduate school, and desperately struggling to complete the book that I hoped would make the difference between being told I had to leave that position or, instead, be given the hand of welcome into the fraternity of those who had safely negotiated that initiation rite. For there can be little question that in the present-day academy tenure is the hardest test that everyone faces in pursuit of an academic career. With both the naiveté and the optimism of younger years, "Black Woman Professor—White University" was a public announcement of my intention to survive and overcome that all-important hurdle. But no one told me then (not that it would have altered my decision) that for all of its difficulties achieving tenure was only the end of one struggle that would lead to another, and another, and another, each increasingly less defined or concrete. I could not then have known that each battle won or lost was a personal down payment, involuntarily made, toward an investment I never realized I was making. No one could have explained (and if someone had tried I would not then have comprehended) what it really meant to be a black woman professor in a white college or university for the long haul. The following incidents, the first of which occurred while I was writing the present piece, illustrate the point.

In my office, I was engaged in conversation with a black woman colleague in the Afro-American Studies Department. She was standing just inside my door. A white male professor from another department (I credit him with complete unconsciousness of what he did) stopped at the door and, without apology, pushed his way past my colleague. Before either she or I realized what had happened, he preempted her presence in *our* space to make a request of me. I had scarcely grasped the politics of the situation before it was over—he was gone and my female colleague had retreated to her office across the hall. There was a moment in the unfolding of this scene when direct confrontation with the professor on his behavior might have served a useful purpose, but the swiftness of that moment and my momentary unguardedness against it aborted the opportunity. It was another everyday incident in our days of such incidents, when white colleagues, without even trying, asserted the privilege of whiteness, especially white male whiteness, over those they perceived to be unequal to themselves by the authority of race and/or sex.

A more insulting incident was reported by a young black woman—a recent Ph.D.—about her job interview at a prestigious eastern college. In a conversation with the search committee, all white, one male member of the group, after remarking on his ignorance of her work, went on to inform her that since she was from the "ghetto" her appointment to the faculty would offer him and the others insight into this element of society. Needless to say, the young woman declined the position, but not before informing him and everyone in the room that she grew up in a black middle-class immigrant family, had attended a prestigious university as an undergraduate, and not on scholarship, and that she had completed graduate school at the University of Wisconsin, Madison, through the same combination of work, loans, and family support that most white middle-class students relied on. One wonders, however, about the effects of such a direct insult on a young black faculty member who had risen from the ghetto to a teaching position in a white well-endowed private college.

Unfortunately, white male professors and administrators are not the only group that offend black women by their racist verbal expressions. White women faculty are equally as guilty. Among their offenses, a favorite that almost all black women faculty have encountered, even from feminists, is a suggestion that resembles the "back to Africa" advice given to many black Americans by overt white racists. The black woman is told by the white woman that she would be happier if she "returned" to a historically black college (in most cases she had not come from one). This advice is further emphasized when the white woman notes that the black woman's contact with the white academy—her education in a white college or university and her subsequent employment by another such institution—gives her (the black woman) added prestige in the historically black college. I received this advice shortly after I was tenured. My Ivy League graduate training, my colleague told me, would make me a "queen" at a historically black college.

Ask any black woman in the white academy about similar experiences in the workplace! Stories abound! The point is that these anecdotes are not isolated or unusual events. They occur daily in many variations in the lives of black women professors. In my first illustration, that I am black and a woman, and that my black colleague was also a woman, and a junior professor at that, were intimately related to our white colleague's actions. One cannot imagine him or any other white male professor barging into the office of a white male colleague, of any rank, and behaving in like manner.

In the second anecdote, one wonders how long it will take—and at what cost to black people—for even (intelligent and educated?) white people to learn that there is no monolith of black people, welfare clients who live in the crime-ridden "ghetto" (which that word denotes when applied to people of African descent)? The young woman in question, one of the most brilliant and articulate former students I have had the pleasure of working with, was, I am sure, impeccably dressed for the occasion. Why a white man automatically assumed that she was a product of the "ghetto" defies imagination. And had she been, how could he not have known that his remarks were insulting and denegrating? The authority of his whiteness is clearly the badge of his arrogance, racism, and ignorance, which he obviously wears with pride.

On one level, the third incident noted is perhaps the most

difficult to cope with, usually because the suggestion is made by a white woman whom one knows and likes reasonably well, and one with whom one must also make alliances in the struggle against sexism in the academy. To step aside from it for a moment, let's consider this conversation. A senior black faculty member in my university recently asked me why she always felt "at home" when she visited historically black colleges as opposed to how she felt in our university, which, technically, is "home" for us. She followed that inquiry with another question: why do we remain in the predominantly white university where many abuses constantly beset our sensitivities?

To the first part of her query I replied that in the white academy our location is always contested spaces even though it is as right-fully our space as that of others there. When we visit historically black colleges, the space is uncontested. In one, our occupancy is conditional; in the other, it is unconditional. In one, there is everything to prove over and over again; in the other, we have nothing to prove. In black-dominated space, we are who we are. In that context we can understand (but never accept) the impulse of the white suggestion that we "return" to the historically black colleges.

To my colleague's second question, I suggested that we choose to remain in these contested spaces because as black women (and men) we know that we have a right to occupy them and will not be driven out by those who would gladly see us go. We have not rejected the historically black colleges, and our anger boils at their implied inferiority by white people. Personally, I never stand as tall or feel as self-assured as immediately after spending a few days on the campus of a historically black college. But this knowl-edge does not make life easier on the white campus, and black women must always weigh the cost of their choices against the balance of energy, will, and the determination to survive with human dignity. Each woman must learn to identify her own limits.

For me, even now, after living this reality for many years and coming to understand much more than I did a decade ago of what it means to be who I am in the place that I am, I find it impossible to conceive of myself in the state of complete "otherness" (as in the anecdotes above) that I represent in the world of whiteness. For what those in my racial and sexual group know but fail to always remember is that the academy is a microcosm of the larger society in which we live and that America and all of Western society remain provinces in which white men (and some white women) of a particular class and with particular dominant ideologies determine the nature of all of our existences. Thus, even without deliberate intentions to enforce dominance over others, the relations between whites and the "other" in white institutions of higher education develop and emerge out of a dynamic that reifies racist and sexist paradigms of power and powerlessness. The question this essay asks is, given this situation, how then has it been for black women, in these last years of the twentieth century, to live, work, and sometimes even claim success in the predominantly white academy?

I see our present in the context of more than two decades of my own constant struggle to minimize loss of personal dignity and find as much fulfillment as possible in my life in the work I have chosen to do. Today, I and many of the black women in the group I spoke of and for in the early 1980s have scaled several resisting walls, and we have lasting scars to prove our efforts. Racism, sexism, and classism are unrelenting adversaries. No skirmish is minor. Each is a major confrontation with powerful forces of tradition, and there is always a price to pay for having been there. Nevertheless, in spite of, or because of our bruises, we are on the other side from where we were a decade ago, and on that side, our white colleagues are forced, even if sometimes only perfunctorily, to acknowledge us as colleagues. For a short time, many of us, reaching this other side, experienced a strange sense of dislocation when, following our positive tenure reviews, we surmised that the "we" and "they" division in which we were positioned in our first years in the academy had disappeared. By virtue of our new standing, some of us thought (and such thoughts were very unsettling) we had become a part of "them," that having fulfilled the requirements of the game as they defined it we now shared their legitimacy. Our discomfiture, however, was hardly warranted. We soon realized that although our status vis-à-vis such things as job security had altered appreciably, we were still excluded from the centers of power vested in the premises of white maleness.

In that respect, the years have taught us that "we" are neither "them" (we have no access to or control of information or economic resources), nor are we who we were, i.e., completely vulnerable in some areas of our lives. Blackness and femaleness insures that we can *never* be them, and we cannot (nor would if we could) return to our early struggles. Experience tells us we occupy our own space: sometimes on the margins of all that goes on around us, oftentimes in the buffer zone between "them" and those who have taken our former places on the lines of anxiety and uncertainty. But always, we are on a battleground trying to determine the nature of the fray and deciding how best to spend our valuable but decidedly depletable physical energies and psychological resources. Today, for the women who have followed us, we hope that we hold the door to professional success slightly more ajar for them than it had been for us. We hope that instead of reinventing our wheel, black women professors now entering the white academy strengthen the positions we set in place.

Yet, for all of these hopes, and although I know that at all levels of their careers black women professors in white colleges and universities continue to work aggressively not to be forced out by many of the difficulties they encounter, I am not as optimistic over material changes in our situation as I was a decade ago. As a consequence, the open-endedness of my "Black Woman Professor—White University" has given way to the collective and infinitely more closed "A Troubled Peace: Black Women in the Halls of the White Academy." The quality of this peace disturbs me. True, over the last decade and a half, such things as open racial hostilities toward black (and other minority group) faculty have decreased considerably among faculties of mixed racial groups. No one, not even the most rabid bigot, wants to be branded a racist. But, appearances deceive. Many of those early hostilities have not dissolved; they have only become more subtle and dangerous. It is infinitely more sophisticated to attack Affirmative Action and like initiatives from behind the banner of " 'quality' without quotas" than to make frontal attacks on minority groups. The result is a continuing dis/ease among black and other minority group faculty within the halls of the white academy.

While in my earlier essay I expressed confidence in collectively finding a solution to some of the problems of race, class, and sex in the academy, today I am pessimistic toward our ever achieving that goal. This reevaluation of the state of black women in the white university admits to grave disappointments, unfulfilled dreams, and deep frustrations on the part of most of the women I know. Nor can they do anything to change the cause of their distress. Change will not come until those responsible for the conditions decide to end the roles that racism, classism, and sexism among white faculty and administrators exert on the lives of others. My pessimism springs from feeling that nothing we have seen over the last twenty-five years indicates such action. While individual white faculty and administrators have made valiant efforts toward change, domination, empowerment, legitimacy, and authority remain in the places they have always been. Minorities and, to a large extent, white women are excluded from these places. After almost two decades of service in white colleges and universities, by dint of race, class, and sex, at best black women and minority group others now experience themselves in the peculiar situation of outsiders within the white academy.[4]

Yet, some people will find it difficult to understand this distress among black women faculty and others. When we stand in certain places (like the major [white] research universities in the country) and survey faculty opportunities in higher education today, no one can deny that some earlier conditions of the work lives of black women educators have changed, and certainly for the better. However, a more critical appraisal reveals the disquieting statistics that even now only a small number of the professoriate in the country are black women, and the overwhelming majority of these are still employed in historically black colleges, not always by their choice. While accurate statistics are difficult to come by, researchers generally estimate that black women compose less than one percent of the faculty in all colleges and universities, and half of that number are still in historically black colleges. For those who wish to enter white institutions, deep-seated social prejudices against blacks and women still work more effectively against black women. These women have an even harder time than black men or white women in gaining access to highly competitive graduate schools and in finding employment in institutions with resources to nurture research careers. In addition, those who are able to enter such colleges and universities on the junior level have a more difficult time achieving tenure because, until they become well known, their work is usually undervalued. Always, when black women attempt to move out of the traditional roles of women in education in the nineteenth and early twentieth centuries, it appears that the odds are stacked against their success. The majority of black women in the academy are part of the negative statistics.[5]

Why then does the world of blacks in higher education look more promising at a first glance from some perspectives? The answer is in the view one gets from a position that easily blinks out the grim reality of most black experiences. From a more privileged place one sees that a number of black women and men have risen above the difficulties outlined above. These scholars (with a few exceptions) were fortunate enough to have gained admission to and to have succeeded in highly competitive and/or prestigious (the two are not always the same) East and West Coast graduate programs in the 1970s and early 1980s. Now they hold appointments, even chair professorships in some cases, in institutions that are recognized as the most desirable in the profession. Everyone has heard that in this time, for all the ubiquitous problems of racial and sexual prejudices in university hiring, every major and hundreds of less-than-major white institutions of higher education in the country are in competition for today's small pool of successful black scholars (especially women), and some are investing generously (postdoctoral fellowships, research funds, reduced teaching loads, generous leave policies, etc.) in some of those whom they identify as the most promising younger black scholars.

However, I suggest that what appears to be an unprecedented "buyers" market for black women and men scholars is anything but the true state of affairs for the majority of the group seeking academic careers outside of the historically black colleges. These well-publicized gestures toward a highly visible small group of brilliant, ambitious, achieving scholars now in well-placed positions in a few institutions signal no major changes in the general status of black women or men in higher education. Most white college and university administrators and faculty, including those who claim a willingness to hire black scholars if only they could find "qualified" ones, or if only they could afford one of the "stars," do not know and cannot comprehend that if such a thing as color/class/race/sex-blind hiring existed, those now excluded would bring tremendous enhancement to the educational mission of their institutions. Instead, they still consider the possible employment of those from these groups as an Affirmative Action duty or, worse, an evidence of their liberal attitudes in educational matters. Never do they see the richness of experience in diversity and openness. Were it otherwise, this update of my first essay would carry a very different tone and title.

Recent controversies over the values of multicultural education have more clearly defined the dragon that lurks at the heart of the problem, which has kept large numbers of people of color out of faculty positions in the majority of white colleges and universities in America, and continues to treat those within as second-class citizens. When the barricades in the struggle for Black Studies in these institutions came down in the 1960s and early 1970s, in response to pressure brought to bear as a result of the Black Revolution of that era, a new area of study entered the academy. And while Black Studies units have had a history of academic and political successes and failures in the white academy, the field opened up the way for a generation of young black scholars to enter these institutions. Those who succeeded defined and developed careers that would have been almost impossible for them otherwise. Other fields—Women's Studies, Chicano Studies, Native American Studies—as well as a host of white ethnic studies programs have benefited from the battles fought by Black Studies in the late 1960s and early 1970s.

Although no active coalition exists between these "Studies" groups except as Ethnic Studies on a few campuses, together they present a force reminiscent of but, collectively, more potentially threatening than Black Studies alone was in the 1960s. In many quarters, the response from those who still promote higher education predicated on the "Great Books" theory or the primacy of Western civilization is an elevation of the tactics of the earlier time. The controversies over the value of a diversified curriculum, now waging on many campuses, and in some popular as well as scholarly journals and magazines, initiated under the auspices of such groups as the National Association of Scholars, are struggles to maintain and privilege Euro-American concepts of knowledge as the only "Truth." They indicate how deeply embedded are the roots of racial, class, and sex prejudices in the centers of white academic power. While sometimes less dramatically experienced, black women engaged these pressures for more than two decades.

Even in those institutions in which they are treated well, black women professors in white colleges and universities are always aware that their presence represents a disruptive incursion into spaces never intended for them, and whatever their ranks, some students, faculty, and administrators are always poised to undermine their professional authority. The vicious obscene attack on a black woman historian at Princeton University by a group of students in the fall of 1990 bears out my point. Under the banner of the secret (for fear of reprisals) "National Association for the Advancement of White People—Princeton Chapter," and claiming the authority of the "Shockley Report," the group distributed flyers, including one in the professor's mailbox, in which Martin Luther King, Jr., Winnie Mandella, the professor in question, and Affirmative Action were called filthy names, and she was singled out as an intellectual incompetent.[6] While this was clearly a racist attack, in addition, on the Madison campus, and I suspect on many others, black women professors (and white women too) have also been sexually harassed by white and black men seeking to intimidate them. Often women are uncertain of how to respond to such racist and sexual outrages—this other kind of rape. Unfortunately, too many women, as in cases of physical rapes, remain silent, internalizing their victimization. This, of course, is wrong.

Women must learn to scream loudly and other colleagues and college/university administrators must be actively involved in the processes that counter such harassment tactics. On the other hand, even when a few black women appear accepted and rewarded on their merits through prizes and awards, praise for good scholarship, and/or appointments to important positions and committees for instance, incidents surrounding them indicate tolerance rather than full recognition of them as equals. Perhaps the low number of available black faculty for positions in white colleges and universities is the clearest indication of the level of threat the presence of black women and black men presents to higher education outside of the historically black colleges.

The small number of black women and men on white college/university faculties is appalling. None of these institutions, to my knowledge, has an aggregate black faculty that is a respectable proportion of its overall faculty population. Even in institutions conscious of the politics of the situation, dozens of departments remain all-white enclaves; and some white colleges and universities still have few black faculty not associated with Black Studies. In the new "hot" market for star black women and men faculty, department heads and university and college administrators blame the small pool of available candidates for the sometimes odiousness of the competition for these faculty, and/or use the numbers as an excuse for the absence of blacks on their faculties. Few, if any, seem to realize they are consciously and/or unconsciously complicitous in maintaining the size of that pool. Nor do they acknowledge the devastating implications of their inertia in attacking the problem at its roots—not at Ph.D. commencements, but at the junior high school level. How otherwise do we account for the state of black graduate affairs such as exists in the English department of my own university? Each fall I receive dozens of telephone calls and letters from across the country from colleagues requesting that I recommend to my new or soon-to-graduate black English department Ph.D. students (usually to teach courses in black literature as part of their workload), faculty positions in the schools of the callers and writers. Had I twenty-five such students in any year, I could guarantee each one a job in the college/university of her/his choice. Yet, in my thirteen years here, the department has had a total of two such graduates from its program, separated in time by approximately nine years. Nor is my university any worse than other comparable Ph.D.-granting institutions with which I am familiar. Why this absence of black graduate students from English departments when there is such a demanding market for them? Is there a connection between discipline departments in white universities and colleges crying out and desperately competing for the few available black faculty and the absence of candidates to fill those positions? In comparison to the numbers of black graduates in engineering, law, and business during the period of my Wisconsin tenure, after more than twenty-five years of Black Studies in the academy, I have no doubt that white colleges and universities have a vested interest in maintaining the miniscule size of the number of black Ph.Ds. in Arts and Sciences. Nor do I deny that engineering, law, and business have been more attractive to black undergraduates for several years. But I am also aware that many potential black graduate students have been turned away from pursuing Ph.Ds. in my discipline by admissions policies that fail to keep up with the currents of the times and thus, ultimately, perpetuate the racist problems of the past.

Black women everywhere suffer race, sex, and class discrimination because they are black and women, and the halls of the academy provide no safe sanctuary. In white universities and colleges, these women experience the workplace as one of society's exclusive clubs to which, even though they have as much right as everyone else to be there, they will never gain full membership— at least, not in the lifetime of this generation of scholars. Given the record of the past, as a group, their numbers will always be small—mere tokens in most institutions. The black women I know complain constantly of overwork: more is expected of them than of others by students, other faculty, administrators, and the professional organizations to which they belong. And that work is infinitely varied, including the expectations that they will assume responsibility for working out the problems that black and Third World students encounter in the academy. Student counseling, academic as well as on psychologically crisis-oriented issues, even for white students, continually appear on the doorstep of the black mother, the great bosom of the world. The women feel sure too (or is this paranoia?) that their performances are more carefully scrutinized than those of some others.

In addition to work expectations of them, black women faculty often find themselves bearing the brunt of jokes and other overt ethnic and gender insensitivities of their colleagues, which does little to enhance their comfort levels among their peers. The energy they give to extra work that serves the needs of their institutions and the psychological toll that coping with the racism and sexism of colleagues demands are barriers to growth and success in the profession of their choice. These problems have a direct relationship to the difficulty many of the women face in completing sufficient research for tenure.

But if the obstacles they face in the white academy are daunting, black women have not been impotent. Looking back over the years since the first group of black women entered this arena, their presence, as has that of all minorities in the same space, has changed the face of American education and revised the premises of previously accepted knowledge to include materials long excluded from such considerations. In their interactions with students and faculty, they have also made major positive impact on many lives. They know that, despite the cost, these years have not been wasted ones.

Still, underlying any possible successes, a troubled peace exists between black women and the various constituencies of the white academy they serve. This state is neither energizing nor creative, for it reflects the wastefulness of marginalized work and devalued selfhood—commodities our world can ill afford to spend this way. White educators must assume leadership and responsibility to deal effectively with the debilitating forces of race, class, and sex that have brought us to this pass. Only then will the troubled peace black women now experience inside these halls dissipate. At that time, to take liberties with the words of the great black woman educator Anna Julia Cooper, the whole *race* of those with rights to be there, with privilege to none, will enter a new space of equality with them and share in opportunities to do the long-neglected work without which the survival of our world will always be in doubt.[7]

Notes

1. Nellie McKay, "Black Woman Professor—White University," *Women in Academe,* ed. Resa L. Dudovitz (Oxford: Pergamon press, 1984), 143–47; and *Radical Voices: A Decade of Feminist Resistance from Women's Studies International Forum,* ed. Renate D. Klein and Deborah Lynn Steinberg (Oxford: Pergamon Press, 1989), 36–41.

2. See Helene Moglen, "Power and Empowerment," *Women in Academe,* 132.

3. *The Norton Anthology of Afro-American Literature,* now in preparation, will most likely be published in 1992. Credit for this landmark project goes to Henry Louis Gates, Jr. of Harvard University. After much lengthy persuasion, Gates convinced Norton that the time had come for the addition of such an anthology to its prestigious list of literary anthologies. The publication of this work will mean that in no part of the world where the English language is taught will anyone ever again have an excuse not to teach Afro-American literature.

4. This is a general statement. I have no wish to discredit the efforts of the many white faculty and administrators across the country who are working to change the situation. Especially, I wish to acknowledge the efforts of Donna Shalala, the chancellor at the University of Wisconsin, Madison, who in a very short time has made the Madison campus a better place for minorities and all women than, only a few years ago, most of us dared to hope would be. But change comes slowly and even painfully to institutions as large as this one. Oppositional forces to Shalala's program for making the campus "user friendly" for everyone have affected progress toward greater equality for all.

5. While overall minority hiring at the University of Wisconsin, Madison, remains well below what it should be, Shalala's "Madison Plan," an initiative to increase minority students and faculty across the campus, has had real success in some areas. When she arrived on the campus in January 1988, there was a total of three black women professors here in a body of more than two thousand. Today, that number stands at fifteen. While black male faculty hiring has not increased dramatically, I suspect that few other white universities of any size have an equal number of black women to Madison's on its faculty.

6. Not only did this flyer make the usual stereotyped accusations against Affirmative Action, the obscenity of the language was shocking. Words like "niggershit" were a prominent part of its descriptive landscape. The group claimed to have sent tapes of "all" of the professor's lectures to New Jersey politicians to apprise them of what was being taught at Princeton under the guise of history. On the positive side, there was an immediate outpouring of support for the professor from angry students, faculty, and administrators.

7. Anna Julia Cooper, *A Voice from the South by a Black Woman of the South* (New York: Oxford University Press, 1988), 31. Originally published in 1892 (Xenia, Ohio: Aldine Printing House), Cooper's often-quoted text reads as follows: "Only the Black Woman can say 'when and where I enter, in the quiet undisputed dignity of my womanhood, without violence and without suing or special patronage, then and there the whole *Negro race enters with me.*'"

At the Receiving End: Reading "Third" World Texts in a "First" World Context

Anuradha Dingwaney Needham
Oberlin College

I N this essay I want to discuss if not the impossibility, then, at least, some very real difficulties in *crossing boundaries* when the objects of one's analyses are works from other cultures.[1] These difficulties are, of course, compounded when one deals with—as I do—works that originate in, or are about, what here is broadly construed as the "Third" world but which are read (or received) in the "First" world. I should specify further that a significant number of works available in the "First" world are from the now largely postcolonial "Third" world and are thus being read in what were not so long ago—and in some instances continue to be—centers of imperial power. The term *postcolonial,* moreover, is deceptive because in the "First" world the imperial mind set is not entirely a thing of a deeply embarrassing past but, with a few variations, even mutations, is a present reality. There are, then, radical inequities in the power the "First" world continues to wield over not only the *material* but also the *discursive* realms within which the "Third" world is framed, and thereby produced as an object of interpretation and knowledge.

Consider, for example, the furor and controversy which followed upon Khomeini's death sentence on Salman Rushdie for writing *The Satanic Verses.* Insofar as the literary establishment and media institutions in the U.S. and several European countries saw it fit to appropriate Rushdie under the banner of an individual's right to "freedom of expression," rationality, and secularism, they, with few exceptions, reproduced the familiar imperializing gesture that automatically conceives of postcolonial "Third" world countries (especially those polities over which Islam is seen to hold sway) as the opposite or other of an enlightened, civilized ethos. The "First" world's willing, aggressive, and ultimately self-aggrandizing move ("I am Rushdie" declared several of the supporters) dramatized what I would call the "First" world's strategic management of an image or representation of the "Third" world that gives it continued cultural power. While some commentaries did locate Khomeini's action in his desire to reassert his power "over the Islamic world," they nevertheless continued to explain it primarily in terms of a gesture peculiarly inherent to, of the very essence of, Islam. Understandably, then, both religious *and* secular Muslims, feeling embattled, reacted defensively—either with counteraccusations or silence.

For my purposes, the responses of my secular Muslim friends and colleagues are particularly instructive. On the one hand, they worried (and were saddened by the thought) that Rushdie had misjudged his audiences and willingly offered himself up for Western appropriation. On the other hand, they conceded that Rushdie had provided a fruitful internal critique that could eventually lead to reform through debate and critical scrutiny of Islam as it is presently constituted by certain ruling and powerful constituencies in, for instance, Iran, Pakistan, Saudi Arabia. But they rightly insisted that such a critique can valuably be conducted only in less inhospitable, less embattled, circumstances. And those of us, Muslims and non-Muslims alike, who witness the daily demonization of Islam in the West, concur. For it remains true, as Edward Said has argued in *Orientalism* and *Covering Islam,* that backwardness and fanaticism are indelibly associated in the "First" world with Islam. In its defense of Rushdie, the "First" world yet again deployed this association, making it well-nigh impossible for any "Third" world intellectual to engage and enter into a conversation on this issue with audiences from the "First" world.

What I have been sketching so far is one instance of the incredible difficulty that attends the reception of a work about "Third" world cultures and its peoples in the "First" world. A productive response can only proceed from knowledge about the subject that does not support and itself arise from hegemonic and coercive control. This did not happen with *The Satanic Verses*.

One of the sad consequences of the kind of difficulty I've been sketching is not only that certain positions cannot be forwarded openly but also that whatever else is of significance is effectively excluded as well and our analysis is impoverished. In all the controversy surrounding *The Satanic Verses,* with discussion focused entirely on two mutually opposing perspectives, concerns about gender, race, and ethnicity, encoded in the *Verses,* were lost, ignored, or elided. Rushdie has gone on record as saying that one of his purposes was to restore/insert women to their rightful place in the history of Islam. Indeed, the *Verses* is replete with images of strong, charismatic female presences, and the representation of

gender itself is a complex and densely imagined effort. Yet, looking at what has been said, one would not believe that gender was
even an issue.[2]

I want to turn now to less spectacular instances of the difficulties
that attend cross-cultural analyses by looking at some of the responses that have been generated by students in a course I teach
on Anglophone literatures of the "Third" world at Oberlin College.[3]

One of the ideas my students and I have explored throughout
the course is whether or not and how various forms of resistance
are enacted in a variety of Anglophone "Third" world texts. My
students are familiar with some aspects of postcolonial scholarship, so they are quick at picking up on some issues: how writing
in the language of the colonizer (English) itself poses some problems; how, though, this language can be used against itself; how
its possibilities can be enlarged. With help from essays I passed
out at the beginning of the course,[4] my students were able to note
and critically scrutinize modes of appropriation by "First" world
audiences; they pointed to specific instances of contest and/or
collusion with colonial/imperial/Western ideologies. Thus, my students bring sophistication and some self-scrutiny to their analyses,
and they bring a great deal of enthusiasm. However, there are
limits as well, and these limits I see as fundamental to the project
of reading across cultures when the culture being decoded is seen
as *unequal* with one's own. In the examples I now turn to, these
limits surface, significantly enough, when 1) women's relationships with dominant ideologies (here colonial, otherwise Western) are involved; or 2) questions of gender constructions are
involved at the same time as those of race and class.

My first example, from *Unwinding Threads*, an anthology of
women's writing in Africa,[5] is the excerpt "My Mother" from
Fadhma Amrouche's autobiography.[6] Fadhma came from a family
of Kabyle village folk; to explain her story to her children, "she
had to explain the Kabyle woman's world." This excerpt deals with
how Fadhma's mother, Aini, transgressed traditional custom
when, on her husband's death, she refused to return to her family,
who then disowned her. Alone, looking after her children, she
became pregnant by a young man, who subsequently denied he
was Fadhma's father. "Kabyle customs are terrible," writes
Fadhma; "when a woman transgresses, it's necessary that she
disappear, that no one see her again. . . . Before French coloniza-
tion, justice was quick. Relatives led the guilty one to the fields
where they beat her. Then they would bury her beside the hill-

side. . . . So my mother sought redress in the French law" (168). In our discussion, some students predictably rehashed how colonialism had *saved* Fadhma and Aini from certain death. Less predictably, quite a large number were angered by what they called Aini's and Fadhma's collusion with colonialism—Aini for seeking redress through colonial authorities; Fadhma for recycling, in her account, the classic polarities of colonial discourse where "native" Kabyle customs are represented as barbaric and the intervention of French law is construed as humane. My students formed this judgment by: 1) eliding or ignoring the severe exclusions and dehumanization that can be seen in this excerpt as a product of certain traditional patriarchal practices which reduce a woman to the status of an object and see her entirely in terms of "property" now considered damaged or sullied and, therefore, as necessary to dispose of; 2) suppressing what follows a few paragraphs later: Fadhma's powerful description (and implicit condemnation) of the oppressive environment in a mission school (a supporting colonial institution) from which her mother quickly removes her:

> From that whole period of my life, I can recall only the tune of the Hail Mary's, a vision of the illuminated chapel. . . . But above all else I see an atrocious picture: a little girl standing against the wall of a corridor. The child is covered with filth, dressed in sackcloth, a little cup of excrement is hung around her throat, and she is crying. A priest is moving toward her and the nun is explaining that the little girl is fractious, that she threw other children's thimbles into the open sewer ditch and had to be forced to climb down into it to recover them. That's why she's covered with filth and is wearing a cup of excrement. In addition to this punishment, the child was whipped until the blood came. When my mother came the next Wednesday, she still found the whip-marks all over my body. She stroked the gashes and had the sister sent for. My mother showed her the marks saying, "Is it for this that I confided my child to your care? Give my daughter back to me!" (169)

In other words, what my students failed to note was that these two women's relationship with colonial authorities and/or representations can be construed less as a matter of collusion than as that of strategic needs and agendas—modes of empowerment (and survival even) alert to the oppressions of both patriarchy and colonialism.[7] (Here it is also worth reiterating that both Aini and Fadhma are outsiders existing on the margins of their community—Fadhma because she's illegitimate and Aini because she has transgressed against Kabyle custom.) My students' failure of insight was predicated on a more fundamental blindness that conceives of colonialism and resistance to it as monolithic, as somehow divorced from, and therefore not affected by, considerations such as gender, race, class, and other diverse material circumstances.

My next example, also from *Unwinding Threads,* is an excerpt from Assia Djebar's *Les Impatients.* Dalila, an educated, independent young Algerian woman, asserts her right to "be herself," to choose her own husband; "What concerns [her] are [her] responsibilities to [herself]" (186); she tries to persuade her docile, traditional sister-in-law to also assert a similar right for herself. This excerpt was, again, construed as Dalila's accommodation to Western values. Thus, while indicting what they called "Western values," my students' critique of Dalila was predicated on the curious assumption that any effort at female independence and emancipation from patriarchal structures is itself a Western project.[8]

The hidden assumption in both examples I've provided construes feminism as a "Western" institution that "native" women participate in only at the risk of assimilating Western or colonial norms. There is also, in the examples I've cited, an uncritical privileging of "traditional" customs or pieties as an authentic site of indigenous culture. The net result, of course, is that the initial polarities "Western/modern" versus "indigenous/traditional" and "colonial" versus "native" remain unchanged—only what gets privileged in any given analysis is switched or inverted.

My final example is Samuel Selvon's *Moses Ascending,*[9] in which Selvon provides an acute and rigorous critique of the systemic racism directed against immigrants to London from the Caribbean, the subcontinent, and African countries. Narrated by an immigrant from Trinidad who has internalized some of this racism, the work nevertheless clearly shows the dominant culture's systemic racism via the accounts of discrimination in housing policies against blacks and other people of color: "And I record with pride that I wasn't one of them prejudiced landlords what put no kolors on their notices" (4); via accounts of police brutality against and constant surveillance of blacks (29–30; 36; 91; 94–97); via the heavily ironized account of the ungodly hours at which blacks are forced to work: "The alarms of all black people in Brit'n are timed to ring before the rest of the population. It is their destiny to be up and about at the crack o' dawn" (5–9).

However, Selvon's book is also one in which women are represented entirely in terms of their sexuality. The primary weapon, for instance, that the only fully developed woman character, Brenda, wields is her sexual power over men. And in a work that is at best ambiguous in its account of Black Power, we nevertheless have Moses present his own grotesque variation on Black is Beautiful in a passage where he celebrates black women's anatomy—a passage that needs to be quoted extensively for a reader to feel the impact of its virulent sexism:

> Blessed be the coming of this new generation of Black Britons, and blessed be I that I still alive and well to witness their coming of age from piccaninny to black beauty. It is a sight for sore eyes to see them flounce and bounce about the city, even if they capsize on their platforms. . . . Be it bevy or crocodile, Women's Lib or Women's Tit, they are on the march, sweeping through the streets. . . . There are no women in the world who could shake their backsides like a black woman. God might give white girls nice legs and high bobbies, but when it comes to backsides, our females are in a class by themselves. It may be that they inherit that proud and defiant part of the anatomy from toting and balancing loads on their heads from the days of slavery . . . thus a black backside merely pedestrianizing. And it is not only up and down, but sideways, and gyrating in circles, and quivering and shivering in all manner of movement. It is not their coming to look at, but their going. It is after they pass you and you turn your head and look that you realize what a great experience you are experiencing. (15)

Now, my students felt that through his "flawed" narrator, one who has internalized a number of Western representations about "Third" world cultures and peoples, Selvon is actually arguing for a crucial distance between his views and his narrator's; hence, Selvon is not guilty of sexism, Moses is. My insistent point, however, was that while Moses' internalized racism is countered elsewhere, in moments when he becomes self-aware and through the judgments of other characters, gender constructions of the sort I've just pointed out are not subjected to a similar irony or counterrepresentation. For this lack we should hold Selvon accountable. But this conclusion my students resisted, arguing, "How can he be so 'politically correct' about racist oppression and not about representations of gender?" This question is, of course, based on the peculiar misconception that knowledge of, and alertness to, one kind of oppression automatically guarantees sensitivity to other varieties of oppression. By this logic, then, just as

sensitivity to racism extends to sensitivity to sexism, sensitivity to
sexism embraces sensitivity to racism. Neither claim, as we all
know, is quite accurate or even provable.[10]

Furthermore, after working with my students extensively in
class, in groups outside class, and individually, I can confidently
assert that most of them would have savaged a white male writer
for the least evidence of sexism or demeaning constructions of
gender. But when it came to Selvon, a writer from the "Third"
world, they were silent and he was exempt from critique. Their
silence, I believe, was in part a function of seeing Selvon's sexism
as somehow part and parcel of his cultural background and was
thus declared off limits. Such caution and circumspection is to be
valued (and I let them know this), but not to make an issue like
this at least a matter for discussion and argument can easily lead to
an unexamined reinscription of a polarity that sets up "us" (i.e.,
from the "First" world) against "them" (i.e., from the "Third"
world).

I began this essay by invoking the difficulties that attend any
attempt to teach and analyze "Third" world texts in a "First" world
context or that may attend any attempt to cross cultural boundaries. I should emphasize, however, that while such analyses are
difficult, they are not impossible to accomplish. But, in order to
attempt them with any sort of theoretical and pedagogical rigor
and to make them work, institutions (in our case, academic institutions) will need to rethink, even reimagine, curriculum and
boundaries that presently constitute, and, thus, demarcate
disciplines, determining, then, how and where those boundaries
can be crossed.

On the matter of curriculum, it's worth remarking that though
in recent years several English departments across the U.S. have
hired people to teach courses on "Third" world literatures, these
courses are, most often, simply tacked on to an already existing
curriculum with its own agendas with which "Third" world literature courses may be at odds. Through the examples I've given, I
hope I've shown why one cannot simply add such courses and
then proceed with business as usual, since, at the very least, these
literatures often demand contexts for and positions vis-à-vis the
power the "First" world wields materially and discursively over the
"Third." English departments, by adding such courses without
reexamining the ideological agendas of their curriculum, tend to
duplicate such power relations. For instance, though listed for the
English department, my course draws only one-third of its students from the English majors. I suspect this happens because,

dealing as it does with materials originating outside of British and U.S. mainstream culture, it is not seen as integral to what students are used to thinking of as the proper study of "English literature." More important, a great deal of what gets done in my class is often not repeated and/or reaffirmed in either the pedagogical practices or interests of my colleagues in general. As a result, little of what my students and I pursue in class enters into the interests and conversations of the larger institutional and disciplinary practices, limiting, then, any real impact of courses like mine within the institution. Yet to avoid some of the pitfalls I have pointed out in my examples, more than the isolated or occasional intervention is called for. Without larger structural changes, I would argue, "Third" world texts cannot be adequately or appropriately studied in a "First" world context: boundaries, for the most part, will not get crossed.

Notes

This essay first appeared in *Women's Studies Quarterly* 18, nos. 3/4 (Winter 1990).

1. This is a somewhat revised version of a paper written originally for a panel on postcolonial issues, which was part of the 1989 MLA forum, "Access to the Academy: Crossing Boundaries," sponsored by the Commission on the Status of Women in the Profession and the Gay and Lesbian Caucus for the Modern Languages.

2. Since this paper was written, Sara Suleri's impressive reading of *The Satanic Verses* has been brought to my attention. In her reading, Rushdie's construction of gender is central to an understanding of his project. See her "Contraband Histories: Salman Rushdie and the Embodiment of Blasphemy," *The Yale Review* 79, no. 4 (1989).

3. Although the following discussion arose from and focuses specifically on student responses generated in my class, the implications of those responses are not restricted to my class alone. Indeed, in various conversations with people from both within and outside the academy, I have been faced with similar responses and/or questions.

4. The essays I passed out included the following: Edward W. Said, "Intellectuals in the Post-Colonial World," *Salmagundi*, nos. 70/71 (Spring/Summer 1986); Fredric Jameson, "Third World Literatures in the Era of Multinational Capitalism," *Social Text* 15 (Fall 1986); Aijaz Ahmad, "Jameson's Rhetoric of Otherness and the 'National Allegory'," *Social Text* 17 (Fall 1987); Benita Parry, "Problems in Current Theories of Colonial Discourse," *Oxford Literary Review* 9, nos. 1/2 (1987); Arun P. Mukherjee, "The Vocabulary of the 'Universal': Cultural Imperialism and Western Literary Criticism," *World Literature Written in English* 26 (1986).

5. *Unwinding Threads: Writing by Women in Africa*, ed. Charlotte H. Bruner (London: Heinemann, 1983). Quotations from "My Mother" are taken from this anthology and page numbers will be cited parenthetically in the text. This procedure will be followed for my quotations from Assia Djebar's *Les Impatients*, also included in *Unwinding Threads*.

6. The full text of Fadhma Amrouche's autobiography, *My Life Story: The Autobiography of a Berber Woman*, is now available in Dorothy Blair's translation for The Women's Press (London, 1988). I should also point out that though my course was restricted to Anglo-

phone literatures of the "Third" world, I smuggled in a few English translations of Francophone works by women writers, and Fadhma's and Assia Djebar's *Les Impatients* are both examples of these.

7. The more detailed account in the complete text of Fadhma's autobiography bears this out. Fadhma, for instance, is most happy when she's at the school, set up by French colonists, getting an education. But she has no illusions about their motives or even the effects of French policies, even though she does revere individuals like Mme. Malaval. See especially the early segments of the first chapter, "The Road to School."

8. To counter this assumption, one need only look at some of the essays in KumKum Sangari and Sudesh Vaid, eds., *Recasting Women: Essays in Colonial History* (New Delhi: Kali for Women, 1989) to come up with examples of women struggling for female independence and emancipation in colonial India. Also, one need only pause and reflect on the example of Fadhma and her mother to realize that such an assumption is, at best, problematic.

9. Samuel Selvon, *Moses Ascending* (London: Heinemann, 1975). Quotations are taken from this edition and page numbers will be cited parenthetically in the text.

10. For examples and analyses of how alertness to sexist remarks and representations do not guarantee alertness to racism and imperialism, see especially Bell Hooks, *Ain't I a Woman: Black Women and Feminism* (Boston: South End Press, 1981) and *Feminist Theory: From Margin to Center* (Boston: South End Press, 1984); Marnia Lazreg, "Feminism and Difference: The Perils of Writing as a Woman on Women in Algeria," *Feminist Studies* 14, no. 1 (Spring 1988); and Chandra Talpade Mohanty, "Under Western Eyes: Feminist Scholarship and Colonial Discourses," *Boundary 2* 12/13 (Spring/Fall 1984).

Toward a Political Economy of Race and Gender

Robyn Wiegman
Syracuse University

I

IN the contemporary academy, as in U.S. culture more generally, race and gender have emerged in recent decades as
important (and contested) categories for refashioning the ground
on which democracy's claim of universal human equivalency has
been made. For feminist theory, whose historical commitment to
reading the economy of gender has outweighed its investment in
an analysis of race, the relation between these categories and the
impossibility of their continued theoretical segregation now constitutes a defining, even if deeply problematized, characteristic of
recent thought. If events at the 1990 National Women's Studies
Association Convention, in which the women of color coalition
withdrew to form its own organization,[1] are any indication, feminism itself faces both a political and theoretical crisis: how to
rethink its relation to issues of race and racism in its broader move
to understand social power in all of its complexity.

Central to this project is not only an unveiling of the ideological
production of "race" and "gender" as signifiers for visually "different" bodies but also an interrogation into the ways race and
gender are routinely collapsed, as the frequency of the phrase
"blacks and women" demonstrates. In a sense, the economy of
visibility that structures popular discourses, where the representational inclusion of "blacks and women" passes as political power
and marks a post-60s culture of balanced bookkeeping, haunts
feminist theory as well. By sliding from the categories of race and
gender as discourses of disempowerment to the identity positions
of "blacks and women," feminist theory often reiterates the
cultural imperative of contemporary U.S. production. That is, it
reads all formulations of cultural "difference" as equivalences
(race = gender, blacks = women) and hence produces a false sym-

47

metry between, as well as within, these categories.[2] Such false symmetries settle rather comfortably within the binarities of domination, enabling a string of seeming specificities—blacks, women, gays and lesbians, etc.—to function as variously exchangeable *others* to a still undisclosed centrality of cultural power. My concern with these equivalences, with the notion that the discrepancies of power in U.S. culture can be "righted" by balancing our system of accounting by adding and exchanging difference, emerges precisely from the confederacy of terms marking this political position. The economy hoped for remains one deeply rooted in the logic of sameness, inextricably bound to a unified, monolithic, and inadequately examined formulation of cultural power.

To some extent, critical debates within "American" literary studies (the term itself demonstrating the unification of a hemisphere into the geopolitics of U.S. domination) replay the fascination with difference as bodies of identity articulated above. In this case, the inclusion of "women's literature" and "African-American literature," for instance, signals a contemporary accounting for specific historical exclusions by refiguring the canon through categories of identity. While many scholars who engage in these canonical debates recognize that inclusion often equals entrance into the master's house, there is increasing resistance to such notions of political transformation and profound skepticism toward strategies that invert or reinscribe the dimensions of domination. Such a reinscription equates a political economy of race and gender with a disparagingly fetishized notion of representation. For here, mere incorporation—the circulation of texts, bodies, and images—becomes coterminous with the dissolution of the structural relations of both sexism and racism. To mark attention to the heterogeneity of social power as the presence of an eccentric body (whether that body be literal, as in departmental hiring practices or textual, as in canonical reassessments) is to collapse difference and identity by relying on the economy of visibility once again. And it is this economy, an economy in which the body is the primary—if not only—locus for thinking beyond sameness, that continues to underwrite race and gender in U.S. culture today.

To draw attention to the way visibility functions is not to dismiss canonical interventions or hiring practices that insist on transforming the academy from its historical locus as bastion of white masculine privilege. But it is to insist that the logic of visibility is a bookkeeping move that can only conceive of differences in unitary and deceptively equivalent formulations: certain bodies are raced, others are gendered, and some are differently sexed. In this way, difference emerges as a highly compromised term, flattened to a horizontal scale and hence incapable of being thought with greater complexity. Indeed, it is the verticality of difference—its intrinsically compounded constitution, its range across, within, and beyond categories of identity—that can subvert the economy of visibility by capturing even the domain of seeming sameness (whiteness, masculinity, and heterosexuality, for instance) as complicated and multiple positionalities themselves. Such a move away from the visible challenges feminist theory by forcing not only an interrogation into its most secure formulation, the category of woman, but into its equally assumed and knowable category, the masculine, as well. For it is here that the vertical configuration would reveal its most troubling conclusion: that for a feminism interested in reading the multiplicity of cultural power and domination, sexual difference cannot be understood as a mere binary of relations nor can it serve as the anchor for all feminist interpretations of the social. To do so inadequately grounds feminism in a theoretical paradigm that takes sexual difference as the primary, even originary, structure for all social differentiation, thereby disabling the ability to read beyond the singular axis of gender.[3]

The inadequacy of this reliance on sexual difference reveals itself most strongly in considering the way race has been theorized, not simply in the isolated present but more significantly in the relationship between the contemporary era and the first decades of feminism's articulation in U.S. culture. In this sense, the pressure today to create a political economy of race and gender that does not merely reinscribe already discernible modes of domination signals a reemergence of interest in these complexities for mainstream feminism and not, as our various historical blindnesses often lead us to believe, a wholly new invention. The very location of feminism's early appearance within the abolitionist struggle as well as contemporary feminism's fashioning of itself in terms of civil rights activism demonstrates the extent to which feminism itself has been and continues to be deeply intertwined with "race" in this country.[4] But where its strength has come from its ability to shape itself along political and discursive lines of black liberation struggle, it is also true that feminism's consistent failure is to negotiate the significance of race within its own epistemological and political categories. Because of this, I want to juxtapose in this essay what appear at the outset as very unlikely

texts—Harriet Beecher Stowe's *Uncle Tom's Cabin* with several essays by Teresa de Lauretis—in order to explore the various ways
that the critical impasses of nineteenth-century feminism have
reconfigured themselves in late twentieth-century feminist
thought.

While the differences between these feminist thinkers are historically and politically immense, it is significant that each conceives of the problem of multiple differences through a politics of
identification. For Stowe, the white woman's ability to sympathize
with the slave, wrought through sentimental narration's reliance
on the feminine as nurturing mother, forges a paradigmatic analogy between gender and race, which in turn enables gender to
function as the site from which all power inequities can be charted
and overcome. For de Lauretis, differences among women (which
constitutes her primary interest) can be negotiated through the
concept of entrustment whereby identification through a symbolic
mother marks the debt held between women and outweighs the
varieties of differences among them. In the process, gender
(being woman) emerges for de Lauretis as the founding distinction for a feminist practice and the question, Which production of
gender? is displaced by the prioritizing of an often undifferentiated multiplicity within women.

In marking multiplicity in this way—as within "women" and not
across the very categories of gender—feminism can still be articulated within its foundational logic of gender, a logic that does not
threaten the patriarchal opposition of masculine/feminine precisely by maintaining the masculine as the unified structure
against which all feminist practice is wed. This logic asserts itself
in Stowe as well, even as her recognition of the racial differences
between free and enslaved men potentially fractures the patriarchal binary of gender. But by equating the African(-Amer-
ican) male with the feminine, as in Stowe's much-discussed
"mothering" of Uncle Tom, her strategy reasserts patriarchy's
logic: the masculine retains its position as the locus of unequivocal
empowerment while the feminine multiplies itself as the inclusive
site of all difference and disempowerment.[5] In de Lauretis's work,
as in much contemporary feminist thought, it is the eradication of
the very question of differences among men that reaffirms the
sanctity of a monolithic masculine and hence underwrites the
primacy of gender as differences within the feminine. In this way,
part of the critical problem taken up and displaced by Stowe and
other nineteenth-century feminist writers—the problem of a
disempowered masculine position and its relationship to the ter-

rain of gender—gets recast in much contemporary feminist theory as no problem at all.[6]

In linking Stowe's strategy to problems at the center of contemporary feminism, I am marking out a topos of similarity that clearly cannot be reduced to identicality. And yet I think that it is important to read the paradigmatic effects of her reading of nineteenth-century configurations of race and gender as part of the historical narrative of feminism to which we are heir, a historical narrative in which the struggle to theorize a feminism irreducible to the binary figures of gender marks the critical difficulty we too share. For this reason, more than the retrieval of a nineteenth-century archive, I want to turn first to Stowe and then to de Lauretis in order to ask: What are the processes of identification that underwrite the transmutation of race into gender? How does a politics of identification function to secure feminist understandings of political bonds in both the nineteenth and late twentieth centuries? And what is the relationship between Stowe's inscription of "race" as contained by the primacy of sexual difference and postmodern understandings of subjectivity, where the risk to explode the boundaries of feminism—of the primacy of sexual difference—is the most necessary and seemingly impossible risk of all?

II

It is perhaps unclear to some why a book that has become so associated with racist stereotypes of African(-Americans)—Sambo, Uncle Tom, and Topsy serving as icons of white supremacist thinking for more than a century—is being upheld here as a major text of nineteenth-century feminist thought. My purpose is certainly not to defend or dismiss the racism of Stowe's novel. But the current political move in U.S. culture to forge a clear separation between nineteenth-century formations of race and racism and those of our own era disturbingly rejuvenates white supremacist logic by cloaking the impact of slavery on the U.S. social, economic, and political systems today. For feminism, any collusion with this dismissal simply replays the historical blindness of the (post-)Reagan years. And yet it is not adequate to chart out the legacy of slavery in order to propose some way of accounting for it either historically or politically—as though the sum of a people's enslavement can be remedied by some contemporary arithmetic. To suspend our condemnation of Stowe, and to read her as indeed we will some day be read, moves us away from the law of the ledger, closer perhaps to the contradictions and complexities that make us rush to cite racism elsewhere but here.

For this reason, it becomes important to recognize that Stowe's attempt to fashion an argument against both slavery and patriarchy is one of the few popular moments in the literary landscape of this nation in which a white woman has sought to grapple, however inadequately, with race and racism. As such an exemplary moment, the novel's turn to the rhetoric of an anti-patriarchal domesticity to simultaneously protest slavery and women's oppression stands as an urgent and disturbing portrait of feminism's early relation to abolitionist struggle. By relying on the figure of the slave to function as vehicle for reading the crisis of slavery as both a product and process of patriarchal domination, Stowe uses her culture's most predominant and contested symbol of oppression as the expression of her own disempowerment. But while this linkage between white women and slaves made visible the legal similarities of disenfrachisement in the institutions of marriage and slavery, it nonetheless glossed crucial distinctions between free white women and both male and female slaves. Such an erasure of difference consequently undermined the potential for political alliance by negating the structural asymmetry within such a configuration of race and gender.

In "Bodily Bonds: The Intersecting Rhetorics of Feminism and Abolition," Sanchez-Eppler establishes the cultural context in which Stowe articulated her system of bodily exchange, arguing that "the problems of having, representing, or interpreting a body structure in both feminist and abolition discourses, since . . . for both women and blacks it is their physical difference from the cultural norms of white masculinity that obstructs their claim to personhood" ("Bodily," 29). This physical difference, based on what I have called an economy of visibility, casts personhood or social subjectivity as constitutive of the flesh, bound to discourses constructing and governing the body. In such a relationship, the binary structures of race (as white/black) and gender (as male/female) are the necessary preconditions for the visible's authority to confer subjectivity—a precondition whose expectation is so overdetermined in the nineteenth century and our own that liminal figures, such as the "mulatto" or hermaphrodite, require complex cultural decipherings in order to simultaneously confirm the normativity of the binary and to recontain its potential disruptions.[7] Through these economies of visibility, the surface of the body as a "raced" and "gendered" terrain is made to speak what lies on its interior. Hence, interiority itself is revealed as the essentialized relation between surface and depth. In this sense, social subjectivity—"personhood"—and interiority—a self-recognized "self"—are collapsed into the discourse of the visible: what culture constructs as the domain of personhood is etched on the body, an etching that reveals and is seemingly indistinguishable from the interior self. For white women and male and female slaves, their visible difference is thus transformed into an interior depthlessness, an eternal lack. This is what stands for me as the radical negation produced by domination and becomes for Stowe the primary articulation site for her narrative linkage between the patriarchal effacement of white women as social subjects and the slave system's negation of Africans as human subjects.

In Stowe's rhetorical universe, the essentialism of this relationship—that interiority is mapped by the flesh, that the reading of the flesh reveals interiority—is heightened by the body's encodement in sentimental narration where the invocation of tears functions as the rhetorical goal.[8] Through the invocation of tears, the reader is drawn into an instance of seeming identification in which, as Sanchez-Eppler discusses, the "physicality of the reading experience radically contracts the distance between narrated events and the moment of their reading, as the feelings in the story are made tangibly present in the flesh of the reader" ("Bodily," 36). In encountering the discursive representation of the inhumanity and suffering imposed on the slave, the reader thus feels and responds to that inhumanity at the level of her own flesh. This decidedly "bodily act" ("Bodily," 36), as Sanchez-Eppler calls it, guarantees sentimental fiction's effectiveness, demonstrating that objective distance has been abandoned for a narrative situated, literally and figuratively, on the reader's body. For the sentimental reader (both those who read the book and those who, like Stowe's Mrs. Bird and Mrs. Shelby, "live" in the book as its exemplary readers), the tearful response to slavery makes possible her identification with the slave, an identification that enlarges her subjective "reality" by matching flesh for flesh. Through this process, the reader's tears and the slave's physical bondage coalesce in a rhetorical figuration that enables Stowe to link race and gender.

Most importantly, however, Stowe's strategy seeks to deny that economy of visibility attendant to the African in nineteenth-century discourses which writes blackness as natural depravity and inherent subhumanity[9]—an economy that equates skin with interiority and thus eclipses the possibilities for social subjectivity or "personhood." Instead Stowe posits the slave's humanity by materializing it at the site of the white reader's body, rendering the white woman's social situation as coterminous in affection, if not in specificity, with the enslaved. In this way, the identificatory process underlying Stowe's utilization of sentimental narration simultaneously refuses the racist economy of visibility inaugurated by imperialism and white supremacy, while portraying patriarchal culture as deeply (perhaps even inherently) dependent upon racial hierarchy. But in eschewing the dominant paradigm of visibility, Stowe's sentimental narrativity paradoxically relies on a second mode of the visible—the manifestation of a seemingly defiant interiority marked by tears—to forge a political alliance between the bodies of race and gender. This alliance's activation through the white domestic gaze and its subsequent location at the white female body demonstrates, I would argue, the theoretical double bind of identificatory politics: transcendence is a one-way trajectory, reasserting and recentering the subjective moment of (white female) articulation. For if the white woman's ability to identify across difference is dependent on forging an equivalence between herself and the slave, the incoherences and asymmetries of nineteenth-century power arrangements have now been converted to an economy of the same.

In doing so, as many readers of *Uncle Tom's Cabin* have noted, the discourse of the sentimental feminine—cast overarchingly as a symbolic and literal mother—becomes the primary mediatory mechanism for linking the white female to both the female and male slave, becomes in other words the moment of their inherent "likeness" and hence the means for transforming both patriarchy and white supremacy.[10] This strategy of the mother, carefully disentangled from an essentialist feminine through the figure of the antimaternal Marie St. Clare, nonetheless requires a number of narrative refashionings of the male slave whose positioning vis-à-vis the feminine is more problematic for Stowe than that of the female slave whose maternity, location in domestic space, and (albeit insecure) domestic relations (both in terms of the white family and her own) are more readily established. Uncle Tom, for instance, though visaged as "a large, broad-chested, powerfully-made man of a full glossy black," possesses not only "a face of grave and steady good sense, united with much kindliness and benevolence" but a "full . . . gentle domestic heart" that enables him to be disaffiliated from the masculine.[11] As Leslie Fiedler writes, Uncle Tom is a suffering heroine, masked by blackface and drag. "Indeed," emphasizes Fiedler, "it is hard to miss the equation . . . Woman = Mother = Slave = Black; or simplifying, Woman = Black, Black = Woman. The final formulation represents most accurately perhaps [Stowe's] perception of the relationship between race and gender."[12]

But in such a perception, the equivalences between black and woman suggested by the form of an equation disguise rather than reveal the rhetorical force of Stowe's strategy. For in endowing Uncle Tom with the Christian, domestic virtues of a pacific matriarchal ideology, Stowe works to literally e-race her African figure and to inscribe instead the moral superiority, heavenly religiosity, and spiritual self-sacrifice she associates with a subtly conquering feminine. Uncle Tom must therefore be "released" from the confines of his black masculine body as the preamble to his purification within the feminine. This occurs in the final horrific scene where transcendence of his body is made complete: "the blows fell now only on the outer man, and not, as before, on the heart" (UTC, 391). Separating the body and the heart, the flesh from its interiority, the masculine from the feminine, Stowe's articulation of identification across difference relies on the transformation of the black masculine ("the outer man") into a white feminine ("the heart"), a transformation that not only releases the white feminine from an essentialized bodily origin but also reconfigures it as the primary terms of and for political alliance. In her attempt to anchor the sign of her text's racial body to a seemingly de-essentialized discourse of sexual difference, Stowe's rhetorical strategy elides the complex overlay of race and gender, transmuting these terms into masculine/oppressor on one side and feminine/all difference and oppression on the other.[13]

My point here, in highlighting the text as I do, is that all male bodies cannot be situated within the category of oppressor, for the binary of sexual difference is inadequate as an explanation for multiple power arrangements. Stowe's response to her own insight into the distribution of power within the masculine—to cast nonoppressor male bodies into a category marked by the feminine—represses patriarchy's most violent internal contradiction by reiterating the terms by which that contradiction can most effectively be veiled: sexual difference. This simultaneously recuperates the potential within the sentimental form to reconfigure relations of interiority, identification, and bodily transgressions. By making race speak gender, Stowe enables the white woman's recognition of the slave's interiority to materialize itself on her flesh (in tears) and to transcend that flesh in subjective identification—a process of identification through which the white woman is disturbingly returned to herself. As Sanchez-Eppler writes, "at stake in the feminists' likening of women to slaves is the recognition that personhood can be annihilated and a person owned, absorbed, and un-named . . . [but] the difficulty of preventing moments of identification from becoming acts of appropriation constitutes the essential dilemma of feminist-abolitionist rhetoric" ("Bodily," 31).

The appropriative nature of these identifications is perhaps best revealed in the trajectory that white feminist thought would take in the postwar period, when the analogy between woman and slave no longer operated within the politically charged field of antislavery crusade. Instead, for white feminists who viewed suffrage as a key marker in the struggle for legal equality, the passage of the Fifteenth Amendment granting black men the vote seemed to signal a shift of cultural power that left patriarchy intact. Claiming that "the black man is still, in political point of view, far above the educated white women of the country," Elizabeth Cady Stanton would assert, "it is better to be the slave of an educated white man, than of a degraded, ignorant black one."[14] Here, Stanton significantly redefines the space of cultural disempowerment, marking the black male's degradation but eliding it nonetheless in a rhetorical move that equates enslavement fully with the white feminine—a reading that perpetuates feminism's inability to extract race and gender from the binary relations of patriarchal logic. Noting how Stanton's strategy assumes "that . . . Black men [would gain] the full privileges of male supremacy,"[15] Angela Davis has aptly characterized Stanton's understanding of the structural link between race and gender as "superficial,"[16] a charge that pressures not simply Stanton but the broader cultural discourse of white feminism and its often rigid devotion to reading racial oppression as coterminous with sexual difference.

III

The problem of paradigms at work in nineteenth-century feminist discourse has revealed itself in the closing decades of the twentieth as perhaps the greatest difficulty not only for feminist theory but for the future of feminism itself. As Davis and other contemporary theorists have discussed, the inability to articulate models that can comprehend the multiple, intersecting and con-

tradictory nature of social hierarchies severely circumvents the
possibilities for constructing a collective feminist subject.[17] Along
these lines, Bell Hooks elaborates:

> Feminist analyses of woman's lot tend to focus exclusively on gender
> and do not provide a solid foundation on which to construct feminist
> theory . . . The idea of "common oppression" [is] a false and corrupt
> platform disguising and mystifying the true nature of women's varied
> and complex social reality.[18]

By asserting the primacy of sexual difference—even as that assertion has functioned as the epistemological center of feminist
thought—feminist theory often continues to miscomprehend the
plurality inherent in questions of race and sexual difference,
either reducing them to one large difference that can be treated,
in all instances, the same or displacing them altogether. Such
simplifications not only disregard the shifting and historically
specific terrain of cultural oppressions, but they also forfeit political and thereotical alliances necessary to a broadly defined and
radically challenging feminist praxis.

In this sense, Stowe's desire to incorporate multiple hierarchies
of oppression and exploitation under the sign of feminism bears
striking resemblance to contemporary feminism's most compelling and troubling crisis. Teresa de Lauretis, whose work has been
vital to ongoing feminist debates, locates this crisis in the burgeon-
ing need to distinguish between "Woman," the monolithic metaphysical category, and "women," the historical, material subjects
constituted not simply in terms of gender but across a range of
subjectivities: race, class, sexuality, ethnicity, nationality, age, etc.[19]
The very ontological and epistemological ground feminism has
staked out around the concept and identity politics of woman are
potentially dissolving in the face of a recognition of subjectivity's
multiple and heterogeneous function. Where Stowe held tight to
humanist discourse and a world view unifiedly defined by gender,
contemporary feminism faces the difficult but crucial task of for-
feiting gender as the solitary category for understanding
"women." Indeed, as Trinh T. Minh-ha seems to suggest in
Woman, Native, Other, the need to articulate subjectivity as multiple
and intersecting—to maintain woman not as superior to but as
interwoven with the racial, ethnic, and cultural signs of native and
other—is a strategy that may postdate feminism itself.[20] This
postdating of the white social bond underwriting feminism in the
U.S. is not the recuperative negation of feminist struggle manifest

in contemporary popular culture's assertion of a "postfeminism" but rather the movement through and beyond the binary of sexual difference that has mapped, in quite opposing but often symmetrical ways, the ideologies of both patriarchy and feminism.

It is this symmetricality, this primacy of sexual difference, that simultaneously makes possible and limits the terms of resistance at work in *Uncle Tom's Cabin* and other texts forging similar strategies—whether in Stowe's century or in our own. Even de Lauretis, for instance, in her call for heterogeneity, wants to define differences *among* women as differences *within* women. As de Lauretis argues:

> For if it is the case that the female subject is en-gendered across multiple representations of class, race, language, and social relations, it is also the case . . . that gender is a common denominator: the female subject is always constructed and defined in gender, starting from gender . . . these differences not only constitute each woman's consciousness and subjective limits but all together define *the female subject of feminism* in its inherent specificity, its inherent and at least for now irreconcilable contradiction.[21]

In choosing to assert the radical multiplicity of *women* and in reading the contradiction of feminism as marked by the competing positions of "female" and "class, race, language, and social relations," de Lauretis deftly articulates a claim to the primacy of gender while embracing feminism's exclusions as contradiction. Such a paradoxical formulation produces a feminism that continues to include—even if "irreconcilably"—difference under the sign "women," thus forging a collective, though internally fragmented, feminist subject that is based nonetheless on gender.

In many ways, the move de Lauretis makes here echoes that of Luce Irigaray and demonstrates an affinity between the relations of sameness and difference in the work of each. Irigaray's claim that "whatever inequalities may exist among women, they all undergo . . . the same oppression, the same exploitation of their body, the same denial of desire"[22] marks women's differences as containable within the category of gender, not as excess to or contradicted by it. Such a move arises from an emphasis by both theorists on the importance of bringing "the difference between the sexes . . . back into play" (*This Sex*, 146) and hence of understanding the extent to which the multiplicity within women has been reduced, like the feminine itself, to the "indifference" of sexual difference. This indifference is evinced most pointedly by the feminine's definitional relation (often referred to as the position of negativity and lack) to the masculine, a relation in which the feminine has no significatory value except in its ability to function as the ground for masculine representation. Given this asymmetry within sexual difference—what Irigaray calls its economy of the same—the very notion of equality between masculine and feminine must be eschewed, for "women merely 'equal' to men would be 'like them,' therefore not women" (*This Sex,* 166). To subvert woman's equivalence to man makes possible a new and wholly other economy of difference, one in which woman emerges as infinitely multiple in herself, no longer bound to the unitary (and hence indifferent) economy set forth by the masculine.

Such a release from the sociosymbolic structure of the masculine leads de Lauretis toward positing sexual *difference* as the "essential difference of feminist theory itself."[23] Continuing, she argues:

> The question, for the feminist philosopher, is how to rethink sexual difference within a dual conceptualization of being . . . in which both being-woman and being-man would be primary, originary forms. This is a question that subverts the categories of Western thought which, precisely, elide sexual difference as primary—as "being there from the beginning" in both woman and man—and relegate it to the status of a secondary difference contained in the gender marking of the being-woman. ("Essence," 17)

What is compelling here is de Lauretis's desire to detach the articulation of the masculine from the bodies of women, to make sexual difference signify as such and hence to unravel the epistemological foundations of gender. But it is precisely the postulation of sexual difference as always and unitarily the privilege of the masculine—and a masculine that seems to know only its difference from the feminine—that disturbs me, for it not only equates the mark of gender with "being-woman," but discounts the possibility that other structures of differentiation may be as essential as sexual difference to feminist theory as well. More pointedly, the various processes through which the masculine represents itself as a cohesive structure (including but not limited to gender) are reified by the seductive myth of masculine sameness on which the articulation of women's difference—and differences from one another—here dwell.

The consequences of de Lauretis's theoretical formulation of the risk of essentialism emerge most fully in the later stages of her essay when she turns to the work of the Milan's Women's Bookstore as a paradigmatic instance of the possibilities for recognizing and working through differences within women. Using the Bookstore's *Non credere di avere dei diritti: la generazione della libertà femminile nell'idea e nelle vicende di un gruppo di donne*[24] as a model for contemporary feminist praxis, de Lauretis explores the practice of "entrustment"—and the central term of its mediation, the symbolic mother—as the means for feminist organization. Specifically, entrustment defines a relationship "in which one woman gives her trust or entrusts herself symbolically to another woman, who thus becomes her guide, mentor, or point of reference" ("Essence," 22). In doing so, a bond is formed "not in spite of, but rather because and in full recognition of the disparity that may exist between them in class or social position, age, level of education, professional status, income, etc." ("Essence," 22). By recognizing these disparities, entrustment enables women to articulate, according to de Lauretis, "a frame of reference no longer patriarchal or male-designed . . . the frame of . . . a female genealogy or a female symbolic" ("Essence," 23). It is this symbolic that emerges in the Bookstore's processes of collective feminist practice as the figuration of the symbolic mother, "a theoretical concept . . . that sustains or recognizes the gendered and embodied nature of women's thought, knowledge, experience, subjectivity, and desire—their 'originary difference'" ("Essence," 25). The symbolic mother thus comes to stand for "the exchange between women across generations and the sharing of knowledge and desire across differences" ("Essence," 25). As a revision of the patriarchally produced mother, the symbol mother of entrustment encodes "the symbolic *debt* each woman has toward other women" ("Essence," 25, emphasis mine).

The debt model invoked here makes the exchange between women an extremely loaded affair, since it is precisely the theoretical impossibility of ever fully repaying the debt to the mother that may ultimately function as the means for securing women's bonds to one another. While this is indeed a shift from an earlier feminist familial model of sisterhood that has routinely been under attack in the past decade, the articulation of the daughter's debt maintains the emphasis on a family metaphor as the defining logic for feminist practice. For me, identification with the mother recalls, however inappropriately or obliquely, the fusion of all differences through the figure of the mother in Stowe's sentimental narrative, marking the feminine as the eternally inclusive site for differences while maintaining a paradigm of cultural power wed to gender. In such a case, the ways in which a mother-centered paradigm escapes the framework of patriarchal ideology remains difficult to imagine indeed.

But the most problematical moment to confront in de Lauretis's description of *Non credere*'s model for female social bonds comes at the end of the essay. Here, she notes that the process of entrustment "makes little space for differences and divisions between—and within—women," in particular race and color which, in the Italian context, she says, "have not been at issue" ("Essence," 31). But where race and color may be indexed as not at issue for Italian feminism, its centrality as a crucial question in U.S. feminism is currently a predominant locus around which debates on the essentialism of our understanding of sexual difference have been waged.[25] By pointing out the inapplicability of this issue for Italian feminism, de Lauretis reveals the fissure in her own theoretical perspective which, while drawing attention to how race may or may not be figured, continues to assert "the notion of essential and originary difference" as a "basic feminist assumption" not only in Italy but "here as well" ("Essence," 32). And it is precisely this basic assumption, de Lauretis contends, that acts as the precondition for any analysis of differences between women, for

without this basic feminist assumption [of originary difference]—basic, that is, to feminism as historically constituted at the present moment—the still necessary articulation of all other differences between and within women must remain framed in male-dominant and heterosexist ideologies of liberal pluralism, conservative humanism, or, goddess forgive, religious fundamentalism. ("Essence," 32)

In other words, only in an analysis thus grounded can "all other differences" emerge from the cover of patriarchal logic. Gender speaks race—even in its seeming absence—here as well.

The significance of the erasure of race cannot be underestimated, for while the sociosymbolic articulation of bonds among women makes possible a transcendence of male-dominated ideologies through the figure of the symbolic mother, the transportation of this politics of identification to the cultural-historical context of the U.S. can only work to further deny the violent materiality of "race" as a determinant of power relations among women. Given the painful history of maternity as a simultaneous marker of the African-American woman's enforced concubinage to both race and gender structures, any hope for a transmutation of patriarchal logic through a symbolic mother brings into question the historical and political relationship between European-American and African-American women—and marks as well the political difficulties raised by readings of the symbolic that seem to discount the landscape of a historical "real." More disturbing, perhaps, is the implicit understanding of race as coterminous with "color" and hence with nonwhite bodies—a theoretical elision through which race can emerge as not "at issue" even as the racial homogeneity of the Italian context may be said to enable the politics of identification mobilized by the symbolic mother. While we may understand the racial context of Italy as significantly different from the U.S., it is precisely that difference which can account for the possibilities of identification based on an originary difference of gender. In the context of U.S. feminist theorizing, then, the indifference to race accorded the European body may well serve as the enabling condition for speaking race within a paradigm of sexual difference once again.

In the process of such speaking, "being-woman" shifts from a biological to a sociohistorical articulation, thereby posing "embodied knowledge" as the precondition for feminist practice. This practice, wed to a code of entrustment and pursued under the aegis of a symbolic mother, is clearly a more complex structure of identificatory politics than that configured by Stowe, and yet the traces of idealism in each of these female-centered and feminine-bonded paradigms are rather arresting in their similarities. In the historically constituted present of feminism in the U.S., a vision of the political that turns us to the originary difference of gender functions more as a return than a transcendence: a return to a political figuration that cannot relinquish a grid of overarching and monolithic male domination, that conceptualizes the terrain of inequality as transgressible through a political process of identification—whether that identification comes from citing a symbolic mother to replace the law of the father, or by guaranteeing the negotiation of differences through the postulation of an originary and essential sexual difference. Indeed, as my discussion has suggested, it is the very seductiveness of identification—of a "you" that can be entrusted as the figuration of "me"—that makes difficult feminism's articulation of its own complex demands for multiplicity and heterogeneity.

IV

In working our way out of the critical impasse established by the binary logics of race and gender, feminist theory may be compelled to relinquish its epistemological tie to sexual difference. This is not a conclusion wrought solely through the context of recent postmodern theorizing, but is rather an interested assessment of the history of feminist thought in the United States. We have everywhere around us and even at the center of our own theoretical paradigms a refusal to read race and gender in ways that demonstrate their complicated, multiple, and inherently embedded relation. By eliding the racial body with the nonwhite and reiterating gender as woman, we cannot begin to understand, let alone create, the kinds of political alliances on which social transformation depends. Most important, perhaps, is the necessity of recognizing how the postulation of political solidarity through even a contradictory and fragmenting structure of gender identification does not enable us to read relations of hierarchy outside of or apart from the domain of the feminine. This, in turn, makes it difficult to render the relationship between the Euro-American woman and the African(-American) male, for instance, with any kind of theoretical complexity. In this sense, the understanding of the force of feminist investigations of race and gender as matters of differences within women leaves intact various structures of (neo)colonial and white supremacist control and falsely inscribes patriarchy as the overarching form of cultural domination.

The counter to this asymmetrical reading of cultural relations necessitates an expansion of feminist theory's gaze to include questions not only of masculine differences but also of disparities that traverse the sacrosanct division of gender, those in which women maintain power over various groups of men. In beginning to make sense out of the way that subjectivity is never fully understandable within a binary grid of oppressor/oppressed, feminist theory encounters a terrain where "difference" can no longer be figured on a horizontal grid. Instead, "difference" emerges as internal to categorical designations, the subversion from within, the very condition that makes difficult any feminist assertion of the broadly configured "Woman" or even "women." As I hope I have made clear, any coherent notion of "Woman" is so thoroughly saturated by racial marking that inculcations of a framework of "Woman/women" become quite inadequate as the foundation for a feminist politics that seeks to escape the historical privilege of its white and Western formulations. To take seriously our desire for this escape entails the pursuit of an increasingly more complicated understanding of subjectivity and social formation, one importantly equipped with the potential for political alliances across the patriarchal abyss of gender.

Notes

I am particularly grateful to Linda Alcoff, Diane Elam, and Ingeborg Majer O'Sickey for reading and discussing previous versions of this essay with me.

1. The June 1990 conference in Akron, Ohio erupted over a dispute within the NWSA concerning the termination of an African-American staffperson, culminating in the resignation of members of the Women of Color Caucus from the organization and the subsequent establishment of the National Womanist/Feminist Woman of Color Association (its first meeting was held May 31–June 2, 1991 in Chicago). Ex-members of the caucus discuss the controversy and their actions in "Speaking for Ourselves," *The Women's Review of Books* 8 (February 1991): 27–30. But as Chela Sandoval discusses in "Feminism and Racism: A Report on the 1981 National Women's Studies Association Conference," in Gloria Anzaldúa, ed., *Making Face, Making Soul Haciendo Caras: Creative and Critical Perspectives by Women of Color* (San Francisco: Aunt Lute Press, 1990), 55–71, the crisis of racism within the organization has a history.

2. Black feminist criticism in particular has been important in forging a critique of feminist theory's difficulty in reading the complex terrain of race and gender in U.S. culture. See, for instance, Angela Davis, *Women, Race and Class* (New York: Vintage Books, 1981); Bell Hooks, *Feminist Theory: From Margin to Center* (Boston: South End Press, 1984); Hooks, *Ain't I a Woman: Black Women and Feminism* (Boston: South End Press, 1981); Gloria Hull, Patricia Scott Bell, and Barbara Smith, eds., *All the Women Are White, All the Blacks Are Men, But Some of Us Are Brave: Black Women's Studies* (Old Westbury, N.Y.: Feminist Press, 1982); Deborah K. King, "Multiple Jeopardy, Multiple Consciousness: The Context of a Black Feminist Ideology," in Micheline R. Malson, Jean F. O'Barr, Sarah Westphal-Wihl, and Mary Wyer, eds., *Feminist Theory in Practice and Process* (Chicago: University of Chicago Press, 1989), 75–106; Valerie Smith, "Black Feminist Theory and the Representation of the 'Other'," in Cheryl Wall, ed., *Changing Our Own Words: Essays on Criticism, Theory, and Writing by Black Women* (New Brunswick, N.J.: Rutgers University Press, 1989), 38–57; and Michele Wallace, "Variations on Negation and the Heresy of Black Feminist Creativity," *Invisibility Blues: From Pop to Theory* (London: Verso Books, 1990).

3. A further consequence of the tie to gender as primary or originary can be seen in Gerda Lerner's *The Creation of Patriarchy* (New York: Oxford University Press, 1986). She argues not only that "the oppression of women antedates slavery and makes it possible" (77) but that "by subordinating women of their own group and later captive women, men learned the symbolic power of sexual control over men and elaborated the symbolic language in which to express dominance" (80). While we may recognize the ability of a discourse of sexual difference to articulate relations that seem, at their most surface level, to exclude women (class and race differences among men, for instance), the linear historical narrative of an originary cultural difference of gender onto which all other systems

have been mapped may obscure rather than illuminate the complex overlay of patriarchy, capitalism, and white supremacy.

4. For a rather positive reading of the feminist-abolitionist connection, see Blanche Glassman Hersh, *The Slavery of Sex: Feminist-Abolitionists in America* (Urbana: University of Illinois Press, 1978); Ellen DuBois, "Women's Rights and Abolition: The Nature of the Connection," in Lewis Perry and Michael Fellman, eds., *Antislavery Reconsidered: New Perspectives on the Abolitionists* (Baton Rouge: University of Louisiana Press, 1979); and DuBois, *Feminism and Suffrage: The Emergence of an Independent Women's Movement in America, 1848–1869* (Ithaca: Cornell University Press, 1978). An important critique of the fusion of feminism and abolitionism is Karen Sanchez-Eppler's "Bodily Bonds: The Intersecting Rhetorics of Feminism and Abolition," *Representations* 24 (Fall 1988); hereafter, "Bodily," cited in the text. For an argument against locating the origins of U.S. feminism in the abolitionist movement, see Barbara J. Berg, *The Remembered Gate: Origins of American Feminism: The Woman and the City, 1800–1860* (New York: Oxford University Press, 1978).

5. For other discussions of the relationship between slavery and patriarchal organization in Stowe, see Elizabeth Ammons, "Heroines in *Uncle Tom's Cabin*," *American Literature* 49 (May 1977); Ammons, "Stowe's Dream of the Mother-Savior: *Uncle Tom's Cabin* and American Women Writers before the 1920s," in Eric Sundquist, ed., *New Essays on "Uncle Tom's Cabin"* (Cambridge: Cambridge University Press, 1986); Dorothy Berkson, "Millenial Politics and the Feminine Fiction of Harriet Beecher Stowe," in Elizabeth Ammons, ed., *Critical Essays on Harriet Beecher Stowe* (Boston: Hall, 1980); Gillian Brown, "Getting into the Kitchen with Dinah: Domestic Politics in *Uncle Tom's Cabin*," *American Quarterly* 36 (Fall 1984); Severn Duvall, "*Uncle Tom's Cabin* and the Sinister Side of Patriarchy," in Seymour L. Gross and John Edward Hardy, eds., *Images of the Negro in American Literature* (Chicago: University of Chicago Press, 1966); Mary Kelley, *Private Woman, Public Stage: Literary Domesticity in Nineteenth-Century America* (New York: Oxford University Press, 1984); Lora Romero, "Bio-Political Resistance in Domestic Ideology and *Uncle Tom's Cabin*," *American Literary History* 1 (Winter 1989); Jane Tompkins, *Sensational Designs: The Cultural Work of American Fiction, 1790–1860* (New York: Oxford University Press, 1985); and Jean Fagan Yellin, "Doing It Herself: *Uncle Tom's Cabin* and Woman's Role in the Slavery Crisis," in Sundquist, ed., *New Essays on "Uncle Tom's Cabin."*

6. While the question of multiplicity and heterogeneity has most often been cast in contemporary feminist theory as a question of differences among women, Eve Kosofsky Sedgwick's *Between Men: English Literature and Male Homosocial Desire* (New York: Columbia University Press, 1985) offers a ground-breaking analysis of the relationship between the discourse of sexual difference among men in nineteenth-century Britain. Other work that has been influential in my thinking about the problem of the masculine in feminist theory includes Susan Jeffords, *The Remasculinization of America: Gender and the Vietnam War* (Bloomington: Indiana University Press, 1989); Kobena Mercer and Issac Julien, "Race, Sexual Politics and Black Masculinity: A Dossier," in Rowena Chapman and Jonathan Rutherford, eds., *Male Order: Unwrapping Masculinity* (London: Lawrence & Wishart, 1988); Tom Yingling, "How the Eye Is Caste: Robert Mapplethorpe and the Limits of Controversy," *Discourse* 12, no. 2 (Spring/Summer 1990). In addition, see my "Negotiating AMERICA: Gender, Race, and the Ideology of the Interracial Male Bond," *Cultural Critique* 13 (Fall 1989), and "Melville's Geography of Gender," *American Literary History* 1 (Winter 1989).

7. Judith Butler's *Gender Trouble: Feminism and the Subversion of Identity* (New York: Routledge, 1990) provides an interesting context in which questions of gender/sexual liminality can be made. By reading Foucault's introduction to the journals of a nineteenth-century French hermaphrodite, Herculine Barbin, Butler explores the way in which

"categories of true sex, discrete gender, and specific sexuality have constituted the stable point of reference for a great deal of feminist theory and politics" (128). She goes on to argue that the gendered body

> has no ontological status apart from the various acts which constitute its reality. This also suggests that if that reality is fabricated as an interior essence, that very interiority is an effect and function of a decidedly public and social discourse, the public regulation of fantasy through the surface politics of the body, the gender border control that differentiates inner from outer, and so institutes the "integrity" of the subject. (136)

This reading of the relationship between surface politics and interiority is suggestive as well of the way in which the text of "race" is inscribed at the level of the flesh. In the United States, the mulatto figure presents the moment of crisis for the public and social discourse of race as a visible economy. For work that explores the historical production of miscegenation, see John G. Mencke, *Mulattoes and Race Mixture: American Attitudes and Images, 1865– 1918* (Ann Arbor, Mich.: UMI Research Press, 1979) and Judith R. Berzon, *Neither White Nor Black: The Mulatto Character in American Fiction* (New York: New York University Press, 1978). Mary Dearborn's "Miscegenation and the Mulatto, Inheritance and Incest: The Pocahontas Marriage, Part II," in *Pocahontas's Daughters: Gender and Ethnicity in American Culture* (New York: Oxford University Press, 1986) provides an important discussion of American literature in the context of ethnicity, miscegenation, and gender.

    8. For further discussion of the sentimental form, see Leslie Fiedler, *Love and Death in the American Novel* (New York: Stein & Day, 1966); Philip Fisher, *Hard Facts: Setting and Form in the American Novel* (New York: Oxford University Press, 1985); and Tompkins, *Sensational Designs*.

    9. For a more elaborate discussion of the context for Stowe's representational strategies, see Goerge Fredrickson's *The Black Image in the White Mind: The Debate on Afro-American Character and Destiny, 1817–1914* (New York: Harper & Row, 1971); Thomas Gossett, *"Uncle Tom's Cabin" and American Culture* (Dallas: Southern Methodist University Press, 1985); Thomas Graham, "Harriet Beecher Stowe and the Question of Race," *New England Quarterly* 46 (December 1973); Richard Yarborough, "Strategies of Black Characterization in *Uncle Tom's Cabin* and the Early Afro-American Novel," in Sundquist, ed., *New Essays on "Uncle Tom's Cabin"*; and Jean Fagan Yellin, *The Intricate Knot: Black Figures in American Literature, 1776–1863* (New York: New York University Press, 1972).

    10. Key essays that explore Stowe's figuration of the feminine include Ammons, "Heroines" and "The Mother-Savior"; Berkson, "Millennial Politics"; and Yellin, "Doing It Herself." See also Tompkins, *Sensational Designs;* and Ann Douglas, *The Feminization of American Culture* (New York: Avon Books, 1977).

    11. Harriet Beecher Stowe, *Uncle Tom's Cabin* (New York: Bantam Books, 1981), 20, 91; hereafter, *UTC,* cited in the text.

    12. Leslie Fiedler, *What Was Literature? Class Culture and Mass Society* (New York: Touchstone Books, 1982), 172.

    13. By reading Stowe's conflation of race and gender through "the primary distinctions . . . between non-Christians and Christians," Yellin explains that "Stowe assigns intellectual superiority and worldly power to the first group and spiritual superiority and otherworldly power—seen as infinitely more important—to the second. In the process, she conflates race and sex. Her first group consists primarily of white males. Her second group includes essentially white females and all nonwhites" ("Doing It Herself," 101).

    14. Elizabeth Cady Stanton, Susan B. Anthony, and Matilda Joslyn Gage, *History of Women's Suffrage*, 2 vols. (New York: Fowler & Wells, 1881), 1:62.

    15. Davis, *Women, Race and Class*, 75.

    16. Ibid., 71.

17. See n.6.

18. Hooks, *Feminist Theory*, 14, 44.

19. See Teresa de Lauretis, *Alice Doesn't: Feminism, Semiotics, Cinema* (Bloomington: Indiana University Press, 1984), 5–6.

20. Trinh T. Minh-ha, *Woman, Native, Other: Writing Postcoloniality and Feminism* (Bloomington: Indiana University Press, 1989).

21. Teresa de Lauretis, "Feminist Studies/Critical Studies: Issues, Terms, and Contexts," in de Lauretis, ed., *Feminist Studies/Critical Studies* (Bloomington: Indiana University Press, 1986), 14. I think it is important to state at the outset of my engagement with de Lauretis's work how crucial her unraveling of "Woman" and "women" has been to contemporary feminist thought and to my own thinking about the issues taken up in this essay. My subsequent critique of the theoretical elisions that occur when investigations focus only on differences among women, then, is not a dismissal of such work but a way of extending our analysis, imploding the bo(u)nds of sexual difference that have paradoxically made possible some of the most significant feminist scholarship in the past decade. Why this implosion is necessary remains the central focus of my work.

22. Luce Irigaray, *This Sex Which is Not One,* trans. Carolyn Burke and Catherine Porter (Ithaca: Cornell University Press, 1985), 164; hereafter, *This Sex,* cited in the text.

23. Teresa de Lauretis, "The Essence of the Triangle, or, Taking the Risk of Essentialism Seriously: Feminist Theory in Italy, the U.S., and Britain," *differences* 1 (Summer 1989):6; hereafter, "Essence," cited in the text.

24. See the Milan's Women's Bookstore Collective, *Sexual Difference: A Theory of Social-Symbolic Practice,* trans. Patricia Cicogna and Teresa de Lauretis (Bloomington: Indiana University Press, 1990).

25. Diana Fuss catalogues current debates on essentialism in the U.S. in *Essentially Speaking: Feminism, Nature and Difference* (New York: Routledge, 1989). Bell Hooks provides an important review of Fuss's text in "Essentialism and Experience," *American Literary History* 3 (Spring 1991).

The Language of Crisis in Feminist Theory

Carla Kaplan
Yale University

FEMINISM'S "CRISIS OF REPRESENTATION"

> Recently the different meanings of feminism for different
> feminists have manifested themselves as a sort of sclerosis of
> the movement, segments of which have become separated
> from and hardened against each other. . . . there are radical
> feminists, socialist feminists, marxist feminists, lesbian sepa-
> ratists, women of color, and so on.
>
> —Rosalind Delmar

ROSALIND Delmar's vision of a diseased feminism, self-con-
sumed by the "sclerosis" of segmentation internal differences generate, is a more anxious version of the widespread
perception that proliferating feminisms threaten to destroy feminism.[1] The apparent impossibility—in the face of these proliferating, vociferous differences—of representing a single, coherent
feminist ideology, movement, or agenda puts feminism (and feminists) in crisis, calling into question the category "women," in
whose name feminism has traditionally pursued its emancipatory
project.

Delmar argues that the "paradox . . . at the heart of the modern
women's movement" is a coupling of a "categorial appeal to all
women" with exclusionary internal practices, and that this leads to
a "set of *crises*" which make feminism's survival an open question.[2]
"Painful fragmentation among feminists," Donna Haraway
agrees, constitutes "the sources of a *crisis* in political identity."[3]
Linda Alcoff also argues that there is an "identity *crisis* in feminist
theory" caused by the fact that "for many contemporary feminist
theorists, the concept of woman is a problem. . . . Our very self-
definition is grounded in a concept that we must deconstruct and
de-essentialize in all of its aspects."[4] Alcoff wonders if this
dilemma "threatens to wipe out feminism itself . . . how can we
ground a feminist politics that deconstructs the female subject?"

(419). Feminist politics, Judith Butler writes, seems to have "lost the categorial basis of its own normative claims. What constitutes the 'who,' the subject, for whom feminism seeks emancipation? If there is no subject, who is left to emancipate?"[5]

Labeling the current climate of conflict a "crisis of representation," as Delmar does, calls attention, first, to the problem of representing unity within difference, and, second, to the problem of representativeness: in the absence of a shared feminist identity, experience, history, goals, or ideology, who speaks for feminism? If no one (or anyone or everyone) legitimately speaks for feminism, no wonder feminists adopt a language of crisis. But this language of crisis does not so much *represent* the current state of feminism as *construct* it in particular—and particularly disadvantageous—ways. It threatens, in other words, to produce the very phenomenon it claims to deplore.

Both feminism's "crisis of representation" and difficulty in agreeing on agenda were recently dramatized for me in a meeting of the governing body of Yale's Women's Studies program in which a half-facetious notion of holding a benefit concert quickly became a heated debate between two factions: those who wanted to invite Holly Near and Ronnie Gilbert, and those who wanted Madonna instead. Ludicrous as this debate must sound, the question of who best represented feminism divided a feminist group that moments before had seemed unified, coherent, and harmonious into antagonistic and seemingly irreconcilable positions on familiar feminist issues: the politics of sexuality and claiming the label "lesbian," the political status of pleasure and desire, the problem of identity, the value of "political correctness," and so on. The only way to "resolve" the problem seemed to be to drop the idea altogether; after all, we couldn't invite them all, we decided. Once we dropped the idea of the benefit and returned to our more serious (and less impassioned) discussion of how to beguile the university into allowing us replacement faculty, at least, to staff our core courses for the coming year, we regained our cohesion as a group and were able, again, to speak comfortably "as feminists," to refer to ourselves as "we," to define ourselves in terms of shared goals and objectives. We solved our fragmentation, in other words, by avoiding the conflict at hand, failing to resolve it. This inclination to solve conflict by leaving practical problems unresolved is not peculiar to this particular group of women. It is built in to the current deployment of a language of crisis in feminist theory.

I am arguing that the proliferation of feminisms is not a "crisis," but that in a number of ways the *perception* of crisis is one. The language of crisis: 1) makes feminism vulnerable to particularly insidious representation and antifeminist attack; 2) constrains feminist readings of women's writing (and probably of women's history, sexuality, economic, legal, and social situatedness); and 3) obscures the racial politics which have engendered so much of the proliferation of different, and differing, contemporary feminisms.

The proliferation of feminist differences which is so often represented as an uncontrollable occurrence of the last few years is historically one of feminism's most salient features. In fact, feminist historiographers have shown that conflict *between* women has been one of the signal characteristics of American feminism throughout the nineteenth and twentieth centuries. As Nancy Cott puts it, such conflict is inevitable: "there is an element of . . . predictability in any fragmentation that follows a united front of women," Cott writes, "for as much as women have common cause in gender issues, they are differentiated by political and cultural and sexual loyalties, and by racial, class and ethnic identities, which inform their experience of gender itself."[6]

If conflict and difference have so consistently characterized feminism, why is a language of crisis so prevalent? Something more than historical forgetfulness is at stake in the current language of crisis. A strong current of nostalgia flows beneath the expression of crisis and its vision of feminism as hopelessly fragmented. Nostalgia for an imagined utopian moment of female solidarity and mutual support. For conflict-free consolidations of women united for social and personal transformation. Nostalgia for a seamless sisterhood. This language of crisis displaces local disputes within feminism, most visibly the disputes over race which have made that dream of seamlessness so palpably illusory.

Throughout the late seventies and early eighties, women of color insisted that "the differences between us did not permit our speaking in one voice."[7] Feminism's putative universality but practical exclusivity prompted many women of color, such as Hazel Carby, to ask white feminists, "what exactly do you mean when you say 'WE'?"[8] This insistence by women of color that "there is a pretense to a homogeneity of experience covered by the word *sisterhood* that does not in fact exist"[9] and that "white women stand in a power relation as oppressors of black women"[10] shocked (and continues to shock) white feminists. Suddenly, it seemed to many self-identified feminists, nothing in feminist theory, practice, or history was untainted by or invulnerable to the paralyzing charge of racism, elitism, blindness, and exclusivity. Strengthened by the force of these initial challenges, anger toward feminism seemed to come from everywhere at once and feminism seemed suddenly under attack. Lesbians, older women, prostitutes, disabled women, "post"-feminists, propornography advocates, and others, articulated their alienation from a feminism, which, they argued, failed them. The perception of being attacked *by other women* contributes to a nostalgic longing for a time when such a thing would be unthinkable. But whereas feminist politics can seem to have constituted a safe haven and refuge for some—disrupted now by out-of-control differences—for others, feminist politics never represented that terrain of safety and support, and, for them, there is no lost golden moment to lament.

The identity politics fueled by these challenges by women of color has, then, a double valence—both emancipatory and compensatory—which may be racially coded. On the one hand, identity politics allowed women of color to emphasize their own particular oppressions "as opposed to working to end somebody else's,"[11] and provided, as Patricia Hill Collins has recently argued, a "self-defined standpoint . . . a distinctive Black feminist consciousness."[12] But, at the same time, identity politics can also fuel nostalgic resistances to change. By substituting a smaller but still definable "categorial appeal" for the one under attack (white, Jewish, middle-class, intellectual, young lesbian-feminist, for example, in the place of "women" or "woman"), identity politics can reinstate—rhetorically at least—a seeming unproblematized sisterhood.[13] This emancipatory/compensatory double valence is further suggested by the absence of a language of crisis among feminist women of color: I find no work by women of color in which it plays a prominent role, which suggests that the illusions which some now see as shattered may never have existed for others, not even as utopian.

The shattering of feminism's illusory solidarity exposed its faultlines and created a "crisis of the concept 'woman'," as Delmar puts it, in which speaking for, as, or on behalf of "women" becomes a dance of impossibilities. Even writers long associated with the project of speaking for silenced and marginalized women have begun to voice a critical uneasiness. Adrienne Rich, for example, has recently written:

I wrote a sentence just now and x'd it out. In it I said that women have always understood the struggle against free-floating abstraction even when they were intimidated by abstract ideas. I don't want to write that

kind of sentence now, the sentence that begins "Women have always." . . . If we have learned anything in these years of late twentieth-
century feminism, it's that that "always" blots out what we really need
to know: when, where, and under what conditions has the statement
been true?[14]

It is precisely this erasure of "always" which dissolves feminism's
illusory subject, according to Judith Butler, Linda Alcoff, and
Sandra Harding.[15] For Butler, "woman" is a "regulatory fiction"
that fixes identity within the hegemonic ground of normative
heterosexuality. Feminist theoretical emphases on gender and political appeals to "women," Butler argues, tend to shore up, not
subvert, the structures of domination which also depend upon
emphasizing gender and women's difference and to foreclose
political consolidations and solidarities. "*Women*," Butler writes,
"even in the plural, has become a troublesome term, a site of
contest, a cause for anxiety."[16] Alcoff asks, "what can we demand
in the name of women if 'women' do not exist and demands in
their name simply reinforce the myth that they do? How can we
speak out against sexism as detrimental to the interests of women
if the category is a fiction? How can we demand legal abortions,
adequate child care, or wages based on comparable worth without
invoking a concept of 'woman'?"[17] Harding argues that we need
to treat the category "woman" with as much skepticism as we have
treated "man." "The problem for feminist theory and practice,"
she writes, is that empirically false dichotomies and categories
"structure our lives and our consciousness . . . [and] we are forced
to think and exist within the very dichotomies we criticize."[18]

But the impossibility of saying "always" and the fictionality of
"women" are not self-evidently linked. Whereas "woman," as a
theoretical abstraction, may need to be deconstructed, the status
of "women" as a political reality may need to be reinforced.
Feminism's subject has not been dissolved, only one, limited and
constraining version of what that subject is. In its place we need a
reformulation which is sensitive both to poststructural insights
and to the challenges posed by the complexities of political work.

The current language of crisis in feminist theory has not
displayed this kind of sensitivity. Notably, for example, none of
the critics quoted above who question—on ontological grounds—
the "categorial basis" of feminism refers to the challenges (often
advanced on experiential as well as ontological grounds) made by
women of color to just this categorial foundationalism. Nor, in
spite of Alcoff's evocation of political issues such as abortion, child

care, and wages, do they balance a discussion of theoretical
viability with a discussion of practical exigencies. My point is not to
criticize other white critics for failing to address or cite black ones
(such critiques are already abundant and to my mind they have
been dead-ended), nor is it to simply reinvoke the familiar theory/
practice dichotomy, but rather to ask if such failures of engagement aren't displaced by a language of crisis which suggests
futility and paralysis. Less the symptoms of crisis, in other words,
such failures may be caused by the false perception that there *is* a
crisis and the language of crisis through which we articulate the
seeming impossibility of speaking across our differences may be
making it easy to stop short of developing the means of doing just
that.

In the late seventies and early eighties the problem of a feminist
standpoint or ground (whether epistemological, experiential, theoretical, or historical) was most often represented as external to
feminism—feminism's vexed relation to patriarchal language, for
example. The problem of "taking a stand as a woman"[19] has come
to seem more a question of whether there is sufficient common
ground to meaningfully speak of a *feminist* standpoint.[20] And the
problems of feminism, as a consequence, appear more internal
and constitutive, less amenable to change and resolution. This
historical shift from the problem of "women" to the problem of
"feminist" occasions some of the failure of engagement with which
I am concerned. First, it falsely conflates the philosophical and
political difficulties posed by the two terms. Second, insofar as
women of color have not always identified with the term "feminist" (for a number of well-grounded historical reasons), it makes
the parameters of the current debate seem doubly exclusionary.

Some have posited that the question is not whether we can
speak of or from a feminist standpoint but, more importantly,
whether we can *act* concertedly from one. But feminists routinely
find themselves in pitched battles over whether to destabilize
gender identity or reaffirm formerly devalued "feminine" traits,
create a "common language" or refuse representation, fight por-
nographic depiction of women or liberate multiple sexualities,
emphasize women's construction in culture and language or fight
for more immediate, concrete and "local" gains: reproductive
rights, legislative protection, political representation.

Even where there is fundamental agreement—for example,
that feminism's categorial base in "women" needs to be analyzed—
there is frequently sharp disagreement over questions of practice
and strategy. Whereas Harding, for example, suggests that we

simply "embrace the instability" of contemporary feminism (648), Alcoff takes the position that we need stabilization and a ground from which to speak. We "cannot simply embrace the paradox" (421) of being unable to speak in "our" own name, she argues. And Butler suggests that we dispense with the very idea of grounding our speech and eschew the category of "women" as imposing "political closure on the kinds of experience articulable as part of a feminist discourse."[21]

I am uncomfortable with all formulations which treat feminism's fragmentation, differences, or internal conflicts as a problem *to be solved,* whether by eschewing self-representation, obliterating the problem-causing differences, or attempting to reconstruct seamless solidarities and sisterhoods. These faultlines are not only constitutive features of feminism, they are also, in a sense, exactly what we have called for in our rhetorical appeals to "difference." But I do not think we can simply "embrace the instability" of our categories and differences either. Our language, self-representations, and reading strategies, as the next two sections argue, reveal how difficult, sometimes impossible, and sometimes impolitic it is to embrace those instabilities. At the same time, they also reveal how necessary it is sometimes to do so.

Pronominal Politics, Valuable Illusions

> If woman seems to be the inessential which never becomes the essential, it is because she herself fails to bring about this change. Proletarians say "We"; Negroes also. Regarding themselves as subjects, they transform the bourgeois, the whites, into "others." But women do not say "We."
>
> —Simone de Beauvoir

> Which identities are available to ground such a potent political myth called "us," and what could motivate enlistment in this collectivity?
>
> —Donna Haraway

> We did not know whom we meant when we said "we."
>
> —Adrienne Rich

The imaginary dialogue I am constructing here[22] is meant to illustrate three problems which are central to what I will be calling feminism's "pronominal politics": first, the political *exigency of saying "we,"* as de Beauvoir expresses it, of speaking as feminists, for women. Second, *the impossibility of saying "we,"* its fictionality, allusions to nothing, as expressed by Haraway. Third, the *inevitability of saying "we,"* as expressed in Rich's determination to evoke collectivity even in the absence of being able to define it.

While feminists often conduct debates over feminism's pronominal politics as if we could choose between these three positions, they are in fact intertwined in such a way that saying "we" may seem impossible, inevitable, and exigent all at once. Both Peggy Kamuf and Judith Butler advocate dropping forms of self-reference such as "feminist" or "we." The "term 'feminism,' Kamuf writes, "operates largely as accepted marker by self-designation," and is "thus a closed system [and we should] . . . drop the name *as a form of self-address . . .* [as a] way of *affirming* the future of, yes, feminism."[23] The appeal to "we," she argues elsewhere, is integral to the structures of power which feminism seeks to dismantle and feminism cannot share in the rhetorical and epistemological operations of those structures—such as faith in the construction of a "delimited and totalizable object" implicit in saying "we"—without reinscribing them.[24] Butler argues that the collapse of "women" and "feminist" as terms is to be celebrated not "lamented as the failure of a feminist political theory." The political exigencies served by rhetorical appeals to "we" are outweighed, Butler argues, by the identity narratives built into them: "the 'us' who gets joined through such a narration is a construction built upon the denial of a decidedly more complex cultural identity—or non-identity, as the case may be."[25] What is striking to me in both Kamuf and Butler's arguments, as in the quote from Haraway, is the centrality given to identity. What are the stakes of transposing political questions of advocacy and representation into a discourse of identity? How do such transpositions ignore the ways in which women currently *are* contending with one another for the designations and meanings of "woman," "feminist," and "we?" Such contention is crucial to sorting out solidarities and sorting through important differences. In the name of philosophically grounded identity, to give up on the process of such contention is to give up on both advocacy and debate around a whole range of key feminist problematics.

It is particularly important to understand this contention as part of a political process because it helps explain why such self-referencing remains crucial even for those for whom it lacks philosophical validity. Without extraordinary caution and even with a substantial amount of syntactical acrobatics, rhetorical appeals to "we" or "us" prove nearly impossible to avoid. Even those who advocate destabilizing feminist categories engage in pronominal politics. Harding, for example, writes that "*we* can learn how to embrace the instability of the analytical categories [of feminism] . . . to use these instabilities as a resource for *our* thinking and practices" (648, emphasis mine). Alcoff, in a sentence I quoted earlier, writes that "*our* very self-definition is grounded in a concept that *we* must deconstruct and de-essentialize in all of its aspects" (emphasis mine). Both statements oscillate between presumptions of identity presumably invalidated by the statements in which they occur and appeals to collective action ungrounded in the collectivity to which they appeal. This oscillation is characteristic of fundamental—and productive—tensions at feminism's core and not something we need to solve by abandoning self-reference nor something we need to apologize for. As part of our political practice and process, such gestures of self-reference need not presume illusory identities nor reify gender nor practice an exclusionary politics. Indeed, the more self-consciously we engage in such gestures and the contestations they inevitably engender, the more we enable our own *productive* destabilizations.

Rather than avoid the feminist "we," then, I am suggesting that we use it, but that we do so as a *proleptic* term, one which points not to an essential reality that preexists or transcends its evocation, but to one which it tries to instantiate. Rich's statement "We did not know whom we meant when we said 'we',," although written in the past tense, illustrates how "we" can work proleptically. Rich's sentence is tricky. The word *we* appears four times. Yet, Rich's rhetoric suggests a strategy not for *finding* a preexisting ground (experiential or ontological), but for building one within discourse and debate. Rich's "we" both seeks to mobilize a constituency and to signal the instability of the referent to which it refers. It acknowledges the complex fact that solidarities both need to be constructed and yet also draw on something prior to their construction. This double-edged rhetorical strategy suggests not that we abandon representation altogether, as Butler has suggested, but that we engage in representations which do not presume a status beyond the provisional and discursive. Representation as hypothesis, in other words, rather than as mirror of reality. As pronominal politics, Rich's rhetoric suggests that we need not feel paralyzed by the fragmentations in which we are engaging and that we can overcome that paralysis without—and this is what allows Rich to avoid a sclerotic vision—trying to heal that fragmentation. Such representations, however, are not "merely" linguistic, as those who fear categorial destabilization have sometimes argued. Indeed, they serve crucial political purposes.

A language of crisis and its concomitant refusal to say "we" or "women" do make feminism vulnerable not only to itself but also to particularly insidious representation and antifeminist attack by opening up a representation gap into which others may safely fall. I can think of no better example of this problem than Camille Paglia. Representing herself as an antifeminist feminist, Paglia has received a great deal of popular press attention for such statements as: "If civilization had been left in female hands we would still be living in grass huts"; "male urination is really a kind of accomplishment, an arc of transcendence"; and "a woman merely waters the ground she stands on."[26] Her views are widely sought on a number of important feminist issues: the canon and tradition ("there is no female Mozart because there is no female Jack the Ripper")[27]; date rape ("aggression and eroticism . . . are deeply intertwined. . . . Every woman must be prudent and cautious about where she goes and with whom. When she makes a mistake, she must accept the consequences and, through self-criticism, resolve never to make that mistake again. . . . The only solution to date rape is female self-awareness and self-control")[28]; popular culture ("Madonna is the true feminist. She exposes the puritanism and suffocating ideology of American feminism . . . Madonna loves real men. She sees the beauty of masculinity, in all its rough vigor and sweaty athletic perfection").[29]

Why is someone who defines feminism as appreciation for sweaty men sought to judge feminism? One answer, of course, is that the press loves Paglia's nastiness. As scholar and polemicist her characteristic moves are ad feminem attacks and crude psychological caricatures. The black artist, for example, is a "vivid, vibrant personality, [full of] dramatic self-assertion and spiritual magnitude."[30] Ivy League humanities departments are full of "lily-livered trash-talking foreign junk bond dealers." The "American personality" is "booming, pushy, manic, facilely optimistic. At its essence, it is infantile in its beaming, bouncing egotism."[31] But, the bulk of Paglia's invective is saved for feminists: "dopey, immature . . . boring, uptight . . . [women who] can't think their way out of a wet paper bag [and are crimped by] solemn Carrie Nation repressiveness."[32] "American feminism," Paglia pronounces,

has a man problem. The beaming Betty Crockers, hangdog dowdies and parochial prudes who call themselves feminists want men to be like women. They fear and despise the masculine. The academic feminists think their nerdy bookworm husbands are the ideal model of human manhood.[33]

No wonder antifeminist men adore Camille Paglia. The only surprising thing is her feigned, I'll presume, surprise that they do:

> You know, I get nothing but letters from men. You know it's ridiculous. Men, men, men like me. Mostly men. Can we have lunch, can we have dinner, can we like, you know, I'll take you to the best restaurant, I mean like that, you know. I have nothing but men, any kind of men—men, men, men.[34]

But if caricatures and vindictiveness attract the media, there is more than this at stake here. While Paglia reassures those who fear feminism by painting feminists as confused, weak, asexual women without power or potential to effect change, she does so by embracing both representational and pronominal politics.

Karen Offen has argued that vulnerability to (external) attack is the gravest consequence of the current "crisis":

> Awash in a sea of competing tendencies and issues that demand solutions, [activists] need a broad-based, dynamic working definition in order to confront and combat the present confusion about and fear of feminism in the public mind. Thereby, activists may reclaim the initiative from our adversaries in explaining what feminism is and is not.[35]

While I am not advocating that it matters whether or not we refute Paglia's claim that we are dopey, immature, sexually repressed hangdog dowdies, a bizarre phenomenon like Paglia does present an important opportunity for us to represent ourselves *to one another* by seizing back the terrain of definition and self-description. The language of crisis helps foster the conditions for the phenomenal success of someone like Camille Paglia by refusing to do what she is only too willing to—namely define and describe feminism—and by suggesting that feminism's golden age is behind us and the current one is dark (racial pun intended) and unhappy. I agree with Ann Anitow's assertion that "in spite of its false promise of unity the [word] 'we' remains politically important,"[36] and would like to take it one step further. Using "we" at moments of crisis is important not because the promise is *false,* but because such gestures of self-designation and representation provide ways to test how that promise has failed and where it might succeed.

HARMONIOUS METAPHORS

Most women have not developed tools for facing anger constructively.

—Audre Lorde

If, as Audre Lorde argues, women lack tools for facing anger,[37] have we used our literature to help fashion those? Do our models of feminist reading affirm conflict or deny it? Is constructing models from feminist reading a helpful practice?

Alice Walker's essay "In Search of Our Mothers' Gardens" draws on many of the key metaphors of feminist theory to advance a now-familiar recuperative enterprise of locating the silenced and devalued voices, lives, and artifacts of marginalized women. Walker movingly reapplies Woolf's Judith Shakespeare parable to the lives of illiterate black slave women: "what did it mean for a black woman to be an artist in our grandmother's time? In our great-grandmother's day? It is a question with an answer cruel enough to stop the blood,"[38] Walker writes. At one point in this argument, Walker turns to the example of a slave quilt to illustrate the ways in which the "lost" arts of her ancestors persist and record their struggles: "though it is made of bits and pieces of worthless rags, it is obviously the work of a person of powerful imagination and deep spiritual feeling. Below this quilt I saw a note that says it was made by 'an anonymous Black woman in Alabama, a hundred years ago'" (239).

In turning to quilting as one of the lost female arts, Walker draws on a privileged feminist metaphor for the stitching together of links between women, both historical and contemporary. This metaphor is given extensive treatment in *The Color Purple* where quilting operates as the only available means of communication and reconciliation between a number of the women characters, as well as the only extant historical record of Celie's life and her children's genealogy. When Corrine suspects Nettie of being the mother of Celie's children and of having slept with Corrine's husband, Samuel, Nettie turns to quilts to force Corrine to remember having met Celie and her fear that Celie might take the children away:

I held up first one and then another to the light, trying to find the first one I remembered her making . . . Aha I said, when I found what I was looking for, and laid the quilt across the bed. Do you remember buying this cloth? I asked, pointing to a flowered square. And what about this checkered bird? . . . She traced the patterns with her finger, and slowly her eyes filled with tears. . . . She [Celie] was so much like Olivia! she said. I was afraid she'd want her back. So I forgot her as soon as I could.[39]

Quilting and weaving, going back to the myth of Philomela, who weaves the story of her rape after Tereus cuts her tongue out, have been symbolic of both the cultural silencing of women and of their ways of subverting and surviving and even recording that silencing. Weaving and quilting also work well as metaphors for the material conditions of many women's lives: the domestic and familial responsibility of stitching together disparate fragments into an aesthetically satisfying and practically useful whole.

Quilting, patchwork, and weaving are also important to the form of much feminist writing. Take, for example, Luce Irigaray's *Speculum of the Other Women,* which weaves together as it deconstructs an array of master narratives. Or Gloria Naylor's *The Women of Brewster Place* and Amy Tan's *The Joy Luck Club,* with their patchwork patterns of different women's stories. Or Mina Loy's poetic collages, structured like enormous crazy quilt runners. Or Monique Wittig's *Les Guerillères,* which Rachel Blau DuPlessis describes as "a form of verbal quilt. We hear her lists, her unstressed series, no punctuation even, no pauses, no setting apart, and so everything joined with no subordination, no ranking."[40]

Blau DuPlessis's own essay, "For the Etruscans," with its brilliant incorporation of many different voices, its dazzling shifts between the autobiographical and the analytical, the personal and social, diary and essay, Fig Newtons and the female aesthetic, is clearly meant to epitomize this "form of verbal quilt." The essay's various arguments for a "female aesthetic" help explain what that may entail: "contradiction," "nonlinear movement," "nonhierarchic," "anti-authoritarian," "anti-phonal many-voices," "a both/and vision," "multiclimactic, multiple centers of attention," "encyclopedic," "apparent nonselection," "mutuality," "porousness," "intimacy."

"For the Etruscans," however, is not truly "multivocal," "anti-authoritarian," "nonselective," or "nonlinear." Indeed, it succeeds, and I do think it is a very successful essay, partly through the very qualities its form would seem to undermine: it is argumentative, linear, cumulative, hierarchical, distanced, and analytical, as well as intimate, multiple, porous, and varied. Given this, I am concerned with its romanticization—and Walker's—of the metaphor of quilting.

I am a quilter. And I principally quilt antique tops, tops pieced together by other women from other historical moments. As I work, these days, on a double wedding ring top made by an anonymous woman in the 1920s, I realize how very *little* I can learn about her (read about her) from the record she has left in her stitching and her fabrics. She liked yellow. She had a good even hand, but was not overly precise (even stitches but poor corners). She was frugal, but probably not poor (new fabric for backings and borders, but old blankets for batting). She must have done a good deal of sewing, or had a friend who did and saved her scraps for her: among hundreds of patches few fabrics are repeated more than twice. I don't know where she pieced, or why, whether she sewed alone or with a friend in the room, her age, where this particular top fit into a lifetime of sewing, what was happening to her when she made it, whether she had children, what she thought of the world, why it wasn't finished. Moreover, and more importantly, I don't like her. I don't feel close to her. For all I know she was a racist and an antisemite. Moreover, I do not recognize Blau du Plessis's politically charged descriptions of form in either her work or in mine. There is nothing random, nonhierarchical, nonselective, all-inclusive, anti-authoritarian, alogical, or spontaneous about a quilt. Indeed, they are extremely ordered, logical, precise constructions, dependent—even when they seem most random—on rigid plans and tight control. The quilt that I am making—that we are making, I suppose—is beautiful and it opens itself to romantic speculations, but I want them to remain speculative and tentative. And I do not want to treat them as either metaphor or model for my feminism.

If I can read very little in the double wedding ring patchwork made by the woman whose quilt I'm completing, the women in Susan Glaspell's story "A Jury of Her Peers" can read a great deal: the story of Minnie Foster's bleak life and oppressive marriage. Glaspell's story demonstrates what Annette Kolodny labels "gender inflected interpretive strategies."[41] The "text" in question is Minnie Foster, in jail for the murder of her husband. As the story opens, the sheriff and county attorney are trying to find (read) the "motive" for the crime, without evidence of which, they fear, the jury may not convict Minnie Foster. Although the house is filled, as it turns out, with motive and evidence, the men are unable to see it.

> "You're convinced there was nothing important here?" the county attorney asked the sheriff. "Nothing that would—point to any motive?" The sheriff too looked all around, as if to re-convince himself. "Nothing here but kitchen things," he said, with a little laugh for the insignificance of kitchen things.[42]

Whereas the men fail to read any meaning in "kitchen things," these insignificant kitchen things reveal to the women how divested Minnie Foster's life was of anything comforting or beautiful, how thoroughly Mr. Foster had deprived her of the conditions for a tolerable life.

The more they look around the kitchen, the more evidence the women see. Most tellingly, Mrs. Peters and Mrs. Hale discover Minnie Foster's quilting, an unmistakable sign of her determination to create and also of her anger and agitation at being denied and erased by her husband:

> Mrs. Hale was looking at the fine, even sewing, and preoccupied with thoughts of the woman who had done that sewing, when she heard the sheriff's wife say, in a queer tone:
> "Why, look at this one."
> She turned to take the block held out to her.
> "The sewing," said Mrs. Peters, in a troubled way. "All the rest of them have been so nice and even—but—this one. Why it looks as if she didn't know what she was about!" . . .
> . . . Martha Hale now scrutinized that piece, compared it with the dainty, accurate sewing of the other blocks. The difference was startling. Holding this block made her feel queer, *as if the distracted thoughts of the woman who had perhaps turned to it to try and quiet herself were communicating themselves to her.* (379–80, emphasis mine)

After they discover the evidence of anger, they immediately find its motive: Minnie Foster's pet canary, its neck wrung, apparently by Mr. Foster. Minnie, the sheriff's wife remembers, was "kind of like a bird herself. Real sweet and pretty, but kind of timid and—fluttery. How—she—did—change" (381). As readers, the women are drawn inside Minnie Foster's life. "Why do you and I *understand*? Why do we *know*—what we know this minute?" (384) Mrs. Peters asks. But it is clear that, given their experiences, *as women,* they cannot help but understand.

Being women makes them not only sympathetic readers, but

collaborative ones. As soon as Mrs. Hale finds the tell-tale evidence that might convict Minnie Foster, she moves to erase it:

> A moment Mrs. Hale sat there, her hands folded over that sewing which was so unlike all the rest of the sewing. Then she had pulled a knot and drawn the threads.
> "Oh, what are you doing, Mrs. Hale?" asked the sheriff's wife, startled.
> "Just pulling out a stitch or two that's not sewed very good," said Mrs. Hale, mildly.
> "I don't think we ought to touch things," Mrs. Peters said, a little helplessly.
> "I'll just finish up this end," answered Mrs. Hale, still in that mild, matter-of-fact fashion.
> She threaded a needle and started to replace bad sewing with good. For a little while she sewed in silence. (380)

Mrs. Hale sews in silence, literally sews silence into the text, replacing Minnie Foster's talking stitches with safer ones.

From a feminist perspective, what's wrong, we might ask, with this model of readership and sisterhood? According to some critics, this is exactly what we need. Shifting from men's to women's writing, Patrocinio Schweickart writes, enables a secondary shift—for the feminist reader—from a "negative hermeneutic of ideological unmasking to a positive hermeneutic whose aim is the recovery and cultivation of women's culture." According to Schweickart, the "woman reader and the woman writer" have a "dialogic" relationship. "The feminist reader," Schweickart writes, succeeds in effecting a mediation between her perspective and that of the writer."[43] Beyond mediation, what we have here is an ethics of merger in which women not only understand one another but co-constitute each other as an "us" opposed to "them," just as the women in this story form a united front against male "justice."

Schweickart's prescriptions accord well not only with Walker and Glaspell's writing, but with Gilman's "The Yellow Wallpaper" as well, a story which has also been used to generate models of feminist reading and feminist practice. Denied a "dialogic" reader, to put the story's problem in Schweickart's terms, the narrator initially turns inward in self-destructive ways and her growing madness, as Kolodny points out, can be ascribed to the fact that she is "isolated from conversational exchanges" (52). Denied a feminist reader, she *becomes* one as she begins to detect and then decipher the figure of another woman, trapped inside the wallpaper of her room. And she goes beyond merely identifying with the trapped figure, merging with her—and thereby liberating her—as her madness progresses. As Mrs. Hale and Mrs. Peters identify with Minnie Foster and the protagonist of "The Yellow Wallpaper" indentifies with the figure in the wallpaper, so feminist readings of "The Yellow Wallpaper" would encourage us to identify with the protagonist. And, indeed, thanks to supportive and sympathetic readings by feminists, this text has been saved, nursed back to health from its historic misreading as merely another horror story of female derangement.

Isak Dinesen's "The Blank Page" and Susan Gubar's essay " 'The Blank Page' and the Issues of Female Creativity" also tell stories about women reading in which sympathetic, uncritical reading is advocated. The story of the blank page is the story of production and reception, writing and reading. It begins with a Carmelite order of nuns, in the mountains of Portugal, who produce, preserve, and exhibit the blood-stained bridal sheets of royal princesses. The blank "page" is an anonymous, unstained framed sheet of white linen, "snow-white from corner to corner, a blank page." The convent sisters, with "eternal and unswerving loyalty" frame and exhibit this sheet along with the blood-stained ones; it is this unstained sheet which most captivates "bridesmaids and maids-of-honor . . . it is in front of the blank page that the old and young nuns, with the Mother Abbess herself, sink into deepest thought."[44]

According to Susan Gubar, it is the sisters' willingness to identify with the princess that matters here: "were the female community less sensitive to the significance of these signs, such stained sheets would hardly be considered art at all."[45] What unsympathetic readers of this sheet would no doubt identify as emptiness is filled with significance by (and for) the interpretive community of women for whom the princess's blank "text" is meaningful. The fact that her act of resistance to the sexual story scripted for her is open to multiple interpretations—did she run away? renounce sexuality? was she not a virgin when she married?—only increases its significance for its audience. This multiplicity of possible readings, which is enabled by the "text's" author's silence, keeps their interest alive and allows them to continue to be collaborative readers, writing in different stories of rebellion. "The resistance of the princess," Gubar writes, "allows for self-expression, for she makes her statement by not writing what she is expected to write" (89). Not writing and keeping silent, moreover, allows for the princess's later recuperation by a sympathetic audience. By keeping quiet, like the absent protagonist of "A Jury of Her Peers" and the mad narrator of "The Yellow Wallpaper" she paves the way for the eventual interlocutor who will seek to hear what it was she did not say.

What, then, is wrong with such models, aside from the danger posed by their prescriptiveness? Let us return to Glaspell's "A Jury of Her Peers." The merger and identification of Mrs. Hale and Mrs. Peters with Minnie Foster eclipses an earlier moment of conflict in the story. Here, both women are represented as sharing in the guilt not of Minnie Foster's crime, but more importantly, of her husband's. Ignoring their neighbor, whose poor lifestyle is considerably beneath their own, the women lend tacit support to the insupportability of Minnie Foster's life. "Oh, I *wish*, I'd come over here once in a while!" she [Mrs. Peters] cried. "That was a crime! That was a crime! Who's going to punish that?" (384).

Kolodny's discussion of this passage suggests that the women's "recognition is itself, of course, a kind of punishment" (57). Kolodny may be right psychologically, but the question of punishment seems to me beside the point. Of greater relevance are questions of representation and resolution. Why do we have elaborate metaphors for male oppression (the dead bird, the bad stove) and female collaboration (the cleaned kitchen, the quilt stitches) but none for the conflict *between* the women? Is that conflict, in spite of its brief mention in the story, one of the truly unspeakable crimes here? I am reading these texts against the grain not only to expose the narratives of conflict they contain, not only to ask why we suppress those narratives in the models we construct from such classic texts, but to ask also what is at stake for us—politically—in constructing such models at all?

These stories, as I have mentioned, are feminist classics. Indeed, they are quickly attaining the status of "older" classics and are on their way to being supplanted by newer ones which may be more permeable to the representation—and therefore the potential working out—of conflict between women. I want to conclude by looking briefly at two of those newer classics, both of which I have begun to teach in my feminist theory class. It is reasonable to ask if we haven't moved beyond the feminist positions earlier classics model and may seem to prescribe. Don't those texts represent positions still bound up with the now discredited mode of speaking of "*the woman* writer," "*the woman* reader," "*the female* artist?" For three reasons, I think that the models represented by these texts, as well as the impulse to generate models, persists. First, as I have shown, using "we," "woman," and "women" is hard to avoid. Indeed, such evocations of similitude and solidarity are on the ascension not the decline in black feminist criticism.[46] Second, we can see the persistence of our desire *for* such evocation even, perhaps especially, where it is most vociferously rejected. The nostalgia underlying the language of crisis in feminist theory expresses that longing for lost coherence. Third, for the transition to new models to be effected, we would need to shift not only the texts and metaphors we privilege, but also the *models of reading* which we bring to them and the habits of generating practices based on those reading models. I am not confident that such radical changes in reading are yet underway.

Nawal El Saadawi's novel *Woman at Point Zero* and Rigoberta Menchú's testimonial *I, Rigoberta Menchú*[47] both tell the story of one woman's resistance to patriarchy and oppression, in Egypt and Latin America, respectively, and both contain problematic structures of narration in which women relate the life stories and political struggles of women considerably less privileged than themselves. In the case of *Woman at Point Zero*, the story of Firdaus's rebellion, resistance, and eventual murder of her pimp is told to the narrator, a female doctor who has escaped many of the social constraints faced by Firdaus. In the case of *I, Rigoberta Menchú*, the story of Rigoberta's development as a Guatemalan revolutionary is told through her Spanish-speaking narrator and transcriber, Elisabeth Burgos-Debray. The relationship between Burgos-Debray and Menchú remains clearly vexed by differences in class, literacy, ideology, power, and authority. These same differences initially vex the relationship between the narrator and Firdaus in *Woman at Point Zero*, but they are made to dissolve there via the medium of narration and because the narrator is a sympathetic and collaborative feminist reader who identifies with her subject to the point of literally losing herself in her.

Overwhelmingly, my students consider *Woman at Point Zero* a better paradigm of feminist resistance than *I, Rigoberta Menchú*, in spite of the fact that Firdaus is executed and Rigoberta goes on to become an active and important revolutionary. Their preferences surprised, then worried me, principally because I realized that in certain ways I shared them. Like my students, I am reassured by the relationship between the narrator and Firdaus, regardless of the outcome of Firdaus's life, and I enjoy that novel's images of female reconciliation and harmony, as opposed to the difficult picture of irreconcilable differences but necessary affiliation offered in *I, Rigoberta Menchú*. I prefer images of sisterhood and solidarity to ones of fragmentation and anger and I enjoy models of conciliation and collectivity, even when I recognize them as nostalgic, idealist, and utopian. I distrust the strength of this preference not because reconciliation is a bad thing or because I am against utopian representation or even wishful thinking, but because I recognize in such readings a *learned* and "politically correct" response to representations of conflict between women and it is this response which I would like to unlearn and so teach my students differently. Perhaps I will never *enjoy* conflict, anger, and struggle in the same way I enjoyed sisterhood, solidarity, and support, but my desires for the one, I recognize, rest on my ability to withstand and work within the other. In the words of Bernice Reagon, "you can do wonderful things in a crisis."[48]

Notes

This essay began as a talk delivered as part of the Women's Studies/Cultural Studies forum organized by Jane Marcus at the 1990 Modern Language Association Convention in Chicago. I would like to thank Jane for providing me with an opportunity to share some of these ideas, as well as Ann Ardis, John Brenkman, Lynne Huffer, and Louise Yelin for helpful conversations and incisive readings of this essay.

1. See Rosalind Delmar, "What Is Feminism?" *What Is Feminism? A Re-Examination*, ed. Juliet Mitchell and Ann Oakley (New York: Pantheon Books, 1986), 8–33. The phrase "crisis of representation" is Delmar's.

2. Ibid., 11, 27, emphasis mine.

3. Donna Haraway, "A Manifesto for Cyborgs," *Feminism/Postmodernism*, ed. Linda J. Nicholson (New York: Routledge, 1990), 197, emphasis mine.

4. Linda Alcoff, "Cultural Feminism Versus Poststructuralism: The Identity Crisis in Feminist Theory," *Signs* 13, no. 3 (Spring 1988): 405, 406, emphasis mine. Future references are cited parenthetically in the text.

5. Judith Butler, "Gender Trouble, Feminist Theory, and Psychoanalytic Discourse," *Feminism/Postmodernism*, 327. See also Marianne Hirsch and Evelyn Fox Keller, eds., *Conflicts in Feminism* (New York: Routledge, 1990), especially the excellent introduction and conclusion to this volume, as well as the essays by contributors, most of whom treat conflict as positive, generative, and constructive, rather than as a crisis.

6. Nancy Cott, "Feminist Theory and Feminist Movements: The Past before Us," *What Is Feminism?*, 58.

7. María C. Lugones and Elizabeth V. Spelman, "Have We Got a Theory for You! Feminist Theory, Cultural Imperialism and the Demand for 'The Woman's Voice'," *Women's Studies International Forum* 6, no. 6 (1983): 573.

8. Hazel V. Carby, "White Woman Listen! Black Feminism and the Boundaries of Sisterhood," *The Empire Strikes Back: Race and Sexism in 70's Britain* (London: Hutchinson, 1982), 233.

9. Audre Lorde, "Age, Race, Class, and Sex: Women Redefining Difference," *Sister Outsider* (Freedom, Calif.: Crossing Press, 1984), 116.

10. Carby, "White Woman Listen!", 214.

11. Combahee River Collective, "The Combahee River Collective Statement," *Monthly*

Review Press (1979), reprinted in *Home Girls: A Black Feminist Anthology*, ed. Barbara Smith (New York: Kitchen Table: Women of Color Press, 1983).

12. Patricia Hill Collins, "The Social Construction of Black Feminist Thought," *Signs* 24, no. 4 (Summer 1986): 747, 748.

13. See Minnie Bruce Pratt, "Identity: Skin, Blood, Heart," *Yours in Struggle: Three Feminist Perspectives on Anti-Semitism and Racism* (Brooklyn: Long Haul Press, 1984) and Biddy Martin and Chandra Talpade Mohanty's response to Pratt in "Feminist Politics: What's Home Got to Do with It?" *Feminist Studies/Critical Studies*, ed. Teresa de Lauretis (Bloomington: Indiana University Press, 1986). See also Mary Louise Adams, "There's No Place like Home: On the Place of Identity in Feminist Politics," *Feminist Review* 21 (Spring 1989).

14. Adrienne Rich, "Notes towards a Politics of Location," *Blood, Bread, and Poetry: Selected Prose, 1979–1985* (New York: Norton, 1986), 214. I discuss Rich's shift away from speaking for the "other woman" in "The Poetics of Accountability: Adrienne Rich's Politics of Location," paper delivered at the Modern Language Association, 1989.

15. While my focus is on North American feminist theory, it should be noted that the writers I discuss here who challenge "woman" as the center of feminist theory and politics are following an intellectual tradition associated principally with French feminism. See especially, Julia Kristeva, "Woman Can Never Be Defined," *New French Feminisms*, ed. Elaine Marks and Isabelle de Courtivron (New York: Schocken Books, 1981) and Monique Wittig, "One Is Not Born a Woman," *Feminist Issues* 7, no. 4 (Winter 1981).

16. Judith Butler, *Gender Trouble: Feminism and the Subversion of Identity* (New York: Routledge, 1990), 3.

17. Alcoff, "Cultural Feminism," 420. Future page references to Alcoff are to this essay and will be cited parenthetically in the text.

18. Sandra Harding, "The Instability of the Analytical Categories of Feminist Theory," *Signs* 11, no. 4 (Summer 1986): 646, 662. Future page references to Harding are to this essay and will be cited parenthetically in the text.

19. Catherine Clément, "Enclave Esclave," *New French Feminisms*, 130.

20. See especially Collins, "The Social Construction of Black Feminist Thought," Sandra Harding, *The Science Question in Feminism* (Ithaca: Cornell University Press, 1986), and Nancy Hartsock, "Rethinking Modernism: Minority vs. Majority Theories," *Cultural Critique* 7 (Fall 1987) and *Money, Sex, and Power: Toward a Feminist Historical Materialism* (New York: Longman, 1983).

21. Butler, "Gender Trouble," 325.

22. Simone de Beauvoir, *The Second Sex*, trans. H. M. Parshley (New York: Bantam Books, 1961), xviii–xix. See also Haraway, "A Manifesto for Cyborgs," 197; Rich, "Notes toward a Politics of Location," 217.

23. Peggy Kamuf, "Parisian Letters: Between Feminism and Deconstruction" [exchange with Nancy K. Miller], *Conflicts in Feminism*, 131–32.

24. Peggy Kamuf, "Replacing Feminist Criticism," *Conflicts in Feminism*, 109.

25. Butler, "Gender Trouble," 339.

26. Camille Paglia, *Sexual Personae: Art and Decadence from Nefertiti to Emily Dickinson* (New Haven: Yale University Press, 1990). See, for example, the following two feature articles: Neil Postman, "Dinner Conversation: She Wants Her TV! He Wants His Book," *Harper's*, March 1991, 44–55; Francesca Stanfill, "Woman Warrior," *New York*, 4 March 1991, 22–30.

27. As quoted by Stanfill.

28. Camille Paglia, "Rape: A Bigger Danger than Feminists Know: Feminists Keep Telling Women They Can Do Anything, Go Anywhere, Say Anything, Wear Anything. No They Can't," *New York Newsday*, 27 January 1991, C32.

29. Camille Paglia, "Madonna—Finally a Real Feminist," *The New York Times*, 14 December 1990, 38.

30. Camille Paglia, "Ninnies, Pedants, Tyrants and Other Academics," *New York Times Book Review*, 5 May 1991, sec. 7, 1.

31. Ibid., 29, 33.

32. Paglia, as quoted by Postman, "She Wants Her TV!", 47.

33. Paglia, "Madonna—Finally, a Real Feminist," 38.

34. Henry Allen, "Camille Paglia's Mad, Mad World View," *The Washington Post*, 15 April 1991, B1, B4.

35. Karen Offen, "Defining Feminism: A Comparative Historical Approach," *Signs* 1, no. 1 (Autumn 1988): 122.

36. Ann Snitow, "A Gender Diary," *Conflicts in Feminism*, 37.

37. Audre Lorde, "The Uses of Anger: Women Responding to Racism," *Sister Outsider*, 130.

38. Alice Walker, "In Search of Our Mothers' Gardens," *In Search of Our Mothers' Gardens: Womanist Prose* (New York: Harcourt Brace Jovanovich, 1983), 233. Future page references will be cited parenthetically in the text.

39. Alice Walker, *The Color Purple* (New York: Washington Square Press, 1982), 168–71.

40. Rachel Blau DuPlessis, "For the Etruscans," *The New Feminist Criticism*, ed. Elaine Showalter (New York: Pantheon Books, 1985), 278.

41. Annette Kolodny, "A Map for Rereading: Gender and the Interpretation of Literary Texts," *New Literary History* 11, no. 3 (Spring 1980), reprinted in *The New Feminist Criticism*, 54. Future page references to Kolodny are to this essay and will be cited parenthetically in the text.

42. Susan Glaspell, "A Jury of Her Peers," *Images of Women in Literature*, ed. Mary Anne Ferguson (Boston: Houghton Mifflin, 1973), 374. Future page references will be cited parenthetically in the text.

43. Patrocinio P. Schweickart, "Reading Ourselves: Toward a Feminist Theory of Reading," *Gender and Reading*, ed. Elizabeth Flynn and Patrocinio Schweickart (Baltimore: The Johns Hopkins Press, 1986), 51, 52, 55.

44. Isak Dinesen, "The Blank Page," *The Norton Anthology of Literature by Women* (New York: Norton, 1985), 1422, 1423.

45. Susan Gubar, "'The Blank Page' and the Issues of Female Creativity," *Writing and Sexual Difference*, ed. Elizabeth Abel (Chicago: University of Chicago Press, 1982), 78. Future page references will be cited parenthetically in the text.

46. See, for example, Deborah E. McDowell, "'The Changing Same': Generational Connections about Black Women Novelists," and Mae Gwendolyn Henderson, "Speaking in Tongues: Dialogics, Dialectics, and the Black Woman Writer's Literary Tradition," both reprinted in *Reading Black, Reading Feminist*, ed. Henry Louis Gates, Jr. (New York: Meridian Books, 1990).

47. Nawal El Saadawi, *Woman at Point Zero*, trans. Sherif Hetata (London: Zed Books, 1983); *I, Rigoberta Menchú, An Indian Woman in Guatemala*, ed. Elisabeth Burgos-Debray, trans. Ann Wright (London: Verso Books, 1984).

48. Bernice Johnson Reagon, "Coalition Politics: Turning the Century," *Home Girls*, 368.

Gender and the Everyday: Toward a Postmodern Materialist Feminist Theory of Mimesis

Teresa L. Ebert

State University of New York, Albany

MIMESIS is in many ways the most crucial site for feminist culture critique. Mimetic fictions are one of the primary domains for the patriarchal organization of everyday reality and the production of gendered subjectivities. Even more important for theorizing feminist political practice and the critique of patriarchy, mimetic fiction is the arena for much of the contestation between opposing feminist theories. The experiential, representational feminism ("gynocriticism," to adopt Elaine Showalter's term) constituting much of Anglo-American mainstream feminism has a deep allegiance to representationalism and mimesis in all discourses but particularly to mimetic fiction as the reliable representation of the reality ("truth") of women's experience. For experiential feminists or gynocritics, literature is the representation, the reflection of the real, and its value or validity, in other words its "truth," derives from the "authenticity" of its reflection of women's experience as "real" persons. This view of realism/representationalism is opposed by textual, deconstructive, antirepresentational feminism ("gynesis," to use Alice Jardine's term),[1] on the one hand, and by materialist, postrepresentational feminism on the other. Despite their differences both textual and materialist feminists call into question the way gynocritics naturalize experience as the referent or ground of discourse and postulate an essentialized gender manifested in that experience.

Experiential feminists participate in the humanist, empirical common sense in which knowledge is based on the "experience" of reality, and experience itself is taken to be "absolute, a given point of departure and its own guarantee"[2] as well as the guarantee of the "real" and especially of gender. In short, gender, for experiential feminists, is the consequence of experience—whether biological or social—and constitutes a stable, recognizable identity

90

specific to the experiences of each sex. In other words, while female identity may be varied and changeable, depending on the specific concrete experiences of particular women, it is not a "floating signifier" nor is it a zone that can be occupied by individuals of different sexes as is posited in poststructuralist theories of gender. Gender, in experiential feminism, is considered to be firmly anchored to the body and its experiences and entails an essential female identity.

However, experience, in humanist empiricism and experiential feminism, is known only through its representation in consciousness and consequently in language. The validity or "truth" of a representation, whether in consciousness or one of its "creations," such as literature, is judged in terms of the authenticity or accuracy of the representation's "reflection" of experience. Marcia Holly, for example, insists that "we judge by standards of authenticity."[3] The "revolutionary" question, she maintains, is the one: "are the truths presented in literature, in fact, *true?*"; and this leads, she argues, to "realism" as the "single requirement" of a "humanist aesthetic."[4] In other words, mimesis—or *verisimilitude,* the fidelity of representations to the experience they reflect—is at the core of experiential feminist criticism which regards literature as well as other cultural narratives (histories, auto/biographies, journals and so on) to all have an essential, recognizable, and verifiable referent—the experience of women—which their language transcribes.

While feminist critics such as Showalter distinguish between the study of woman as reader, writer, or critic as very different kinds of critical activities with different subjects (e.g., images of women, the traditions of women's writing, or the histories of women's lives), we can see that the test of "truth" and of the "reality" of these various critical modes is always and inevitably the experience of women. Thus we can adapt Showalter's term "gynocriticism" to encompass the entire range of feminist criticism—whether formalist, thematic, or historical—concerned in some way with the authentic and accurate representation of women's experience in literature and its traditions.[5] Gynocriticism, in short, is the critical form of experiential feminists: whereas experiential feminists seek to rectify the exclusion of women from full participation in society and the omission of women from history, gynocritics redress the exclusion and misrepresentation of women in literature and its traditions. Gynocriticism is thus a mimetic criticism. It is preoccupied, on the one hand, with the *verisimilitude* of representations of women's experience in texts (literary, historical, and critical), and, on the other, postulates a secure, knowable, reliable (and, for some, even a direct, largely unmediated) relation between the woman reader/writer and the text expressing (or misrepresenting) the "reality" of women's lives.

Gynocritics subscribe, for the most part, to the traditional view of mimesis set forth by Eric Auerbach in his classic study *Mimesis*, which Edward Said has called "one of the most admired and influential books of literary criticism ever written."[6] "Modern realism," for Auerbach, is "the serious treatment of everyday reality" in which "everyday occurrences are accurately and profoundly set in a definite period of contemporary history."[7] Auerbach's views in a sense elaborate on George Eliot's famous manifesto on realism, in chapter seventeen of her novel *Adam Bede*, in which she declares the realistic writer is always "ready to give the loving pains of a life to the faithful representing of commonplace things." The representation of the commonplace is the literary enactment of the "personal," of everyday, intimate feelings and occurrences. The reunderstanding of women's experience—the commonplace, personal happenings of their lives—and the recognition and articulation of women's everyday reality in the social and cultural practices in which it has previously been suppressed, marginalized, hidden or unspoken is for experiential feminists a political act: "the personal is political." Thus voicing women's experience in literature, its traditions and institutions in accurate and "true" ways is considered a profoundly political act by gynocritics. For these feminists, mimesis as "the serious treatment of everyday reality," to quote Auerbach again, is seen as the necessary and only valid—in other words "authentic," "faithful" and "true"—way of articulating women's experience. So much so, they fail to recognize that mimesis is itself a literary and cultural "convention," a historical product of the discourses of culture. Instead they take mimesis to be a norm of universal exactitude: the truthful, accurate, and verifiable portrayal of the "way things are" or were—the direct, unmediated expression of women's everyday lives.

Mimesis in this traditional, humanist sense is the making "present"—*re-presenting*—what is absent: mimesis not only voices the (absent) experience it stands for but, even more important for gynocritics, also renders visible previously "unseen" and excluded experience. The "seen" is, of course, itself a political category whose politicality is suppressed by gynocriticism. When gynocritics talk about the unseen being made visible, they are in fact referring to the unseen being represented mimetically. Non-mimetic representations (abstract art, experimental fiction, innovative film, nonrepresentational dance) are not among those arts that enable the unseen to achieve the status of the "seen." Mimesis—as the (re)discovery and articulation of the heretofore excluded and unspoken personal reality of women's lives in social situations—is seen as political, liberating, and inherently feminist by gynocritics since the excluded it represents is precisely what patriarchy has rendered silent and invisible: women's everyday experience in all its dense details.

Experiential feminists thus reclaim realism in the face of the prevailing antirealism of much contemporary writing. But since what is accepted as realism varies with changing historical conditions, the form of realism that is recognized as an accurate and authentic representation of women's experience is continually contested among gynocritics. The crucial question here is not the particular form of "realism"—even Holly admits "realism . . . might take any form"[8]—but that it is *read,* in other words accepted, at a particular historical moment as an accurate and "true" representation of the experience it refers to. The increasing fragmentation of contemporary life and the articulation of the previously excluded, "nonrational" aspects of women's daily lives or of African-American experience, for example, has meant that such literary innovations as collage and multiple, shifting points of view and fantastic events (e.g., Woolf's *Mrs. Dalloway* or Morrison's *Beloved*) are increasingly viewed as more "real" than the traditional coherent plot and unitary point of view of previous modes of realism (e.g., Austen's *Emma* or Brontë's *Jane Eyre*).[9]

Regardless of whether a particular mode representing experience is considered more or less authentic or "real" than another, the defining criteria of mimesis shared by gynocritics is the "fact" that the representation expresses what are recognized at a given historical moment as attributes of "real" experiences of "real" women *outside* the text. And these "real" referents guarantee the validity or "truth" of the representation: the experience or female identity articulated is one that can be collectively recognized and shared by writer and readers alike; in short, it is assumed to be *universal.* The mimetic representation of women and their experiences is thus a mode of idealism: it articulates the "essential" features of women's lives and identities across class, race, and even time. This idealism, or more accurately what Catherine Belsey calls an *"empiricist-idealist* interpretation of the world,"[10] *essentializes* gender: whether it is seen as the result of experience,

biology, social roles, or the like, gender is taken to be the fundamental attribute and thus the "truth" of individuals. While the
specific features of femininity or masculinity may be seen to vary
culturally, the "fact" of one's femaleness or maleness is taken as
given and transcultural. It is viewed, in effect, as the "transcendent," idealist quality of individuals—or in a more experiential
terminology—one's femaleness (or maleness) is a shared, recognizable quality common to other members of the culture. In other
words, empiricist-idealism *cognitivizes* gender and the experience
assumed to produce it: our lived "experience" of our gender is
seen as mediated through our mind or consciousness, and language is, for the most part, still regarded as a mere transparent
and nonproblematic instrument of our consciousness—a "translation" of our perceptions of the "real."[11] Mimesis itself, in spite of
commonly held beliefs, is thus a mode of cognitivism which ultimately dematerializes the depicted phenomena. The naturalized
relationship seen to exist between representations and our perceptions or experience of the "real"—between representations
and the gendered experiences they reflect—only serves to further
essentialize (cognitivize) gender: in other words, turn it into a
matter of mind rather than socioeconomic materiality.

   For gynocritics, then, mimesis represents women as possessing a
recognizable, knowable "essence" of female experience, and
therefore of female identity, that is always "present" and available
despite the diversity of concrete experiences and daily details
manifesting it and even though some of its features may change
culturally and historically. In articulating women's voices, mimesis
not only makes women's essence present to themselves but also to
the patriarchal culture that would exclude them, and the function
of gynocriticism is to amplify women's "true," essential voices,
chastise "false" voices (particularly male misrepresentations of
female voices), and liberate silenced, marginalized and oppressed
voices. For most gynocritics, then, mimesis is considered the necessary and only valid mode for the expression of women's experience and identity, and therefore it is not only synonymous with
literature but also with liberation. All the more so, because
gynocritics tend to equate femaleness with feminism itself: to be a
woman—that is, to have an essential female identity and experience—is in and of itself to be a feminist, and to re-present, to
speak one's femaleness, is seen as a subversion of male traditions
that exclude women's experience. Opposition to patriarchy is thus
defined solely as opposition to men's experiences and tradition—
to male representations—and not as a fundamental transforma-

tion of the system of gender on which patriarchal exploitation is based. Mimesis, then, is considered to have a liberating function in this opposition precisely because it is the means through which women are assumed to make themselves present in literature and its institutions.

But this equation of women, their experiences and their writing with feminism—rather than a theorization of feminism as the political act of transforming the patriarchal production of gender itself—means women (and men) have to adhere to the already given conditions of their gender. And gynocritics consider any opposition to this ideological essentialization of women and re-ification of mimesis as antifeminist: an act of bad faith against one's own femaleness and complicitous with the male tradition. Thus Showalter denigrates opposing critics, especially textual or deconstructive feminists like "Hélène Cixous and the women con-tributors to *Diacritics*," as going around "in men's ill-fitting hand-me-downs, the Annie Hall of English studies."[12]

But by reifying mimesis as the only authentic and reliable repre-sentation of women's voices, experience, and identity, gynocritics ally themselves with the very regime of truth that has for so long successfully suppressed the politics of representation in culture. Mimesis is representation—a cultural practice—and as such a po-litical undertaking. The task of feminism is to demystify the politics of all kinds of representation and not to naturalize some of these and thus place them beyond the reach of a feminist culture critique. As Nelly Furman argues, "When feminist critics focus their interest on women's experience of life and its 'picturing' in literature, what is left unquestioned is whether literature con-ceived as a representational art is not *per se* a patriarchal form of discourse."[13] However, to claim as Furman does that mimesis is "*per se* a patriarchal form of discourse" is itself an essentializing move and erases the historicity of both mimesis and patriarchal discourse. Rather we can say that insofar as mimesis operates to produce and secure gendered subjects and naturalize "femaleness," it does so on behalf of patriarchal ideology and in support of patriarchal social relations. Moreover, gynocriticism acts to valorize and essentialize gender differences, especially women's experiences and identity; in doing so it legitimizes the patriarchal symbolic order and becomes in effect a *patriarchal feminism*.

In opposition to gynocriticsm, what I call textual or antirepre-sentational feminism—that mode of feminism deeply influenced by the deconstructive readings of Derrida and the psychoanalysis

of Lacan—has carried out a sustained critique of mimesis, representation, and an "essentialized" female identity. Textual feminism, as in the writings of Hélène Cixous, Luce Irigary, Alice
Jardine, Shoshana Felman and Jane Gallop, participates in, and is
to a large degree synonymous with, the postmodern delegitimation of the "paternal" master narratives of Western culture, a
process that Jardine has called "gynesis."[14] Textual feminism or
gynesis engages in the poststructuralist deconstruction of the fundamental concepts of Western humanism, such as identity, representation and the real, which form the founding assumptions of
gynocriticism. In doing so, textual feminism displaces the very
idea of woman as a "real" referent or "essential" identity and
instead rewrites woman as a rhetorical category, a textual effect.
"Woman," in gynesis, according to Jardine, "is neither a person
nor a thing, but a horizon . . . a reading effect, a woman-in-effect
that is never stable and has no identity." Woman in other words is
the conceptual, textual "space" of the Other excluded from the
dominant patriarchal modes of knowing in the West: woman is
the "'nonknowledge,' what has eluded" these master narratives,
"what has engulfed them," the "other-than-themselves." Woman,
for textual feminists, is thus the name of "what has remained
impossible for man to think."[15] She is not the biological other but
rather the *unrepresentable* other that exceeds the discourses of
patriarchy: she is the *absent,* unspoken Other.

The textual retheorization of woman as the excluded Other of
discourse and thus as a mode of writing rather than as the agent
of "real" experiences fundamentally deconstructs the basic pre-
cepts of mimetic feminism and the dominant (and for gynesis,
paternal) modes of knowing on which it depends, particularly the
prevailing notion of "truth." "Truth in the West," as Jardine points
out, "has always been defined as 'exactitude of representation',"
other words as mimesis, and it is mimesis that gynesis displaces.
Thus "the true," as Jardine argues, "can no longer be linked to
traditional notions of experience-in-the-world." In fact experience
is itself discursive in gynesis, and, like woman, is retheorized as
"that process which exceeds mastery, as the 'silence' of discourse,
as that which disturbs the subject-present-to-itself."[16] If not only
woman but experience as well lose their "reality," becoming the
excluded Other, the *unrepresentable,* in gynesis, then the naturalized, liberating link gynocritics find between mimesis, experience, and women is radically deconstructed.

Realism, as we have seen, is for gynocritics the representation of
identity in which women and their experiences are reflected accu-

rately (resemblance with the real). Mimesis makes women *present* and visible; it is the place where women speak for themselves. For textual feminists, on the other hand, realism is quite the opposite. It is the *illusion* of presence, the trope of resemblance that functions to conceal the movement of *différance:* the slippage of signification that destabilizes all representations (of the real), exposing their "emptiness," their absent center. Textual feminists, in short, participate in the post-Saussurian, antirepresentational theory of signification in which signifiers refer not to some "real" outside language but merely to other signifiers in an endless chain of significations. Signifiers, in other words, refer not to some content but to the absences or differences among signifiers. Realism thus does not represent "real" women and their experiences, nor can it present women to themselves or to men. Rather for textual feminists, "woman" is the *absent,* excluded Other of realism: the *unrepresentable* of mimesis. As Shoshana Felman argues, woman is "the *realistic invisible,* that which realism as such is inherently unable to see."[17] In other words, for gynesis, women are the "unsaid," the supplement necessary for mimesis to produce itself.

Realism is a regime of truth, in effect an ideological discourse, which secures its "representations" as "real" by excluding or suppressing that which threatens to undermine their seeming "naturalness." In other words, it delimits the boundaries of the "representable" or intelligible and thus of the "real." For gynesis the subversive "unreal"—in other words the excess of signification it cannot master—is woman. As Felman points out, realism

> postulates a conception of "nature" and of "reality" which seeks to establish itself, tautologically, as "natural" and as "real." Nothing, indeed, is less neutral than this apparent neutrality; nothing is less "natural" than this frontier which is supposed to separate "the real" from "the unreal" and which in fact delimits only the inside and the outside of an ideological circle: an inside which is *exclusive* of madness and women, i.e., the "supernatural" and the "unreal."[18]

Thus mimesis, which experiential feminists take to be the "natural," "neutral" reflection of the "real," is for textual feminists deeply complicit with paternal master narratives. The "belief in simple referentiality," common among American feminists, Jane Gallop argues, is "ultimately politically conservative, because it cannot recognize that the reality to which it appeals is a traditional ideological construction, whether one terms it phallomorphic, or metaphysical, or bourgeois, or something else."[19]

To say that woman is excluded and unrepresentable, however, does not mean mimesis does not try to *simulate* her. The "representations" of woman put forth in mimesis are, textual feminists argue, merely the specular image of the male: the reflection and guarantee of male identity as Felman so aptly demonstrates in her critique of the Balzac short story "Adieu." Thus "if a 'woman' is strictly, exactly 'what *resembles* a woman'," in other words a simulation, then "it becomes apparent," according to Felman, "that 'femininity' is much less a 'natural' category than a rhetorical one, analogical and metaphorical."[20] For textual feminists then, "woman" is a paradoxical matrix of various discursive processes and not a coherent identity: she is a textual effect of simulation "represented" as the specular other and guarantee of the male in mimesis as well as the space of the excluded Other: the unrepresentable "Real" of mimesis.

Obviously for textual feminists to say that woman is the unrepresentable "Real," they do not mean a concrete "real" person that language can only incompletely "represent" or reflect as experiential feminists might interpret the concept. Rather the "unrepresentable" is the excess of signification that the prevailing (patriarchal) modes of knowing or master narratives, including mimesis, cannot recognize or make intelligible and therefore is marked as a negative category, namely the "unreal." However, that which is left out as "unreal" according to deconstructive feminism is an excess: a transgressive force of subversion. Excess is thus not an "extra" but a surplus that subverts the economy of signification underwriting mimesis. Woman in gynesis becomes the *name* for this metaphysically/ideologically unknowable Other. Moreover, by "Real" textual feminists do not mean an empirically verifiable entity "out there" but rather the Lacanian "Real," which, according to Jardine, "is certainly not history—nor 'reality,' nor a 'text'." Instead the "Real" for Jardine, annotating Lacan, "designates that which is categorically unrepresentable, nonhuman, at the limits of the known; it is emptiness, the scream, the zero point of death, the proximity of jouissance."[21] Similarly Felman defines the "Real" as "a radically decentering resistance; the real as, precisely, Other, the unrepresentable as such, the ex-centric residue which the specular relationship of vision cannot embrace."[22]

The notion of the "Real" put forth in gynesis contests the materialist politicization of the "Real" argued for in this study. The "Real," I contend, is the *effect of history*. While it is not directly "knowable" or "representable," in other words it *exceeds* the dominant signification, it is not the mystified, transcendental realm of gynesis. Rather its *effects* are intelligible; they affect social practices in patriarchy and are constantly manifested in social struggle, that is, in "reality." What is unrepresentable, what surpasses significacation is always already embedded in history. In order for excess to be designated excess, in other words, in order for excess to be intelligible *as excess,* it needs to be the surplus of that which exists economically and socially—what is in history. That which exists, of course, varies from one site to another; from one symbolic order to another; from one class, race, gender to another, and therefore is always the subject of struggle. What we take to be reality then is always contested by other "realities," which have been marginalized, and as such what we assume to be the "real" (the dominant "reality") is always already "supplemented" and thus put in question by other realities. This is another way of saying that contrary to gynocritics, the real (the dominant reality) is never *true* (in the universal sense they intend) because it is traversed by other realities; nor is it stable since it is the outcome of social struggle.

If the unrepresentable "Real"—the matrix of these contesting realities—is not a rhetorical or cognitive category (the empty space of Lacanian desire) as textual feminists argue but the *effect of contestations in history:* what then is "Woman" whom gynesis gives as the *name* for this "unreal" Other? Moreover what is the excluded Other—the resistance—to patriarchy if it is not woman? These questions are at the core of the contestations between textual feminism and the postmodern, materialist feminist critique I am developing here, and the answers have profound consequences for what is proposed as revolutionary, counterpatriarchal practice in the two theories. By postulating woman as the unrepresentable excess, as silent, resisting other to male dominance and phallocentric narratives, textual feminists put forth woman as the *Other* of patriarchy itself. But such a move, to my mind, mystifies both woman and patriarchy as rhetorical and cognitive categories thereby removing them from social struggle. Moreover it leaves intact the entire economy of gender—merely reversing its terms—according to which patriarchy is organized. As I have argued elsewhere, ideology produces "Woman" as Other to male hegemony and *represents* this opposition as resistance to patriarchy in order to conceal the forbidden Other, the actual threat to patriarchy: the unspeakable *nongendered Other.*[23] The unrepresentable Other opposing patriarchy then is *nongender;* while woman, who is *named* as this oppositional Other, is instead the *gendered other always already contained within patriarchy.* Whether she is theorized as an experiential entity or rhetorical space, woman is the necessary supplement on which patriarchy depends. Nongender, however, is not a mystified realm of emptiness but an opposing economy of signification organized *Otherwise* than around gender, and it is unrepresentable not because it is the reified category of the Other but because it has been suppressed and excluded through social struggle—through the repressive operations of the dominant ideology and hegemonic social relations.

Gynesis or textual feminism, then, reverses the hierarchy of the patriarchal economy of gender but without transforming that system: it intervenes in patriarchal power relations but without overthrowing them. In fact, emancipation by overthrowing patriarchy cannot be the outcome of textual feminism. Like all other modes of deconstruction, textual feminism operates with the assumption that the critique of a system of signification must always take place from within that system; it is in other words an immanent critique. As such it always already uses the very system that it "critiques." The reason for textual feminism's (and deconstruction's) privileging of immanent critique is that it regards any critique made from other sites to be essentially a "transcendental" critique: a critique that violates the terms of the system and is thus an exercise in violence; it imposes alien values on the system by not respecting the system in its own terms. However, no system operates in its own terms: its own terms are always those which the perceivers of the system, depending on their own ideological and historical situationality, attribute to the system. The point of political critique is exactly this demystification of a system's "own terms": where do they come from and WHY? This is a crucial question because textual feminism—like all deconstruction—is a critique of HOW (how the system operates) while the political critique is a critique of WHY (why the system exists, what interests does it serve). So when I say that textual feminism is unable to transform patriarchy, I am not pointing out some neglect, weakness, or oversight of gynesis. On the contrary, this is a philosophical commitment on the part of textual feminists. No system, according to textual feminism/deconstruction, can be overthrown because that which overthrows is regarded to be already a part of the system to be overthrown. We are, in other words, always *in* our practices, and there is no way we can achieve a critical distance from ourselves. In fact any critical distance is suspected by deconstruction as an expression of a desire for TRUTH, a metaphysics of presence. However, materialist feminism regards this logic to be essentially an updating of the logic of liberal reformism and considers deconstruction to be the latest expression of liberal pluralism on the part of European intellectuals.

Gynesis is nonetheless an important critique and delegitimation of patriarchal modes of knowing, particularly mimesis and the "representation" of woman. But it is a formalist and immanent critique—one that critiques the system in terms of the system itself—rather than a political critique: a critique that interrogates the system in terms of the interests it serves and the economic and political regime it underwrites. Textual feminists have undertaken the necessary problematization of "woman" and dissociated her from an anatomical referent. In doing so they have de-essentialized the rather naive empiricism of experiential feminism in which woman is an unproblematic signifier for a fundamental, already existing "femaleness" (whether this is ascribed to biology or to a collective set of experiences). At the same time in reducing woman to a floating signifier of difference that names the site of exclusion, woman becomes a rhetorical space anyone can occupy regardless of their "gender." Consequently, many of the proponents of gynesis are "masters," men like Derrida and Lacan, whose writing has served to merely "reform"—to update while still maintaining—the existing structure of patriarchal power-knowledge relations. To retheorize woman as a signifier without politicizing signification itself as the site of social struggle and the arena for the ideological production of subjectivities is merely to inscribe women in an erotics of signification while erasing her as a historical subject. By situating woman entirely within the jouissance of textuality, gynesis removes woman from social conflict and negates the material social relations producing woman as a historical, gendered subject within patriarchy. It mystifies political conflict as textual difference and abolishes social transformation in an endless play of floating signifiers and textual gaps: substituting the pleasures of the text for a politics of the text-world.

Thus, writing the feminine body, for Cixous and other textual feminists, enables woman to leave "opposition, hierarchizing, exchange, the struggle for mastery . . . all that comes from a period in time governed by phallocentric values" and become part of "an 'economy' that can no longer be put in economic terms."[24] Woman, in short, enters a libidinal economy that renders her body one of "free" (unrestrained) desires. But this "free" body of desire is merely the vehicle of the amorphous, voracious, desiring and devouring of pleasure required by a consumer culture. This transcendent, mystified body of gynesis is unharnessed, unconstrained, and above all *not produced:* it simply *is;* it *exists* in its own essence, that is, in its (gendered) desires. But this only leaves woman back where she has always been perceived to be: outside the economic, outside social relations and thus outside the arena of social transformation. In other words, the body of woman put forth by textual feminists, notably Cixous and Irigaray, as the sensuous referent anchoring subversive writing and materializing the textual, is a *libidinal body* and not the *body in social conflict.* The materiality of this body is the commonsensical materialism of libidinal desire and its tangible appendages: breasts, lips (vulvar and oral), vagina and so on. It is not the materialism of social relations that, for example, Marx inquires into in *The German Ideology:* the social relations producing the body, its historically produced desires and their intelligibility in the patriarchal economy of gender. *Écriture féminine* reduces the political and social to an erotics of the libido: for textual feminists, woman's "libido," as Cixous says, "will produce far more radical effects of political and social change."[25] But this is mere mystical empiricism; how such radical changes are to be brought about except through desire/ing is never theorized.

By diverting women's attention away from "emancipation"—the collective, economic and political end to the extraction of surplus value and exploitation in power-knowledge relations according to gender—and toward "liberation"—personal freedom attained through the force of the libidinal body—textual feminism, in effect, legitimates the oppression of women. The subtle, complex moves of deconstructive feminism through the mazes of textuality as difference and unmasterable slippages of language eventually ends in the rather commonsensical resurrection of the old, tired humanist subject through the assertion of a neoreferentialism. This neoreferentiality anchors the text and therefore "stabilizes" it (in spite of the rhetoric of rupture and instability so valorized in textual feminism) in the libidinal body. Once more the self, this time in a postmodern disguise, emerges as the independent originator of meaning, change, and its own sexuality. Such a move again eclipses the radical alternative: the politicization of signification (situating it in social struggle) and a theorization of subjects as *historical* agents (not "free," individual agents) produced by and participating in ideological contradictions and contestations and therefore able to engage in transformative practices. It thus turns out that Showalter's more recent appropriations of *écriture féminine* as part of gynocriticism have a basis after all in the retrograde politics of textual feminism: in its neoessentialist privileging of the libidinal (feminine) body and resurrection of the autonomous, amorous subject with her independent "free" will or rather independent "free" desire. Gynesis, in the end, is merely the flip side of experiential feminism.

Nor is textual feminism's antirealism a politically transformative alternative. Writing the feminine, textual feminists argue, is the writing of undecidability, and thus they claim it is antirealist and subversive. But the antirealism of gynesis is more a formal displacement of realism than a process which inaugurates emancipatory practices by overthrowing the regime of mimesis. According to Cixous, feminine writing disrupts patriarchy by fracturing the authority of self-present representation and breaking the "rhetorics, regulations and codes" of the Law of the Father organizing phallogocentric modes of knowing. To write the feminine for textual feminists is to subvert the hegemony of mimesis—which is the discourse of the exclusion of woman—through gaps, absences, discontinuities, repetitions, and especially parody (the device which unleashes the repressed textual pleasure) in order to make a space for woman to speak. Thus "woman's *seizing* the occasion to *speak*," is, for Cixous, "her shattering entry into history" and into mimesis: thereby rupturing representation itself and exploding those discourses that have silenced her. This means for Cixous that "a feminine text cannot fail to be more than subversive . . . to blow up the law, to break up the 'truth' with laughter."[26] Thus while experiential feminists reclaim realism as the liberating expression of women's experience, textual feminists undermine it. But they do not overturn or abolish realism's reproduction of an engendered—and thus exploitative—reality.

Moreover, for textual feminists to valorize the antimimetic (feminine) text as subversive and to denigrate the mimetic text as reactionary and patriarchal is as essentializing as the experientialist feminists' claim that the mimetic text is liberating. Mimesis, I propose, is neither reactionary nor liberating *in and of itself*, nor is antimimesis subversive *in and of itself*. The politics of a text or of representation is not determined by the "essential" features of a particular mode of representation of textuality but by the *uses* to which they are put: how they operate within a particular ideological organization of signification at a specific historical moment. The politics of representation is a question then of the *effects* produced, especially the kinds of subjectivities generated. The issue of mimesis for a postrepresentational feminist cultural critique is how is mimesis (as both a writing and reading practice) situated in the patriarchal economy of signification: in other words what are its *effects* and consequences in terms of transformative practices in writing/reading texts of culture; what subjectivities does it produce and how are these related to the ideological imperatives of patriarchy (does it resecure or contest patriarchal hegemony)?

Mimesis is itself self-divided, sliding and unstable. But the instability of mimesis does not come from the fact that it is a textual product; rather it derives from the fact that it is an ideological apparatus. Mimesis, like any signifying practice, is divided by the contradictions of the symbolic order and social relations which make it intelligible to begin with, and its alterity, gaps, and absences are the effects of the social conflicts and slippages in ideology itself. The discontinuity between "text" and "reality" is not, contrary to deconstructive feminism, an inherent quality of textuality, i.e., difference, but the effect of inconsistencies, aporias, and discontinuities of ideology, which always represents itself as a self-same discourse of coherence, identity, and continuity. The kinds of incoherences and discontinuities of ideology vary from one social formation to another as do the types of aporia and differences that readers of texts find in them. If difference, incoherence, and discontinuities were inherent (ahistorical and permanent) features of textuality itself, then "differences" in texts would remain the "same" all throughout history. The history of reading and reception, however, contradicts this: each social formation produces subjects who read different differences in texts depending on how those texts are situated in relation to the conditions of production in any given historical moment.

Mimesis is a historical strategy in the discourses of culture, and its features, effects, and uses vary from one historical period to another, from one symbolic order to another, and are determined by class, gender, and race, that is, by social struggle. Thus what is accepted as realistic—commonly assumed to be faithful to everyday experiences and consciousness—by one group may seem quite unrealistic to another. Toni Morrison's novels may seem full of fantastic, "unreal" events for white middle-class (male) readers, but they may not seem so extraordinary for African-American readers. Morrison has commented on the everyday reality of her childhood growing up in an African-American family, saying, "We were intimate with the supernatural."[27] Thus much of the "fantastic" in her novels can be read by some readers as "authentic" representations of everyday life filled with "decoding dream symbols . . . signs, visitations, ways of knowing that reached beyond the five senses."[28] Nor are realism's political effects always conservative and reactionary. Mimesis in non-Western, third-world literature is often revolutionary: it has been used to contest and overturn the prevailing common sense valorized in the conventional and oppressive modes of antirepresentationalism that have supported the dominant social relations.

Similarly, antirealism and experimental avant-garde writing are equally historically determined and just as much ideological apparatuses as mimesis—antirepresentationalism can be used as easily to conserve and resecure patriarchy as to contest it. In fact, for postrepresentational feminists, the avant-garde, deconstructive play of the antirealist gynesis operates to revive and resecure patriarchy by removing reading/writing practices from history, by substituting textual differences for economic, social, and historical contradictions, and by mystifying woman as a rhetorical category, as inaccessible Other. In the end the textual feminist critique of mimesis and the subversive writing of *écriture féminine* participate in the *re*novation of patriarchy by *de*legitimating traditional, dysfunctional forms of patriarchy while *re*legitimating gender differences and the opposition masculine/feminine on which patriarchy depends. They do so by means of new discourses and languages more responsive to the shifting contemporary world. Gynesis, in other words, engages in the postmodern resurrection of patriarchy to meet the changing demands of late-capitalism and risks being a patriarchal feminism.

Again, the question of mimesis for feminist culture critique is not whether mimesis is essentially patriarchal or whether antirealism is revolutionary, but what are the *uses* of mimesis: how does it operate in the patriarchal economy of signification and production of subjectivities. In the postrepresentational theory of mimesis I am articulating here, representation is not considered the *reflection* or imitation of something else, that is, of experience or the extradiscursive "real." Rather, representation is theorized as the ideological *production* of "reality": the production of the meanings and significations that are *made to stand for* or *seem* to stand for an unknowable "real" and make it intelligible at a given historical moment. And the political economy of representation should be sought *not* in the slippages of signifying systems but in examining how certain forms of representation preserve and render natural the interests of certain classes and gender. Representation is always already inscribed in the political, economic, and ideological practices within any given social formation and functions to legitimate the validity, unavoidability, and historical necessity of those practices. In other words, the practices of the social

formation take place within a specific symbolic order which orga-
nizes significations in such a way that they support that social
formation. The effect of representations, then, is to *naturalize* this
economy of significations by (re)presenting them as "grounded"
in "real" referents—and thus as not only the ineluctable "way
things are" but the way they ought to be *always*—and to produce
the subjectivities necessary to continually (re)secure the authority
of the symbolic order and the social formation it supports.

Given the fact that any social formation is an ensemble of
conflicts and contestations, it follows that there can never be just
one set of representations—an essential, verifiable reflection of
the real—or mode of representation. However, ideology does put
forth a dominant set or mode of representation which establishes
the agenda of the real according to the hegemonic economic and
social relations. This dominant representation is always contested
by conflicting representations put forth by opposing classes, marginalized races, and the "second sex" in order to transform the
agenda of the real and the subjectivities and social relations it
secures. Thus the production of representations can be
hegemonic or oppositional depending on the position of the ideology determining them and the social relations they legitimate.
Any ideological production of representations, then, is fissured
not only by the struggle over conflicting ways of organizing significations but also by the contradictions within the ideology itself.
This is another way of again saying that representation is neither
an imitation of something which exists prior to it (mimesis from
Plato to contemporary gynocriticism), nor is it the effect of formal
systems of signification as in gynesis. Rather representation, in my
view, is the very site of social conflict, and those representations
that determine the "real" are those that validate the dominant
ideological, political, and economic practices of the social formation.

We can then theorize mimesis as that form of (ideological)
representation which operates through a fetishization and reification of the *everyday* to naturalize a historically specific economy of
signification and the social relations it underwrites. In late-cap-
italist patriarchy, the symbolic order that mimesis legitimates is
obviously patriarchy, and mimesis operates to secure its hegemony
and to suppress ways of organizing the economy of signification
otherwise than according to the phallus. Specifically mimesis acts
to reproduce and secure gendered subjectivities by (re)presenting
the maleness or femaleness of an individual as embedded in the
very factuality of daily experience and thus as "actuality," as the

inevitable "way things are." In doing so, mimesis not only puts forth the historically specific constructions of gender as universal, transhistorical and "natural"—that is as a "fact" of experience if not biology—but more important it conceals the actuality of gender as signification, that is, as ideological representation and thus open to contestation and change. By reifying the details of daily experience as the intractable "real" and then putting forth (ideological) representations as authentic, "true" expressions of this "real," mimesis becomes the most effective cultural site for the (re)production of the patriarchal political economy of signification as the "real" and for perpetuating its hegemony. In fact, mimesis has become so effective and pervasive an agent of the patriarchal symbolic order that it is the dominant mode of knowing informing nearly all cultural practices from the discourses of common sense to economic practices. And the mark of the success of the dominant ideology in recruiting complying subjectivities is that the majority of readers of literature have come, by and large, to view mimetic fiction as synonymous with literature itself.

Mimesis claims to be the expression of the sensuous immediacy of experience, of the facts and details of daily life, which it puts forth as the very concreteness of reality itself. However, for postrepresentational feminists, "daily life" (the object of our commonsense "experience") is not produced out of "daily life" itself (that is, life as derived directly from the structure of the world "out there")—as empiricists, notably gynocritics, believe—rather the everyday life is produced by ideology: it is mediated by practices in the social formation. In other words the seeming sensuousness of experience and the facticity of reality are *ideological effects:* they are the results of ideological representations—mimetic constructions—of the significations of the symbolic order as "natural" as "there" as "what is." The experience of the everyday, then, is not direct but the outcome of social knowledge—knowing the codes of culture. Materialist feminist cultural critique acknowledges the necessity of daily practices (unlike gynesis), but it contests the THERENESS of the everyday (unlike gynocriticism) and demonstrates that this thereness—which is the equation of objectivity and the reality of realism—is not in the world itself but in the discourses of patriarchy. We can thus read Roland Barthes's "reality effect" not just as a formal or semiotic operation but as an ideological one. Barthes has argued in his essay "The Reality Effect" that the function of seemingly "insignificant," "useless details" in mimetic narratives—those descriptions of facts, things, features, events and so on which are "not justified by any purpose of action or communication"—guarantee the "plausibility" of the narrative and "denote what is commonly called 'concrete reality'." In signifying "the category of the 'real,' and not its various contents,"[29] these "useless details" signify "realism" itself. But more than that, I would argue, the everyday details pervading realistic texts function ideologically to establish the *credibility*—that is the *reality*—of the (ideological) representations assumed in the narrative. They function to authorize as *what is* the gendered subjectivities and meanings produced by the text and represented as the "real" (or at least an "authentic" expression of the "real"). Moreover the suffusion, even surplus, of daily details in mimetic fiction functions to make the "real" seem plentiful, complex and above all *present*.

To fully understand the authority of mimesis in the patriarchal symbolic order, we need to distinguish the different operation of ideology in diverse discourses of culture, for example, in popular and mimetic narratives. In popular literature the imaginary—or more precisely its ideological simulation in the symbolic—is explicitly articulated and foregrounded, and ideology operates in these narratives to interpellate the reader into gendered subjectivities through the fusional identity of the reader with overt articulation and reification of imaginary ("ideal") figures, notably the phallic figure. But from the perspective of mimesis these imaginary or "ideal" figures, such as the detective or romance hero, seem simplistic, stereotypical, clichéd, or mythic. They lack the particularity, individuality, uniqueness, and complexity of "real" people; in other words, their representations lack sufficient "realistic" details to give them plausibility. Mimetic fiction, on the other hand, subordinates the imaginary to the primacy of the everyday in order to resecure and embed gendered subjectivities in the fabric of daily life with a high degree of verisimilitude that puts its representations beyond easy questioning by the reader. This produced "density" of mimetic fiction serves to relegitimate and replenish ideological simulations of the imaginary, especially the phallic figure, by investing these simulations with sufficient details and thus "reality." Mimetic fiction is thus not only the affirmation of the "visible," the everyday; it is also the carefully contained insertion of the imaginary—or rather simulations of the imaginary—in the everyday thereby refurbishing and renewing the necessary ideological identities needed to interpellate readers into gendered subject positions. We can better theorize these ideological operations of mimesis by mapping the political economy of its relations on the semiotic square (see Figure 1).

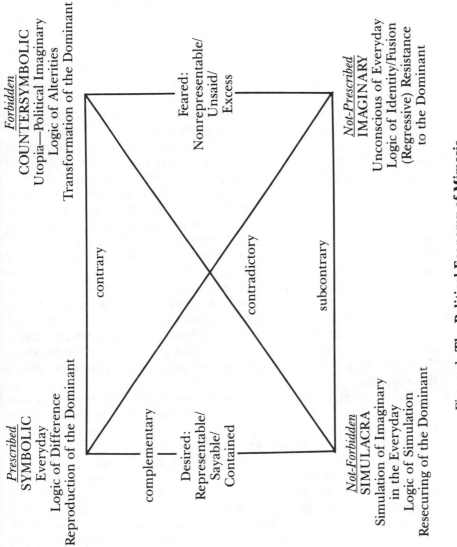

Figure 1. **The Political Economy of Mimesis**

First, in the prescribed or privileged relation, mimesis represents itself (or more accurately, ideology represents mimesis) as the reflection of the symbolic order. The symbolic order, again, is the production and division of reality according to the Law of the Father, which is the logic of difference: the injunction to differentiate or divide subjectivities and significations in terms of the phallic signifier, in other words, to engender. The symbolic order is the intrusion of the "third term"—language, the Father, difference—in the undifferentiated (imaginary) relation to identity and unity with the Other (Mother) preceding the individual's entry into language and thus social reality or the everyday. As the arena of the everyday, the symbolic order is characterized by difference, multiplicity, and complexity: the privileged features of mimesis. Thus details, characters, and events in mimetic fiction acquire plausibility and authority according to the degree of diversity, complexity, and differentiation they are given. The symbolic order is also marked by loss, division, and alienation, but these features function to undermine ideological hegemony. In fact they indicate the contradictions in the symbolic order that dispel the "naturalization" of ideological representations of reality, especially gender. Thus in order to reproduce and secure that everyday reality put forth by the symbolic order and to interpellate individuals in the relations necessary to maintain it, ideology must mask the absences and lack in the reality of the everyday and instead (re)present it as a plenitude and a presence: a plenitude of facts and details and the irrevocable and thus unalterable presence of facticity itself. But presence and plenitude are features of the imaginary, which is contradictory and thus supplementary to the symbolic.

The imaginary constitutes the unconscious of the everyday and is governed by the logic of identity or fusion. It is the arena of the repressed longing for the object of desire, for the Other with which the individual seeks to fuse in a relation of unity and wholeness. The imaginary is thus the "unreal" space of presence, plenitude, and unity. Moreover it is the excluded, nonrepresentable excess of desire of the everyday and thus a resistance to the symbolic. But such resistance is regressive in that it is based on the nostalgic desire for a return to the presymbolic, for an immersion in the unconscious, for an escape from the symbolic. To the degree that gynesis theorizes the Other in opposition to the symbolic and mimesis, and as the imaginary unconscious of the everyday instead of as the political imaginary or countersymbolic, textual feminists risk engaging in a regressive resistance rather than a political transformation of patriarchy. The countersymbolic—which is the forbidden contrary to the patriarchal symbolic, the utopian way of organizing reality *otherwise* than according to the phallic signifier—is governed by the logic of alterity rather than identity and is thus transformative rather than regressive. The countersymbolic is the fundamental threat that patriarchy has to exclude and render unknowable, unspeakable, and unrepresentable.

In order to conceal the political imaginary and harness the plenitude and fusional identities of the unconscious imaginary, ideology needs to simulate these imaginary relations on the level of the symbolic. In other words ideology must invest its representations of the everyday—that is, of reality—with simulations of imaginary identities in order to endow them with the illusion of presence, wholeness, and inevitability. Such representations are, of course, simulacra. Simulacra function, on the one hand, to *replenish* those representations of the everyday which have begun to lose their seeming "naturalness" or fullness and to reveal their lack. They also operate, on the other hand, to render imaginary identities—such as the phallic figure—credible, plausible, and thus effective in the symbolic arena by embedding them in details and presenting them as highly differentiated and complex rather than stereotypical entities. In other words simulacra represent the imaginary figures they mimic as authentic reflections of the "real," thereby naturalizing and legitimating them. Simulacra thus resecure the dominant by validating and replenishing ideological representations necessary to construct the patriarchal real and to interpellate individuals into gendered subject positions. Moreover the effectivity of simulacra in harnessing imaginary unities and using them to represent a plentiful and ever present, transcendent and irrevocable "real" is crucial in the ideological suppression of the threatening alterities and transformative oppositions of the countersymbolic. For if the "real" can be convincingly put forth as always already "there," as an unchanging whole despite its diversity of details, then it will seem immutably the "way things are." Obviously in theorizing simulations as necessary modes of representation and as always already ideological, I am contesting Baudrillard's notion of simulation as the displacement of representations and as unanchored signs.[30] Nor are simulations a form of radical activity in a consumer society; rather the increasing use of simulations in late-capitalism is a result of ideology's need to redouble its efforts to resecure the symbolic as it is put in crisis.

To critique how mimesis operates on behalf of patriarchal ideology to produce gendered subjectivities, I want to first examine the reification of everyday details and the way these are represented as a plenitude and irrevocable "thereness" in which individuals are firmly fixed. Mimetic fictions obviously are diverse and complex texts. Unlike popular fictions, which frequently follow readily recognized formulas and are overtly repetitious in their effects, mimetic fictions present themselves as unique and distinctive. However, for all their diversity, mimetic fictions are also alike in their ideological operations and effects. The foremost of these is the representation of everyday details as a self-evident presence, an immediate marker of the real—Barthes's "reality effect"—through which the narrative is naturalized as anchored in reality and in terms of which individuals are interpellated into an unquestionable maleness or femaleness.

As indicated on the semiotic square mapping the political economy of mimesis (Figure 1), the primary operation of mimesis is the representation of everyday reality in terms of the logic of difference of the symbolic—in other words the patriarchal injunction to differentiate, to line up on one or the other side of the phallic divide. Mimesis reproduces the symbolic in the everyday through a representation of difference not as absences and gaps but as a profusion of acts and details with which the individual is portrayed as having an *immediate* (that is an imaginary) connection or identification. In other words the individual is represented as immersed, contained, and encompassed in a fusional relation with the seeming fullness and presence of details put forth by mimesis as the reflection of the plenitude of the real. By representing difference as a multiplicity, mimesis participates in the ideological suppression of difference as opposition, contradiction, and struggle over alternative modes of signification and subjectivities. The everyday, which is the arena of conflict and contestation, is thus assumed by mimesis in an ideological operation as an (imaginary) plenitude: a "natural" fixed, immutable unity. The "real" is thus presented to us as a seamless web of pluralities in which differences are reduced to mere diversity, and threatening contradictions, conflicts, and alterities are suppressed and concealed.

Differences in the symbolic order and the everyday are represented as always grounded on an underlying unity—whether the unity of a life, the times, a period, or humanity itself. Ideology interpellates individuals into this seamless plurality, this seeming "natural" order, fixing them in their "natural"—that is their gendered—place by representing them as inescapably immersed in the "unified" web of the everyday with which they are fused in an imaginary identification. The everyday reality of difference and plurality of details, of unique individuality, is in itself the ideological representation of an imaginary unity through the singular detail which is made to stand for the whole. In other words, the unity of the "ideal"—the imaginary object of wholeness and completeness—lies at the heart of the empiricism of the everyday and is the ground ideology puts forth to anchor the innumerable details of daily life and invest them with "meaning." In mimetic fiction, then, the singular, diverse, and unique details and the different entities they constitute in the narrative stand for "ideal"/imaginary figures. Thus the very different, distinct, and individualistic women in a mimetic narrative stand for the single imaginary "ideal" *woman*. This imaginary gendered figure of *essential* femaleness (or maleness as the case may be) is the "significance" ideology attempts to invest in the innumerable different men and women represented in the text and the diverse details constituting them. The reader's engagement with singular details and identification with unique individual characters in mimetic fiction is an ideological interpellation: an imaginary fusion with the seemingly "natural," "ideal" gender they stand for and essentialize in all their particularity.

No matter how different individual texts of mimetic fiction may be, we can find instances of this ideological production of the everyday as a unitary plenitude, in which the individual is fixed in "natural," immutable gendered positions, on nearly every page of any text one reads. To demonstrate how pervasive this ideological operation is, I will examine two politically opposed and seemingly quite different mimetic texts: John Updike's *Couples* and Marge Piercy's *Vida*. Beginning with *Couples*, I want to critique the scene portraying the formal dinner-dance/wake held the night Robert Kennedy was shot. It is a scene like many others in Updike's numerous texts in which the subjects—both the subject of the text (the character) and the subject spoken by the text (the reader)[31]—are immersed and fixed in the concrete profusion of details surrounding them:

> The fashion that fall was for deep décolletage; Piet, arriving at nine, was overwhelmed by bared breasts . . . Entering the Thornes' living room he saw naked shoulders and flaringly bared bosoms floating through the candlelight, haunting the African masks, the gaudy toss pillows, the wickerwork hassocks and strap-hinged Spanish chests and faded wing chairs. . . . Marcia Little-Smith, in a braless orange bodice, displayed, as she reached forward, earrings shuddering, to tap a

cigarette into a copper ashtray each dent of which was crescental in
the candlelight, conical tits hanging in shadow like tubular roots loose
in water. Georgene wore white, two filmy breadths of cloth crossed to
form an athletic and Attic binder, her breasts flattened boyishly, as if
she were on her back. . . .

Bea Guerin drifted toward him with uplifted face; her bosom,
sprinkled with sweat, was held forward in a stiff scarlet carapace like
two sugared buns being offered warm in the metal vessel of their
baking. "Oh Piet," she said, "isn't it awful, that we're all here, that we
couldn't stay away, couldn't stay home and mourn decently?" With
lowered lids he fumbled out a concurrence, hungering for the breasts
that had risen to such a roundness their upper rims made a dimpled
angle with Bea's chest-wall.[32]

The passage is saturated with an abundance of very different,
distinct, and singular "bared breasts." This detailed enumeration
of dissimilar breasts manifests the multiplicity and variation of
women's bodies in daily life and stresses the "uniqueness" and
physicality of each woman's breasts: their differing weights,
shapes, and sizes. The passage also specifies the diverse color,
style, and fabric of each woman's dress, the way it covers, confines,
or displays her breasts. Such specific, quotidian details as well as
the emphasis on their difference and multiplicity operate to establish the credibility and "reality" (the existence in daily life) of these
representations of breasts which are not so much self-evident
aspects of the female body as they are imaginary objects of intense
male desire, or "hungering," as Piet is described.

Moreover the passage is also filled with details wholly unrelated
to breasts, bodies, or clothes, such as "the African masks" and "the
gaudy toss pillows." These details seem quite insignificant, but on
closer examination they make an important contribution to the
"reality effect" of the portrayal of breasts. Most are common
ordinary items, and those that are not (the African masks, for
instance) merely serve to mark the individuality and difference of
the everyday. All these objects are put forth as physical, solid, and
unquestionably "there"; they anchor the "flaringly bared bosoms
floating through the candlelight" in a seemingly concrete physical
reality "out there" by lending the floating breasts the same apparent solidity, physicality, and irrevocable "thereness" of the "strap-
hinged Spanish chests and faded wing chairs." They give the
representations of breasts the authority of the empirical.

The imaginary object of desire, the "floating" breasts, then are
simulated in the symbolic—that is in the everyday—in all their
particularity and represented as having the same "realness," "nat-

uralness," "thereness," and physicality as the "wickerwork hassocks." The quotidian particularity of these descriptions operates to conceal the ideological production of breasts as signifiers and to "naturalize" and "objectify" their "significance," representing it as empirically "real" and repressing its historical constructedness. Yet the "significance" of everyday details in mimesis is always ideological: they stand for simulations of imaginary, "ideal," identities ("femaleness"), no matter how much mimesis puts them forth as evidence of empirical reality. Therefore despite their seemingly irrefutable "realness," the breasts are signifers of the sexual, anatomical other, the not-male, the female, required by patriarchy and in opposition to which men take their place as other, as male. Through the mimetic reification of details, breasts are thus ideologically constructed in the everyday as the "real" physical mark of otherness—that which is most visibly different from male—and thus as the irrefutable "detail" fixing "women" (those with breasts of whatever size or shape) in their gendered place of not-male, of female.

On the other hand those who "hunger" for all these different, diverse breasts—it doesn't matter so much which ones, just breasts in all their plurality and paradoxically their imaginary essence—receive the imaginary reassurance that they "possess" the phallus ideology opposes to breasts: to desire breasts is to make the (absent) phallus seem present. In fact this resecuring of "male" subjects—both the subject of the text (notably Piet Hanema) and the subject spoken by the text (the reader)—as the *possessor* of the absent phallus through an imaginary fusion with the sexual, genital other is the primary ideological operation and thematic concern of Updike's *Couples*. After all, woman in patriarchal ideology is the guarantor of the phallus. The narrative is the enactment of Piet's continuing efforts to reach an immediate, complete sexual merging with woman, with the not-male, and thereby confirm the phallus as concretely, physically present for him. Moreover such representations affirm men as the privileged subjectivities in patriarchy and the "desirers" while again fetishizing women (or the anatomical parts that stand for them) as the "objects" of desire: the solid, physical "things" to be possessed, penetrated, used, and consumed.

The diverse women depicted here in all the particularity of their very different anatomies as well as their individual tastes, movements, and relation to their sexuality/breasts (in other words their personalities), all *stand for* the same imaginary identity: the *essential* (ideal) "Woman." Whether this essential "Woman" is read as the imaginary object of sexual desire or the very principle of "femaleness"—either biological or experiential—she is always taken to be NOT-MALE, or more positively, "female." In other words, these singular women, from the voluptuous Janet to the athletic Georgene, are as much representations of the non-male as any popular romance heroine. The detailed particularity of mimetic representations, however, gives these simulations of the gendered other much greater credibility and authority in the arena of the everyday.

But such ideological representations are contradictory. On the one hand, they require the singularity of details, the individual difference of women in the everyday to make them seem plausible and "real." On the other hand, these very differences and particularities disrupt the imaginary identity and wholeness ideology tries to simulate in the everyday. Updike's narrative resolves this contradiction by foregrounding the imaginary "ideal" underlying empiricism: all these highly differentiated women are, in effect, the same woman. They are substitutable and replaceable, a series of interchangeable women whose *significance* lies not in their individuality but in their essence: their femaleness which is the "transcendental signified" endowing all signifiers (individual women) with the same meaning and sexual plenitude. When asked what he thinks is most "wonderful," Piet answers, "a sleeping woman . . . because when she is sleeping . . . *she becomes all women*" (252, emphasis mine). In other words, her singularity is suppressed, and she becomes the "ideal" woman (the transcendental signified) with whom he can find an imaginary fusion. However, when the demands of a specific woman's daily particularity and difference shatter the illusion of imaginary connection, he leaves her and moves on to the next one whose "difference" is still enticing and not yet intrusive, substituting this next one with still another one when her daily material practices and physical concreteness ("the goosebumped roughness of her buttocks, the gray unpleasantness of her shaved armpits" (454), disrupt his imaginary connection.

The reassertion of the authority of everyday "reality" over the sexual imaginary in *Couples* demonstrates the way ideology utilizes the multiplicity and diversity of mimesis to enact its contradictory needs and at the same time represent these as "complexity." On the one hand, ideology needs to simulate and harness the imaginary in the symbolic in order to naturalize the everyday: to render it seemingly immediate, inevitable, and whole and to invest its details with fullness and presence. On the other hand, fomenting imaginary relations threatens to release a regressive desire for identities that may disrupt some operations of the symbolic order. It is important to point out here that the ideological contradiction over the simulation of the imaginary in the symbolic is rooted in social struggle. These simulations enable ideology to naturalize and resecure the everyday "reality" it constructs in order to legitimate and reproduce the social relations necessary to patriarchal capitalism. Thus while the disruptions caused by the imaginary may offer resistance to certain practices in the symbolic or render specific patriarchal agents (like Piet) ineffective, they are regressive rather than transformative. They are always ideologically constrained simulations that harness desire and direct it toward gendered identities, thereby reinforcing the fundamental economy of patriarchy instead of contesting it. Mimesis is thus a crucial site of ideological operation since its pluralism allows for diverse ways of expressing and containing this contradiction. It enables varying degrees of simulation of the imaginary while offering different ways of constraining it and reasserting the primacy, "presence," and hegemony of the everyday. In fact the multiplicity of these seemingly endless instances of ideological infusions and containment of the imaginary in the everyday is what gives mimetic narratives their sense of complexity and diversity.

In Marge Piercy's feminist novel, *Vida,* on the other hand, the hegemony of patriarchal ideology is at least partially contested and the narrative attempts to disinvest concrete, individual men of their imaginary potency and to locate them firmly in the everyday, in the "reality" of experience. The novel is a wholly mimetic narrative informed by an experiential feminism that attempts to contest male dominance and the institutionalization of patriarchal authority in the state. It puts forth as the main subject of the text an increasingly feminist member of the radical left underground, Vida, and the most valorized subject in the text is her sister, Nadine, a mother and radical feminist lesbian. *Vida* thematizes male domination and tries to expose male oppression and exploitation of women by showing men "the way they really are"; in other words by firmly fixing them in their everyday particularity. In doing so, each man represented is largely disinvested of any imaginary significance as a phallic figure. At the same time they are *reinvested* with the imaginary presence, facticity, and inevitability of their concrete, individual maleness. Men are depicted as singular, individual, and empirical. The mimetic representations of each man continually set him in the "thereness" of his body and his actions but even more important in the concrete, sensual details of Vida's experience of these.

For instance, in an early description of Leigh, Vida's husband and lover of many years, Piercy does not depict an imaginary phallic figure but rather a concrete man who is knowable through such daily details and specific practices as gaining weight, the cut and color of his clothes (a "Bush outfit in black corduroy")[33] and the question of who shopped for them. Moreover the men are shown in terms of varying degrees of oppression, ranging from the dominating, violent Kevin through the leftist, egotistical somewhat chauvinistic Leigh to Joel: "a truly new breed of human being, a man untouched by macho roles, vulnerable and open, gentle and emotional as a woman" (89). Yet each man, in all his difference, stands for an essential irrevocable "maleness" that is always opposite from women's own essential "femaleness." Thus despite her very different politics, Piercy ends up essentializing maleness and femaleness as completely as does Updike. This is not to say, however, that Piercy valorizes maleness in the way Updike does, but she does reassert its inviolability nonetheless.

The men in Piercy's novel are in large part objects of sexual desire, and Vida engages in sexual relations with a number of them—as many if not more than the number of women in Updike's *Couples,* which is known for its promiscuity. However, unlike the ideological imbuing of sexual intimacy with imaginary unity in Updike's *Couples,* Piercy's narrative reduces the imaginary fusion of the sexual encounter and instead embeds sexuality in the everyday details and concrete occurrences of the physical and emotional experience. Unlike the "brilliant glimpses" in *Couples* of Piet's sexual union with Foxy in which he "lost himself on the slopes of her presence" (213), Vida's sexual encounters never leave the quotidian "thereness" of the body's physicality: the particularity of differences constituting the everyday/symbolic overwhelm any imaginary identification. Piercy's displacement of the imaginary identity of the phallic figure in the physicality, the immutable "thereness" and singularity of individual men—their "weight," "pressure," "dense hairiness," "bones jutting," and "hammering of his penis in her"—is a means of liberating women from the tyranny of patriarchal ideology, which defines women in terms of their sexual fusion with the imaginary phallic figure men are made to stand for, as in Harlequin Romances.

But such liberation is individual and personal and occurs on the level of the everyday, in other words, within the patriarchal symbolic, and is not *emancipation,* which is the freeing of all from the system of oppression according to gender. Such individual liberation is always limited and constrained by the patriarchal construction of the everyday. Piercy's representations put forth the inadequacy, limitations, and oppressive traits of specific men and the sexual politics they practice—Joel's infantile jealousy, Kevin's physical abuse of women, and Leigh's selfishness. But her fidelity to mimesis and careful delineation of the men's particularity and concreteness endows these individual men with the fullness, presence, and inevitability of the everyday—in other words, patriarchal reality—and in so firmly establishing their difference from women she reifies them as the embodiment of an essential masculinity of otherness. She thus rejuvenates gender differences and reasserts the concrete power of men in the everyday.

The imaginary, however, is not wholly absent in Piercy's reification of the everyday: it is invested in women. In displacing the phallic figure and the symbolic father, Piercy substitutes for it the mother figure, who is the imaginary object of desire with whom Vida seeks an imaginary identity. This desire to regain a bonding and fusion with the mother figure is made specific and represented in daily reality in terms of Vida's longing for her "real," biological mother, Ruby, from whom she is separated by the patriarchal authority of the state and then by her mother's death. It is an imaginary unity expressing a shared, essentialization of women's experiences and bodies: "He could not comprehend her link with Ruby, based not on politics but on a shared hard-luck childhood; on shared complicity; on shared bodily continuity— the same breasts, the same legs and green eyes; the same deep driving energy, in Ruby dissipated in endless chain smoking, cleaning, pacing, in Vida harnessed but the same force" (303). Since this desire to reunite with the mother is largely unfillable in the everyday, Piercy manifests this imaginary unity in daily life in terms of a "sisterhood" among women—including Vida's relation to her "real" sister, Natalie. This sisterhood, like Vida's link with her mother, is based on a bonding generated by women's essential shared femaleness: their "shared complicity" in the experiences of patriarchy and their similar "bodily continuity"—the inevitable "fact" that their breasts, legs, and vaginas are so different from men. The experiential feminist ideology Piercy puts forth in *Vida* may attempt to contest male domination and to substitute a resisting ideology based on a simulated imaginary unity of women in terms of their essential female experiences. But as long as it does not challenge the way patriarchal ideology constructs reality, it ends up participating in and promoting the inevitability of the everyday reality and gendered subjectivities patriarchy constructs. Piercy displaces the phallic figure in the particularities of the everyday, on the one hand, and through the imaginary potency of the mother figure and sisterhood on the other. However, in doing so she rejuvenates and further reifies the essentialization of gender—male and female—on which patriarchy depends. Thus through the operation of mimesis which reifies the everyday and imbues it with imaginary presence and potency, Piercy resecures the very domination of patriarchy she attempted to contest.

It is only through a critique of the ideological (re)production of representation and the political economy of significations and subjectivities it generates that it is possible to intervene in these ideological representations and demystify the "realities" they produce. The transformative practice for a counterpatriarchal feminism thus can only be a culture critique that interrogates the continued production and naturalization of a political economy of gender and its relations of exploitation and points the way toward an overthrow of the patriarchal symbolic and the social formation it legitimates. A postmodern feminist culture critique is thus a political practice seeking to "produce" the everyday in terms of the "utopian" countersymbolic—the nonexploitative way of organizing significations and subjectivities *Otherwise* than according to the phallus—thus to legitimate and secure the suppressed social formation contesting patriarchal capitalism.

Notes

1. While Alice Jardine articulates a gap between "gynesis" and feminism and uses gynesis primarily to describe the works of male poststructuralist theorists, gynesis is also an apt term for textual feminism which not only critiques phallogocentrism but also rewrites feminism in terms of poststructuralism. Alice Jardine, *Gynesis: Configurations of Woman and Modernity* (Ithaca: Cornell University Press, 1985).

2. Paul Hirst, *On Law and Ideology* (Atlantic Highlands, N. J.: Humanities Press, 1979).

3. Marcia Holly, "Consciousness and Authenticity: Toward a Feminist Aesthetic," *Feminist Literary Criticism: Explorations in Theory*, ed. Josephine Donovan (Lexington: University Press of Kentucky, 1975), 40.

4. Ibid., 39.

5. Some of the by now classic examples of the gynocritic study of women's experience whether in terms of images and themes of women in literature or the lives and tradition of women writers include such anthologies as Susan Koppelman Cornillon, ed., *Images of Women in Fiction: Feminist Perspectives* (Bowling Green, Ohio: Bowling Green University Popular Press, 1972); Arlyn Diamond and Lee Edwards, eds., *The Authority of Experience: Essays in Feminist Criticism* (Amherst: University of Massachusetts Press, 1977); Ellen Moers, *Literary Women* (Garden City, N.Y.: Anchor-Doubleday, 1977); Elaine Showalter, *A Literature of Their Own* (Princeton: Princeton University Press, 1977); and Sandra Gilbert and Susan Gubar, *The Madwoman in the Attic: The Woman Writer and the Nineteenth-Century Literary Imagination* (New Haven: Yale University Press, 1979).

6. Edward Said, *The World, the Text and the Critic* (Cambridge: Harvard University Press, 1983), 5. The critical discussions of mimesis are too extensive to cite here. For a useful overview of the major theories of mimesis, see Wallace Martin, *Recent Theories of Narrative* (Ithaca: Cornell University Press, 1986), esp. chap. 3.; George Levine, *The Realistic Imagination* (Chicago: University of Chicago Press, 1981); and Colin MacCabe, "Realism: Balzac and Barthes," in his *Tracking the Signifier. Theoretical Essays: Film, Linguistics, Literature* (Minneapolis: University of Minnesota Press, 1985).

7. Erich Auerbach, *Mimesis: The Representation of Reality in Western Literature*, trans. Willard Trask (1946; reprint, Princeton: Princeton University Press, 1953), 491, 485.

8. Holly, "Consciousness and Authenticity," 39.

9. The argument for the "realism" of innovative forms is made by such writers and critics as Raymond Federman, "Surfiction," in his *Surfiction*, 2d ed. (Chicago: Swallow Press, 1981), 5–15 and Sharon Spencer in *Space, Time and Structure in the Modern Novel* (New York: New York University Press, 1971).

10. Catherine Belsey, *Critical Practice* (London: Methuen, 1980).

11. Perhaps one of the most important recent discussions of the debate over essentialism is Diana Fuss, *Essentially Speaking: Feminism, Nature and Difference* (New York: Routledge, 1989). But I find that Fuss's own critique of essentialism and her argument that anti-essential constructionism "operates as a more sophisticated form of essentialism" (xii) are also based on a form of cognitivism that erases the social and historical production of cultural categories and knowledges. Moreover, her claim that "essentialism is embedded in the idea of the social and lodged in the problem of social determination" (6) is based on her reading the social ontologically rather than historically.

12. Elaine Showalter, "Toward a Feminist Poetics," *The New Feminist Criticism*, ed. Showalter (New York: Pantheon Books, 1985), 140, 139.

13. Nelly Furman, "The Politics of Language: Beyond the Gender Principle?" in Gayle Greene and Coppélia Kahn, eds., *Making a Difference* (London: Methuen, 1985), 67.

14. See, for example, Hélène Cixous, "The Laugh of the Medusa," in Elaine Marks and Isabelle de Courtivron, eds., *New French Feminisms* (Amherst: University of Massachusetts Press, 1980), 245–64; Cixous and Catherine Clément, *The Newly Born Woman*, trans. Betsy Wing (Minneapolis: University of Minnesota Press, 1986); Luce Irigaray, *Speculum of the Other Woman*, trans. Gillian Gill (Ithaca: Cornell University Press, 1985); and Irigaray, *This Sex Which Is Not One*, trans. Carolyn Burke and Catherine Porter (Ithaca: Cornell University Press, 1985). Kristeva's work is on the boundaries of textual feminism, especially her focus on the libidinal body, which is associated with her concept of the semiotic "chora"; see her *Revolution in Poetic Language*, trans. Margaret Waller (New York: Columbia University Press, 1986). For criticial discussions of the theories of *écriture féminine*, see especially Toril Moi, *Sexual/Textual Politics: Feminist Literary Theory* (London: Methuen, 1985); Chris Weedon, *Feminist Practice and Postructuralist Theory* (Oxford: Blackwell, 1987); Nelly Furman, "The Politics of Language: Beyond the Gender Principle?"; Ann Rosalind Jones, "Writing the Body: Toward an Understanding of *l'écriture féminine*," in Judith Newton and Deborah Rosenfelt, eds., *Feminist Criticism and Social Change: Sex, Class and Race in Literature and Culture* (New York: Methuen, 1985); Parveen Adams, "A Note on Sexual Division and Sexual Differences," *m/f* (1971), 51–57; Parveen Adams and Jeff Minson, "The 'Subject' of Feminism," *m/f* (1987), 43–61; Beverley Brown and Parveen Adams, "The Feminine Body and Feminist Politics," *m/f* (1979), 35–50; Jane Gallop, *The Daughter's Seduction: Feminism and Psychoanalysis* (Ithaca: Cornell University Press, 1982).

15. Jardine, *Gynesis*, 25, 34.

16. Ibid., 147, 150, 151.

17. Shoshana Felman, "Women and Madness: The Critical Phallacy," *Diacritics* 5, no. 4 (Winter 1975): 6.

18. Ibid.

19. Jane Gallop, *Thinking through the Body* (New York: Columbia University Press, 1988), 98–99. While Gallop argues here against referentiality, most of her writing in this book as well as much of her recent work is a return to referentiality. Her neoreferentiality is perhaps most obvious in her essay "Beyond the Phallus" in which she is "insisting on the penis . . . the masculine body" as secure referent and anchor of meaning in opposition to the abstract phallus (*Thinking,* 131).

20. Felman, "Women and Madness," 8.

21. Jardine, *Gynesis,* 122, 122–23. For a detailed discussion of Lacan's theory of the "Real," see Ellie Ragland-Sullivan, *Jacques Lacan and the Philosophy of Psychoanalysis* (Urbana: University of Illinois Press, 1986), 183–95. Although Ragland-Sullivan does not elaborate on the implication of Lacan's views on the real for postmodern feminism, her discussion provides a good starting point for such an extension. Also see Fredric Jameson's interpretation of Lacan's view of the real in his "Imaginary and Symbolic in Lacan: Marxism, Psychoanalytic Criticism, and the Problem of the Subject," *Yale French Studies* 55/56 (1977), 338–95 and in his *The Political Unconscious: Narrative as a Socially Symbolic Act* (Ithaca: Cornell University Press, 1981).

22. Felman, "Women and Madness," 10.

23. For further discussion of these issues, see Teresa L. Ebert, *Patriarchal Narratives* (forthcoming); Ebert, "The Romance of Patriarchy: Ideology, Subjectivity, and Postmodern Feminist Cultural Theory," *Cultural Critique* 10 (Fall 1988); Ebert, "Detecting the Phallus: Authority, Ideology and the Production of Patriarchal Agents in Detective Fiction," *Rethinking Marxism* (forthcoming); Ebert, "The Difference of Postmodern Feminism," *College English* 53, no. 8 (December 1991).

24. Cixous, "Laugh of the Medusa," 264.

25. Ibid., 252.

26. Ibid., 256, 250, 258.

27. Quoted in Jean Strouse, "Toni Morrison's Black Magic," *Newsweek,* 30 March 1981, 54.

28. Ibid.

29. Roland Barthes, "The Reality Effect," *French Literary Theory Today: A Reader,* ed. Tzvetan Todorov, trans. R. Carter (Cambridge: Cambridge University Press, 1982), 12, 14, 16.

30. See Jean Baudrillard, *Simulations,* trans. Paul Foss et al. (New York: Semiotext(e), 1983), passim.

31. See Kaja Silverman, *The Subject of Semiotics* (New York: Oxford University Press, 1983), 44–53.

32. John Updike, *Couples* (Greenwich, Conn.: Fawcett, 1968), 310–11. Future page references will be cited parenthetically in the text.

33. Marge Piercy, *Vida* (1979; reprint, New York: Fawcett Crest-Ballantine, 1981), 28. Future page references will be cited parenthetically in the text.

Feminist Literary Criticism and Cultural Studies

Laurie Langbauer
Swarthmore College

THIS essay grows out of a discomfort with a prevailing tendency within theoretical discussions of cultural studies. That
problem is similar to one implied by the word *culture* itself, which
in its earliest sense has to do with cults and worship, authority,
transcendence. We know that that term—*culture*—has always appealed to conservatives from Matthew Arnold to William Bennett,
precisely to those people who are themselves bothered by
"women's," "African-American," "gay," by those other adjectives
that up to now through great struggle have been allowed in the
academy to modify "studies." In the minds of its proponents,
cultural studies may not be meant to appropriate or synthesize
such other areas, but in the minds of (some) administrators that
seems to be its attraction, which is precisely why I would like to
think about the *dangers* of synthesis. Despite its great promise,
cultural studies as it has currently been theorized (especially given
the unexamined influence of groups like the Centre for Cultural
Studies at the University of Birmingham, and the critics associated
with it—Stuart Hall, Richard Johnson—who explicitly value synthesis, coherence, unity) betrays a homogenizing tendency—one
at odds with the very multiculturalism it wishes to foster.

To expose the bias toward unifying, if not totalizing, in cultural
studies, I want to examine another term—not *culture* but *the everyday*. Like much recent theory (feminism included), cultural studies
depends on an unexamined use of this term to ground its approach. My goal is not so much to explore the way this ground is
unstable, but to ask what that instability tells us: how is the category of the everyday a figure for our complex relations to culture
and ideology? For the hidden forces that shape and control us, as
well as for our negotiations within such structures?

One thing that gets unsettled when we expose the everyday as a
shaky and unstable ground is cultural studies' desire for its own

coherence and inclusiveness. Inclusiveness, that is, can involve exclusion—it is hard to imagine a model of it that doesn't. By questioning what we mean when we invoke the everyday, I'm arguing for an ongoing struggle to try to imagine just such a model, a practice that will need to highlight the ways it too keeps sacrificing the difficulties and evasiveness of difference in favor of consistency and pattern. Although this goal seems unreachable (and that's important), the emphasis on it is crucial. Such an emphasis perhaps distinguishes diversity from pluralism in the various politics we construct. At any rate, questioning what we mean when we invoke the everyday is one way to continue that—never resolvable—venture.

The everyday is the accepted critical shorthand for everything quotidian, mundane, or ordinary, everything that carries our sense of daily life but seems unremarkable. Part of the problem of treating the everyday as some referential bedrock is how often and easily its meaning shifts—it has been made to refer to everything from forgetfulness to bureaucracy to walking or housework (think of Freud, Lefebvre, de Certeau), and the list goes on.[1] Instead of trying to define the term, what interests me is the way approaches that buttress themselves with the everyday give different meanings to it. Rather than repeating the unexamined but rhetorically powerful invocation of the everyday as a stabilizing ground, I want to look at the ways that the term can do double duty, contradicting such use. To establish the everyday not as essential but as a construct puts into question the supposedly fixed, universalizing order that rests on and controls it. That is, to use the everyday as a way of opening up just what we mean by culture exposes the extent to which—whether we locate the cultural whole we imagine in the collective or in power—theories of culture tend to totalize and hence to exclude. To argue against totalization is not perhaps to return to a wishful deconstructive emphasis on liberating contradiction, if only because the story told by the everyday is not one of freedom or autonomy but one in which its actors can only (as de Certeau might call it) "make do" within the structures that determine them.

At least, that may be why the everyday has been so haunting a tale to various feminists working to transform the totalizing pressures within feminism itself, to uncover the differences among women. By turning very briefly to texts by Raymond Williams, Virginia Woolf, Alice Walker, and Paule Marshall, I will argue that the everyday has been useful for an important oppositional feminist critique, useful as one site on which to locate difference, to expose the racial homogenization that continues within our gender analyses; in that critique, the everyday becomes a figure for how disparity and division, rather than harmony and integrity, make up culture. Just as power isn't only total and constraining, to these feminists the everyday isn't simply empty and exhausted. Its resources lie in its intransigence, the way its bare anonymity, its reduction to the ordinary, provide a literary heritage for writers such as Walker and Marshall, who find in the daily practice of ordinary black women a way to make do and make over the forms that also constrain them. To them, the everyday, as the figure both for the hidden forces that shape us and for the energies that stray within, or make over, such forces, becomes also the representative figure for a kind of doubleness. And this understanding of the everyday provides a model to help make over approaches that ignore or repress doubleness. To insist on a split within culture—finding resources within its strictures—is one way to counter a universalizing sweep that tends otherwise to deny such practices, exclude certain voices. This view of such doubleness within culture is at odds with one implicit understanding of culture in the field of cultural studies itself that comes to stand for culture, that presents itself *as* a field, a network of synthesis and assimilation. In this essay, I will argue that, in revising such assumptions, cultural studies, and feminism, will have to revise themselves.

In an early essay, "Culture Is Ordinary," Raymond Williams expresses a vision of culture, which, despite disclaimers, still informs much contemporary cultural criticism. For Williams in that essay, to say culture is ordinary is to talk about how culture "mean[s] a whole way of life": "the questions I ask about culture," he writes, "are questions about our general and common purposes."[2] E. P. Thompson then, and Stuart Hall and Mary Poovey now, have criticized the way such "humanist" ideas of commonality repress difference "in order to produce the illusion of a unified, totalizing, universal truth."[3] But the dynamic Hall shows operating on Thompson and Williams—where the "dimension of struggle and confrontation between opposed *ways* of life" becomes subordinated to an overall totality that explains it, where "discontinuities of an unexpected kind"[4] are made explainable as part of an organizing pattern—continues to organize current (supposedly "post-structural") definitions of cultural studies (Hall's and Poovey's included); although such essays pay lip service to a poststructural emphasis on inescapable contradiction, insoluble conflict—difference itself—the implicit rhetoric of cultural studies continues to present it as a collective and unifying field, one that works by "synthesis" that will undo exclusion and separation.[5] In "What Is Cultural Studies Anyway?", all of Richard Johnson's careful qualifications, for instance, his recognition of the problems of universalizing, evaporate when he writes: "perhaps we need ways of viewing a vigorous but fragmented field of study, if not as a *unity* at least as a *whole*."[6]

For feminism, if culture is ordinary, it is important that it mean something else. Different feminisms in different ways have persistently exposed that the supposedly universal, the general, the common, actually impose themselves through exclusion, marginalization, oppression. And "culture" has been one of the monoliths that has excluded women most. Yet it is precisely to expose, if not to undo, such exclusions that various feminisms too (perhaps current cultural studies has learned it from them) proclaim that culture is ordinary. Michèle Barrett, for instance, locates feminist politics precisely in this recognition. "Feminism," she writes, "has politicized everyday life—culture in the anthropological sense of the lived practices of a society."[7] Like Williams, by locating culture in the everyday, such feminists hope to rob it of its capital "C," to define it as a shaping practice rather than the province of a privileged elite. Yet such feminisms are especially useful, I think, when they do more. The problem for feminists may not be women's *exclusion* as much as it is the denial of difference that leads to that exclusion in the first place.

Yet, within feminism, as within Williams's work as well, such a notion of the everyday—and of the practices and culture founded on it—can also deny difference. Critics interested in history have seen the history of feminism as only recently beginning to emerge from its own limited view of a unified women's culture. In reflecting on cultural studies, Poovey writes that "in the 1970s . . . some women of color and lesbians argued that feminism itself involved significant exclusions—that feminism systematically repressed the differences among women in order to reify a single homogenized entity—Woman—which could be opposed to (the also falsely homogenized entity) Man."[8] Such reemphases begin to heed the call of black critics like Hazel Carby, who writes: "Feminism has to be transformed if it is to address us. . . . In other words, of white feminists we must ask, what exactly do you mean when you say 'WE'?"[9]

One way Carby suggests that white feminists (like myself) confront this question is to recognize the differences between the "day-to-day struggles" of white women and black women (and also the different struggles within these groups).[10] If culture is ordinary, then we need to recognize how the day-to-dayness—the everydayness—that makes up the ordinary is itself not stable; part of what makes the everyday the normalizing vehicle of power that feminists influenced by Foucault have seen it to be may be the assumption that it is the same for everyone—a fixed referential truth rather than a construct that changes with a shift in context.[11]

Carby asks white feminists to investigate how their own forms and structures invisibly deny difference and carry racism. One way to do so might be by uncovering differences within the category of the everyday. An important text for many kinds of feminism, Virginia Woolf's *A Room of One's Own*—Nancy Armstrong calls this text Woolf's meditation on "what it means to be a woman in culture"[12]—links women and culture with the everyday; it is a text that, like Williams's, "talk[s] of the common life which is the real life."[13] In taking this route to give women's struggles a pattern, an integrity (think of the synthesizing force inherent in the climax of androgyny that ends Woolf's text), Woolf's text too imposes a homogenizing vision of woman. But "the crumpled skin of the day" (24) Woolf wishes to fling into the hedge is not so easily skimmed off; the supposedly deep commonalities between women are disturbed within that text by "puzzles that one notes in the margins of daily life" (35). For Woolf finds that there is something about the everyday that disturbs ideas about it—unsettling her own desire "to feel the usual things in the usual places," making it "impossible for me to roll out my sonorous phrases about 'elemental feelings,' 'the common stuff of humanity'" (95). Woolf's shift of attention to the everyday, to "ordinary people in the street" (67), especially women's "infinitely obscure lives" (93) (obscure because so ordinary), opens up a vision of difference that goes beyond and calls into question the blanket conclusions about women and culture she wishes to draw. That recognition of a difference that inhabits our own desire for unity has been useful to various feminists in helping to call into question the single vision of woman and culture that Woolf's text also propagates.

Of *A Room of One's Own*, Adrienne Rich writes: "Like Virginia Woolf, I am aware of the women who are not with us because they are washing the dishes and looking after the children. Nearly fifty years after she spoke, that fact remains largely unchanged. And I am thinking also of the women whom she left out of the picture altogether—women who are washing other people's dishes and caring for other people's children."[14] To include those women left out altogether not just by cultural history but, worse, by feminist revisions of it like Woolf's, Alice Walker (in "In Search of Our Mother's Gardens") quotes Woolf in order to revise her prose, to insert into and write over it the everyday reality of black women in America, silenced by dominant culture, yet for each of whom "being an artist has been a daily part of her life"—for instance, a poet like Phillis Wheatley, who, far from having a room and five hundred pounds of her own, "owned not even herself."[15] Walker's notion of the everyday involves not so much a specific content, as it does a form, or an impulse. It is not just these anonymous women's songs—for many of them remain unrecorded—but *"the notion of song"* (237); not just their stories—for many of them remain unfinished—but the urgency of them (240): that is the legacy Walker tells us their daily lives leave African-American women writers like herself. "Torn by 'contrary instincts,'" Wheatley's "struggling ambivalent lines" (236–37) record the difference of these women's struggles. And Walker too begins her own essay from a place of division to record the ongoing strain out of which she must still write: an epigraph (from Marilou Awiakta's poem "Abiding Appalachia") that reads: "Creation often / needs two hearts" (230).

That the everyday is the medium in which such differences get registered is Paule Marshall's point in her own statement about literary heritage, "From the Poets in the Kitchen." She too brings to our attention "unknown bards" like Woolf's Judith Shakespeare, but these are not the sisters of a privileged literary hierarchy, but, like Walker's, "a group of ordinary housewives and mothers" even more invisible.[16] Immigrants to Brooklyn from Barbados, negotiating the "strange customs and laws" of an alien culture (7), such women infuse an artistic practice Marshall will imitate in her writing with tactics learned from the struggles of their own workaday lives: "Using everyday speech, the simple commonplace words—but always with imagination and skill—they gave voice to the most complex ideas. Flannery O'Connor would have approved of how they made ordinary language work, as she put it, 'double-time,' stretching, shading, deepening its meaning. Like Joseph Conrad they were always trying to infuse new life in the 'old old words worn thin . . . by . . . careless usage'" (9). Locating their art in all that is left to them, conserving, turning-over, the used-up and worn-out, infusing new life by accepting the ordinary *as* ordinary distinguishes this everyday practice, just as "common speech and the plain, workaday words that make it up are . . . the stock in trade of some of the best fiction writers"

(3). Marshall connects this heritage to standard literary culture, exemplified by O'Connor and Conrad, but only to insist that what is best *there* is most like the "rich legacy of language and culture" that comes from the everyday life of these black women (12).

The complexity of the everyday for Marshall, the way it works for her double-time, is to introduce a notion of "fundamental dualism" (9) of unresolvable opposition and contradiction into an otherwise closed language and culture. And "it wasn't only what the women talked about—the content—but the way they put things—their style" (7), Marshall writes. For Marshall too, the everyday becomes not so much its content (the trivialized banalities of endless drudgery that black women especially are made to perform) but the styles and tactics derived from it.[17]

What Barbara Christian calls "the tone of the commonplace" informs black women's writing, she argues, as a way of "making space," of keeping that work from being "reduced to a stereotype."[18] Although the concentration on the ordinary she describes can be part of a realism fully as conventional as the heroic mode she sees black women writers refusing, her point is more complex than this qualification allows. In using the everyday to attempt to gesture to a "space" outside the homogenizing structures of a culture that ignores them (whether or not this gesture can ever be successful), African-American women writers interrogate the notion of culture as totalizing, the notion of the ordinary as single and common to us all. By "making space," the everyday undoes a monolithic idea of culture by suggesting how the same space can be inhabited simultaneously in different ways. What distinguishes "commonplaces" from "stereotypes" for these writers may be that the commonplace for them makes space within the supposedly unchanging patterns that give stereotypes their oppressive force.

One important version of feminist struggle—taken by Catherine Gallagher, say—has been to emphasize such patterns as determining, to show how the level of the everyday is exactly where dominant structure seems most entrenched and totalizing: "the woman's liberation movement . . . forced us to see that the more 'personal' and 'mundane' the issues, the more resistance to change we encountered,"[19] she writes. A version of the everyday that emphasizes the importance of conflict and difference instead supplies a notion of struggle that is itself in conflict with an understanding of the everyday as unifying, of culture as total. To say culture is ordinary, is everyday, then, is to gesture to the very divisions and differences in our understanding of the terms like *ordinary, everyday.* Our struggle to keep feminism and cultural studies from being reduced to monolithic stereotypes will indeed need to involve such everyday struggles.

Notes

1. See Sigmund Freud, *The Psychopathology of Everyday Life*, trans. Alan Tyson, ed. Angela Richmond, vol. 5 of *The Pelican Freud Library*, ed. James Strachey (New York: Penguin Books, 1975); Henri Lefebvre, *Everyday Life in the Modern World*, trans. Sacha Rabinovitch (New Brunswick, N.J.: Transaction Books, 1984); and Michel de Certeau, *The Practice of Everyday Life*, trans. Steven Rendall (Berkeley: University of California Press, 1984).

2. Raymond Williams, "Culture Is Ordinary," *Resources of Hope: Culture, Democracy, Socialism* (New York: Verso Books, 1989), 4. See also "a culture is common meanings" (8) and a writer's job is "with making those meanings common" (18).

3. Mary Poovey, "Cultural Criticism: Past and Present," *College English* 52 (1990):619.

4. Stuart Hall, "Cultural Studies: Two Paradigms," *Media, Culture, and Society* 2 (1980):61, 60.

5. Ibid., 72. Similarly, although Poovey's essay explicitly aligns itself with a poststructural deconstruction of terms, its aims of dissolving the conventional opposition between different cultural representations (622), of making visible (and perhaps undoing) exclusion (623), of calling into question the disciplinary division of knowledge, along with departmental segregation and specialized scholarship (623), as well as her muted call for collective action at the end of the essay (624), all carry the implicit burden of cultural studies as an integrating and unifying field.

6. Richard Johnson, "What Is Cultural Studies Anyway?" *Social Text* 16 (Winter 1986/87):41.

7. Quoted in Patrick Brantlinger, *Crusoe's Footprints: Cultural Studies in Britain and America* (New York: Routledge, 1990), 136.

8. Poovey, "Cultural Criticism," 619.

9. Hazel V. Carby, "White Woman Listen! Black Feminism and the Boundaries of Sisterhood," *The Empire Strikes Back: Race and Racism in 70's Britain* (London: Hutchinson, 1982), 233.

10. Ibid., 215, 219.

11. For one reading of women's relation to the way power comes from the bottom up, in terms of daily normalizing practices, see Nancy Armstrong, *Desire and Domestic Fiction: A Political History of the Novel* (New York: Oxford University Press, 1987).

12. Ibid., 242.

13. Virginia Woolf, *A Room of One's Own* (New York: Harcourt Brace Jovanovich), 117. Future page references to *A Room* will be cited in the text.

14. Adrienne Rich, "When We Dead Awaken: Feminist Writing as Re-Vision," in her *On Lies, Secrets, and Silences* (New York: Norton, 1979), 38.

15. Alice Walker, "In Search of Our Mothers' Gardens," *In Search of Our Mothers' Gardens: Womanist Prose* (New York: Harcourt Brace Jovanovich, 1983), 242, 235. Future page references to "In Search" will be cited in the text.

16. Paule Marshall, "From the Poets in the Kitchen," in her *Reena and Other Stories* (Old Westbury, N. Y.: Feminist Press, 1983), 4. Future page references to "Poets" will be cited in the text.

17. For more on the way the everyday gives voice to such complex and subtle ideas, see

Bell Hooks's discussion of the phrase "Halfway, I'm just halfway" as an example of the theory and abstraction in everyday (African-American) speech; Bell Hooks, "Feminist Theory: A Radical Agenda," in her *Talking Back: Thinking Feminist/Thinking Black* (Boston: South End Press, 1989), 39.

18. Barbara Christian, "Ordinary Women: The Tone of the Commonplace," in her *Black Women Novelists: The Development of a Tradition* (Westport, Conn.: Greenwood Press, 1980), 71, 73, 71.

19. Catherine Gallagher, "Marxism and the New Historicism," *The New Historicism*, ed. H. Aram Veeser (New York: Routledge, 1989), 42.

The View from Elsewhere: Utopian Constructions of "Difference"

Daphne Patai
University of Massachusetts at Amherst

T HIS essay is about the obvious, and about how the things we consider obvious quietly fade into invisibility. I want to argue that it is precisely the obvious that needs to be made visible, and that in order to recuperate the obvious we need to find a vantage point, a place from which the obvious loses its obviousness and is stripped of its quality of that-which-goes-without-saying.

In her influential article "Archimedes and the Paradox of Feminist Criticism" (1981), Myra Jehlen likened the feminist search for a position from which to exercise its radical skepticism to Archimedes' search for a fulcrum for moving the world. Unlike Archimedes, whose search was doomed to failure by the need to find "a standpoint off this world altogether," feminists, Jehlen argues, need a "terrestrial fulcrum" that would position them "at once on and off a world." Women's Studies programs, according to Jehlen, merely created enclaves incapable of having an impact on the male discourses and disciplines that continued to constitute the norm. Thus, the problem for feminist scholars was one of surmounting their "alternative footing,"[1] that is, their isolation. Jehlen proposed a way out of this dilemma, at least in the arena of literary criticism, through the adoption of a radically comparatist method, one that focuses on contradiction.

My argument, by contrast, is that we already have available to us a virtual Archimedean fulcrum in certain kinds of fiction—utopian speculations—and that we should make use of it. The "thought experiments" set in motion by utopian fiction provide readers with an imaginative experience of an alternative reality. To look for a new "position" in our actual world, in which most positions are already overdetermined, is perhaps to disregard the important role of the imagination in shaping our sense of the possible. In other words, the experience of reading a utopia and immersing oneself in its alternative social constructions does locate the reader, however temporarily, in an "elsewhere," an elsewhere that provides a unique vantage point from which to view and appraise patterns of invisible obviousness in our own world. Such imaginative experiences, because of their potential consequences in our apprehension of everyday life, have great importance, for the shift they allow in our perception of the obvious can both restore our capacity to be startled and renew our resolve to act.

The obviousness of the concept of "difference" between women and men is what I wish to call into question in this essay. This concept permeates contemporary feminist discourse. It has undergone a variety of lexical treatments, but always it has remained at the heart of feminist debate. In legal theory, in literary criticism, in political, philosophical, even biological analyses of gender, our basic categories have remained constant. We ask: shall we emphasize "sameness" or "difference?" In the realm of law, the practical consequences of adopting one or the other of these categories are readily apparent. To deny difference by stressing sameness may lead to women's relinquishing of, for example, spousal support in the event of divorce. But to accept difference may lead to reinforcement of the traditional gendered division of reality, for emphasis on difference can justify the exclusion of women and/or stimulate protectionist rather than egalitarian provisions, for women in the workplace, for example.[2] In literary criticism, this discussion is in some sense replicated: to point out the double standards and benightedness of traditional male devaluation of women writers can easily lead to an "equality" argument (or at least a "comparable worth" argument), i.e., that women can join the canon, that women writers are just as good as men, that the failure to recognize their equal value is predominantly the result of sheer prejudice, vested interests, privileging of male subjects and modes, dumb canonical paradigms, and so on. And such a position of course incurs the same risks as the "equality" or "sameness" argument in law: it fails to challenge the very structure of the preexisting situation, and merely, modestly, hopes to insert women into it.[3] In opposition to all this, the argument for "difference" challenges the notion that "joining 'em" is an appropriate strategy or desirable aim, and insists instead that women write differently, must be judged differently, and that the male paradigms do not need to be extended but totally rejected.[4]

What gives shape and meaning to the whole critical debate today is above all the fact that it is a *political* assault, an effort to

make visible the political nature of earlier judgments that successfully clothed themselves in the mantle of neutrality, of things-
in-themselves. This assault is, of course, motivated by a desire to
disrupt a particular discourse that takes itself as the "natural" state
of correct judgments. There is no point, here, in rehearsing the
familiar arguments about whether we need to expand the old
canon, create a new canon, or do away with canons altogether. I
want, rather, to call attention to the obvious. *The powerful group
need never engage in this kind of discussion.* All it need do is try to
maintain its centrality and power by resisting attacks, deflecting
questions, and thwarting redefinitions. In fact, even without
much active resistance its past power is its most effective ally in
maintaining its position, for the traditional exercise of power is
rarely perceived as such; it is usually experienced, instead, as the
way-things-are.[5] Its definitions determine what is legitimate (in
life, in law, in art) and nothing is simpler than demonstrating the
self-interested position from which challenges to those definitions
are launched. For, not surprisingly, it is "outsiders" who most need
to initiate such attacks. Feminist thought has emphatically not
resolved the problem within the arena of literary criticism, nor,
indeed, elsewhere.[6]

   The vocabulary, shifts, and moves in the long-standing debate
about women's difference have been analyzed in detail by Ann
Snitow in a recent essay.[7] Snitow refers to the "great gender
divide" or "feminist divide"—that is, the way in which arguments
over difference and sameness keep reappearing in varied guises
as feminist thought progresses, and reappearing not only between
divergent positions but *within* particular positions as well, as is
apparent already as early as in Mary Wollstonecraft's writing in
1792. Catharine Stimpson's terminology of "minimizers" and
"maximizers," as Snitow points out, was an early second-wave
version of this divide in theoretical discussions of gender: are we
to minimize or maximize women's "difference" from men?[8] More
recently, we have used the terminology of essentialism versus
social constructionism to cover much the same ground. Equality
and difference, Snitow states, is the "oldest, certainly the most all-
encompassing" name for the divide (213), with difference theory
tending to emphasize the body (and the unconscious), while
equality theory deemphasizes the body and confides in a self not
circumscribed by gender (213). Snitow's point is that feminist
theorists "keep renaming this tension, as if new names could
advance feminist political work" (206), and warns us that new
names can make us forget the frequency with which we have

named this split before. I would add that these acts of naming and renaming do not get us very far in resolving a fundamentally political problem. Whatever the terminology, lines of political allegiance in fact break down, for among the maximalists, essentialists, or embracers of difference we find not only feminists wishing to insist on difference while merely inverting the evaluative labels (attaching a positive sign to femaleness and a negative one to maleness), but also male antifeminists making much the same arguments in an effort to perpetuate their own privileged positions. Claiming "difference"—as we shall see more clearly later—is a game anybody can play, and for the most diverse purposes. It leaves quite untouched the further problem of what to do with that difference or what is presupposed by such a claim.

The crucial point to be noted here is that all these discussions of difference are themselves grounded in political disparities. That is, it is impossible even to name "difference" without implying a comparison and without inadvertently privileging the unmarked term of the comparison. Difference, in other words, is a problem for the group that carries the mark of difference; it is not a problem for the unmarked group that is taken to be the norm. In our context, difference is a problem *for women*—but it is a problem created for women *by men*. I take this to be the meaning of Simone de Beauvoir's famous phrase, "One is not born a woman." Instead of committing ourselves uncritically to arguments about difference, whether celebrating it, deploring it, or declaring it to be a misunderstanding, we need to note how the entire discussion is framed and structured. This apparently trivial detail—that the debate is framed in this particular way at all—signals the relative existence of power on one side and powerlessness on the other. That is why in our world it is not men who have a stake in challenging the idea of men's "difference"; it is not men who have to argue for their sameness in relation to women; it is not men who engage in an elaborate self-definition, always vis-à-vis a higher-status Other. Quite the contrary, it is men who are far more likely to embrace the notion of difference, thereby naturalizing and neutralizing what they might otherwise have to confront as a position of domination maintained against the very political principles many of them (at least in our supposedly liberal democratic society) espouse. Virginia Woolf noted in *A Room of One's Own* that the libraries were full of books about women, but that "men" appeared far less frequently as subjects of books. This does not, of course, mean that there is more interest in women than in men or that work on women has enjoyed more impor-

tance; on the contrary, what Woolf's remark reveals is that men
were (and are) the norm and that this problematizes the existence
of "women" who thereby turn into subjects of investigation, "subjects" in a dual sense. While women become *the* sex, *the* problem
("What *do* women want?" asked Freud in disingenuous befuddle-
ment, as if we were another species), whose status and very being
are in need of endless discussion and negotiation, all that men
need do is the habitual: reality already supports their position in
every way.

This process can be better understood by utilizing the insights
of ethnomethodology. As Dean MacCannell puts it: "In the actual
operation of social life everything appears firmly attached to its
meaning. . . . Ordinary reality remains intuitively obvious in the
way it is structured. The social world is simply saturated with
meaning in such a way that does not call attention to itself as it is in
the process of becoming meaningful. This is its most mysterious
and its most social quality."[9] In the case of gender inequalities,
whether they are seen as rooted in inherent biological differences
or in social habit becomes much less of an issue once one focuses
not on "difference" but on power. For it is always, and only, the
out-group peering in, its nose pressed to the glass, whose characteristics and status undergo detailed scrutiny. It is this group that
is "different," and must cajole, convince, and present reasons for
its claims to a change in status. And, precisely because of their
habitual powerlessness and the supposition that they should be
unseen and unheard, outsiders are stalked by what I term "surplus visibility," which makes any space they do occupy, any voice
they do raise, appear excessive and unwarranted. The absence of
power—which has a remarkable ability to legitimize and naturalize itself—makes challenges to it invariably appear as instances
of special pleading, hence easy to delegitimize.[10]

Difference, to repeat, is in our world a problem for women, not
for men. Only women, in television ads, need to declare, with
touchingly contrived smiles of pride and conviction: "Because I'm
worth it!" It would be ridiculous for a man to make such a
statement; the words themselves, in a man's mouth, would seem
oxymoronic, evoking a comical image of powerlessness and lack
of confidence, for why say what is believed by most people and
confirmed by everyday social interactions? In this sense, women's
"difference"—understood as a damning inferiority—is pa-
thetically embedded even (or particularly) in noisy claims to the
contrary.

Similarly, even as we argue about the nature of women's difference, we cannot help but reproduce the very problem we are seeking to escape. For the fact remains that we are indeed positioned in certain ways by current reality, and our efforts to transform the situation are often puny compared to the unfathomable power of What Is. In this regard, it is important to move from a vocabulary of gender "roles" to one of gendered "positions." As Bronwyn Davies and Rom Harré point out, the term *role* is usually embedded in traditional perspectives that see gender positions as static and fixed. But discourse (not to mention political and social life) in fact "positions" individuals, through everyday interactions, in particular ways that need to be analyzed and challenged.[11] Whether we argue for equality or difference, then, we must observe that it is *men* (and their power, which includes the power to define reality, reproduce their perspectives, and impose those perspectives as neutral) who are always the reference point. How, then, can we move out of this frame?

I want to suggest that a first step toward escape is to see that this is precisely what it is: a particular frame, held in place by routine gender practices and a traditional gendered discourse. The women's movement knew this a decade or two ago—when the idea of the male as the norm lost its obviousness and stood displayed as the ideological expression of power that it is. This recuperation of the obvious was extremely important as both an intellectual and a political move for women. But in the increasingly sophisticated discussions of difference since that time, this simple political perception has tended once again to be lost. How else could feminism have given itself heart and soul to the discussion of difference while not remembering to attend to the political implications of that very discussion?

There is a body of literature that helps us to see the obvious, the unnoticed, the habitual, in our gendered positions. I mean utopian fantasies cast as sex-role reversals.[12] By a simple shift in perspective, these reversals make the workings of power instantaneously visible. In the world of the sex-role reversal, hierarchy prevails but it is women who rule. Thus, "difference" becomes a problem for men and it is men who must strive for political gains by arguing that their "difference" should not lead to disempowerment, men who put forth arguments to counter women's claims about men's biology and socialization, about nature and culture. It is men who anxiously attend to every word proffered by the women on whom their livelihood and well-being depend, their very body language revealing their inferior status; it is men who complain about being left out, about not being taken seriously, about their limited job opportunities and tedious house-hold routines. And it is men who grow weary of women's ego-centric sexual practices and demeaning arguments about male biological inferiority, and men whose sexuality and body image are suppressed and distorted. To imaginatively live, for some hours or days, in these societies in which gender power is reversed has a startling effect: one returns suddenly aware that from the point of view of those imaginary societies it is our own world that rests on a bizarre sex-role reversal, one in which men rule, and that we take this as "reality."[13]

This is why I consider the argument about difference to be a game either side[14] can play, a game whose meaning comes en-tirely from a given political framework and not at all from the details of biology. No such argument can tell us anything about what men or women "are," for it enables us to see only what we already know: that certain groups in a given society occupy cer-tain slots, a position which both invites and constrains them to perpetuate the prevailing reality, and that challenges to domina-tion can and will occur in fairly predictable ways and will encoun-ter predictable obstacles.

Power inequalities are not readily done away with by acts of verbal contestation. The very arguments we make about power, like the arguments about gender that clearly derive from them, always take place in a context in which the devalued pole is already on the defensive.[15] Hence discussions of the inferiority of women are much more commonplace than discussions of the superiority of men. Men do not need to argue about whether their power resides in what they *are* or in what they *do*—although certainly they will respond to such questions when challenged. Women do need to engage in this discussion. Sex-role reversals highlight these maneuvers. In the scholarly literature, we would have to go to many different texts to acquire knowledge of pre-cisely how language, child-rearing habits, body posture, clothes, manners, education, religious beliefs, legal codes, household rou-tines, sexual practices—and all the many other ways in which domination of one group by another translates into aspects of everyday life—both sustain and display gender inequality. But any fairly simple sex-role reversal will reveal many of these interlock-ing mechanisms of gender domination even to a rather un-sophisticated reader. Such is the power of focusing on the unfamiliar, which suddenly brings the obvious back into view.

Nor did it take late twentieth-century arguments to suggest such a reversal to feminist writers. Well over one hundred years ago, Annie Denton Cridge, in her short text *Man's Rights, or, How Would You Like It?* (1870),[16] imagined a matriarchal society in which it is men who are obsessed with their appearance, who are trivialized and overworked. Cridge's oppressed men are deprived of political power with perfectly plausible arguments from nature such as that set forth by an elegant and confident woman speaking against men's demands for their civil and political rights: "Again, how well Nature knows the superiority of woman and the inferiority of man, inasmuch as she has chosen woman for maternity" (31). And since nature is harmonious, woman's physical superiority is reflected as well in her mental superiority. Thus, it makes sense for men to take on all household and childcare tasks not immediately associated with childbirth, both to compensate for their biological inferiority and to ease the burdens of their obviously superior mates. Like many other feminist writers working in this genre, Cridge keeps readers from taking this as mere satire, for she lets her narrator (a dreamer from our world) comment: "I thought in my dream that I was greatly dissatisfied with the lady's speech, and I did pity the little gentlemen on the platform who were forced to hear so much about their inferiority" (31). Because Cridge sees that not only women's private roles but also their public roles need changing, her reversal is played out in both the individual household scene and the civic forum, allowing her to offer her readers an estranged look at their own reality through the dominant women's reactions to the peculiar spectacle of men claiming public spaces.[17] In this way, Cridge turns our habitual perceptions on their heads. When, at the end of the book, her narrator tells her hosts that in her own world it is men who rule, her words are greeted with the kind of incredulity that expresses the unquestioned conviction that the-way-things-are is the only way they can be.

Over one hundred years later, the Norwegian writer Gerd Brantenberg wrote *Egalia's Daughters,* originally published in Norway in 1977 and translated into English in 1985. The brilliant arguments for male biological inferiority set forth in this novel are so totally convincing that readers may well find themselves wondering how women had ever been bamboozled into believing the contrary—and this, of course, is the point.[18]

In Brantenberg's imaginary country of Egalia, the familiar notion that biology is destiny is radically exploded precisely by the thoroughgoing reversal of gender roles and all the multifaceted signs of power that characterize our patriarchal society. Language is a key element in this reversal, as Brantenberg introduces us to a world in which wim rule and do the "important" work of the world—as businesswim, seawim, fisherwim, and so on. "Moulding Mothers" are an ideological touchstone, and expressions such as "the huwom race," "what the Lucy!", and "well I'll be a daughter of a dog!" abound. The national poet of Egalia is Walta Whitman; and there is a Sparksist movement, based on the analysis of class society set forth by one Clara Sparks.[19] Virtually everything that characterizes and defines Western patriarchal society finds its analogue and reversal in this imaginative tour de force. The oppressed menwim wear "pehos"—penisholders—an analogy with the Norwegian word for brassiere, "brystholder," which is seldom spoken out loud but usually shortened to BH, a not so embarrassing euphemism, explains Brantenberg.[20] While such a scenario has its predecessors—especially with regard to dress codes, behavior, and social power (staples of the sex-role reversal repertoire)—it is in her fascinating treatment of sexual behavior that Brantenberg most effectively challenges arguments from biology.

Egalia's gender ideology is, like ours, based on the notion that anatomy is destiny: thus it is male biology that makes Egalia's menwim inferior to the ruling wim, that consigns menwim to the status of housebounds, eager to earn fatherhood-protection from their sexual partners, the exploitive and domineering wim. Turning the woman-is-to-nature as man-is-to-culture argument entirely on its head, Brantenberg's matriarchal society subscribes to the profoundly reasonable conclusion that, in a world in which such an opposition between nature and culture exists, it is men who are closer to nature and hence less valuable to civilization, for only in males are sexual pleasure and procreation intimately linked: orgasm accompanies ejaculation.[21] Women's superiority, in terms of evolutionary development, is, according to this view, manifest in their characteristic separation of procreation (through intercourse) from sexual pleasure (orgasm). But this reconstruction of a biological argument for "natural" inferiority in fact thoroughly deconstructs biology as a relevant category in determining gender power, for nothing is simpler for Brantenberg than to demonstrate with unrelenting logic the social construction not only of gender roles but even of sexual behavior on the most intimate level. Hers is the only such novel I know of that takes the reversal directly into that last bastion of biological thinking: the bedroom.

In Egalia, then, it is the menwim who must prove they are taking their contraceptive pills and must get special dispensation if they wish to become fathers; it is the wim who use men for their own sexual pleasure (vigorously rubbing against the supine man-wom's thigh, hand masturbation while grabbing his penis, etc.); it is the wim who impose their sexual demands on tired menwim who'd rather go to sleep; it is the menwim who haven't had an orgasm in ages and rarely even get an erection. This last point is of particular interest: since the wim have defined male erection as unnecessary for their own pleasure, and since the tradition of wim's dominance prevents the menwim from being able to formulate (even to find the language for) their own sexual desires, patriarchal society's biological "facts"—that is, erection and constant sexual responsiveness (the supposed male norm in our society)—cease to be such in Egalia. Instead, the key element highlighted in Brantenberg's fiction is none other than the matter of power based on domination: who is dominant? who is in a position to use whom?

The instrumental view of males is the norm in Egalia: menwim are sexually controlled, molested, abused, and raped by wim, who then blame the victims for being provocative or for being in the wrong place at the wrong time. The menwim, thoroughly responsive to female power, are at the wim's mercy; hence accomplished and powerful older wim are "naturally" considered attractive by many young and ambitious menwim; and, if the sexual allure of power fails, harassment and economic power are always an alternative. If a manwom impregnates a wom and she is not willing to give him fatherhood-protection, it is he who is disgraced and her word that is credited (unless, of course, he can prove that he has duly taken his contraceptive pill—a monthly public act). It is he who must worry about livelihood and abandonment. In such a society, the fact that women but not men give birth is a further source and evidence of women's power and of men's powerlessness. "Naturally," childbirth is revered and rewarded (and dissociated from subsequent childcare), while the workplace is geared entirely to the needs and life patterns of the wim.[22]

Brantenberg does not challenge the fundamental biological facts. She does not "liberate" women from their unique reproductive potentiality; rather, she sees that the social meaning of pregnancy is the real issue, and that this is linked not as cause but as rationale to women's inferior position in patriarchal society. Not all sex-role reversals accept male and female biological roles in reproduction as the inevitable ones. But what is of particular interest, in the texts that do, is precisely the entirely reasonable and logical arguments that can be made on behalf of a reversal of political roles, of dominant and dominated, based upon familiar biological "facts." Do I need to say that these writers are not positing such a vision as a genuine utopia—are not, that is, suggesting that domination as a political instrument must exist—but are offering instead a satirical portrait of their own societies, with the intent of making their readers question categories that are normally accepted and taken for granted, and doing this in large part through the use of humor? Brantenberg herself has commented on this: "the idea is so simple, and it simply came up, because all arguments to maintain patriarchy are stupid. And although stupidity may lead to cruelty and tragedy, it is also laughable."[23]

It is not only feminist writers such as Brantenberg who depict the penis as the "weakest limb." Even some nonfeminist and antifeminist writers of sex-role reversals, whose works are intended ultimately to reaffirm the rightness or inevitability of our familiar gender patterns, find themselves positing excellent biological arguments for women's political and social superiority. Thomas Berger, for example, in his satirical novel *Regiment of Women* (1973), presents the gynocratic argument that men's political inferiority is related to their very physiology, for they have external genitalia easily vulnerable to pain and attack, and this cannot fail to hinder their movements and ability to act in the world.[24]

Can we get beyond such arguments about biology and society? These ways of formulating the problem, as Snitow notes, continue to exist within the heart of feminism; this is why, for example, there is no feminist consensus on such key topics as reproductive technologies or pornography. Objecting to Linda Alcoff's claim that we must transcend the dilemma by developing a third way, Snitow argues that no transcendence, no third course, is possible: "The urgent contradiction women constantly experience between the pressure to be a woman and the pressure not to be one will change only through a historical process; it cannot be dissolved through thought alone."[25]

But the sex-role reversals I have described clearly show that this problem is not one of terminology or definitions (what is "woman," "man," "difference"?), but of political power. When men are dominant, women are trapped in a constant oscillation, as Snitow shows, between sameness and difference as stances from which to pursue their claims. If women were in power—as they are in the alternative societies set in motion by the fictional technique of sex-role reversal—it would be "man" and its meanings that would be subjected to the same argumentation, splits, divides, and tensions. One has to back away from the entire discussion for this to come into focus. Why is it not a pressing issue for men in our society to determine whether "man" has meaning predominantly in a social or biological sense? Because men already enjoy a privileged position and it is only women who, in combatting them, are perpetually forced to question, redefine, and reposition themselves.

In an earlier article, entitled "Beyond Defensiveness: Feminist Research Strategies," I urged that we simply posit women as the norm in our discourse and as our center of reference, and proceed from there.[26] I was struck, at that time, by the pitfalls of an eternally combative and oppositional stance (a stance fatally marked by the condition of "Other"). But I was not then acquainted with the insights offered in the work of an important British writer of feminist utopian fiction who repeatedly addressed these very issues. Katharine Burdekin (1896–1963) published ten novels, under her own name as well as under the male pseudonym "Murray Constantine," between 1922 and 1940. Burdekin envisioned both masculinist and feminist futures, and wrote two novels that are mirror images of one another in this respect. One is the masculinist dystopia *Swastika Night*, written in 1936 and first published in 1937 with "Murray Constantine" as its author.[27] In this astonishing novel, depicting Europe seven hundred years after a victory by Germany's National Socialists, Burdekin identified the key element in fascism as the "cult of masculinity." The counterpart to *Swastika Night*, composed, I believe, before Hitler's increasingly aggressive stance compelled Burdekin to imagine a possible Nazi future, is entitled *The End of This Day's Business*. Written in about 1935 but not published until 1989, this novel is set four thousand years in the future, when women rule the world in peace and harmony and only one price is exacted by this rule: the subjection of men who, ignorant of their own history and denied access to the language of learning, lead inconsequential lives in their pleasant separate sphere. Lacking late twentieth-century terminology such as "sexual objectification" and "the feminine mystique," Burdekin nonetheless depicted the existence of such phenomena among her disarmed and disempowered males.[28]

In Burdekin's work, important themes in later novels are often prefigured in earlier ones. The sex-role reversal of *The End of This Day's Business* is first evoked in a passage in an earlier work, the pacifist novel aptly named *Quiet Ways*, published in 1930. Here

Burdekin for a brief moment sets forth a vision of a different way of being, in which "woman" is not a category perpetually subjected to defamation and in need of analysis and defense. Helga, Burdekin's six-foot-tall, 160-pound heroine, is described as self-contained in a way that a conventional misogynist male acquaintance, a man appropriately named Carapace, finds intolerable. The scene is recounted from the man's point of view and through his reactions the reader is made to see the gender work routinely done by women, even as they attempt to contest male power, and the unsettling effect on a man when a woman merely refrains from engaging in these routines. Burdekin contrasts Carapace's "hominism" (a term she probably borrowed from George Bernard Shaw) to Helga's "feminism":

> Carapace despised women who aped men, but that at least was flattering. This heavy impenetrability [of Helga's], this self-sufficiency, this almost contemptuous absence of mind when men were speaking was a portent. It was new and dangerous; it threatened, if it became at all general, to upset the world far more than the ordinary type of feminism which concentrates on votes and professions. Carapace was a passionate hominist, and his spiritual home was Greece in the age of Pericles. His sensitive soul was for ever being pricked and scraped by twentieth-century ideas of equality. But Helga did more than prick and scrape him; she lacerated him. For the first time in his life he felt femininity to be not flippant, weak, fundamentally indecent and contemptible, but a massive, patient, immensely powerful thing. His revolt was tinged with fear. He was deeply afraid that Helga did not believe herself inferior to Alan [her husband], and if women like this became common what in God's name was to happen to the world? Would they not bring up their daughters in their own calm sense of superiority, a sense, not less dangerous, but rather more, because it made no noisy assertions. Would they not bring up their young sons to think themselves of less absolute value than the girls? Carapace's brain, racing into the future, saw a complete reversal of the accepted order of things. Son worship abolished, and daughter worship set up in its place. Women being brought up to thank God they were not men. Boys brought up to wish they were women. There was no limit to the horrors that might come if women once really lost their sense of inferiority. And that it could be completely missing he had the proof before him.[29]

I cite this passage at length not out of a desire to promote a quietism that could be (mis)interpreted as acquiescence to a masculinist reality. Rather, what strikes me about it now, as I emerge from the still-raging debates over sameness and difference, is the refreshing sense of space conveyed by the early part of this passage—its evocation of a kind of inner buffer zone in which a woman is genuinely, if momentarily, outside the reaches of endless argumentation framed entirely in terms of male power and women's perpetual need to contest it. Carapace, in a flash, senses the threat that such a way of being poses to an androcentric reality. Assuming as he does the inevitability of hierarchy, he at once jumps to the conclusion that such independence in women would lead to a mere reversal that would alter the positions of the individual players but not the terms of the game. What he sees, in other words, is that male power is not an absolute and unchangeable fact, but a relation that depends upon women's subordination. In a 1934 novel entitled *Proud Man* (published under the pseudonym), Burdekin would go on to argue that revolutionary efforts are doomed to failure if they cannot be more than "reversals of privilege."[30] She brings this argument to life in *The End of This Day's Business,* which addresses the political problem of domination—this time by women—in a world much like that of Carapace's nightmare.

We, meanwhile, knowing the terms of our situation in the real world, must react against them. But it seems to me that, if our reactions remain caught within the structures and concepts made available to us by the "patriarchy," we have gained little. Can we not believe somewhat less vehemently in the reality of concepts such as "essentialism" and "social constructionism," and instead reserve a space for ourselves in which these particular positionings are not the sum total of our experience or existence? I do not, after all, experience my "difference" until it is imposed upon me from outside. As long as I continue to engage in our habitual discussions of that difference—whether attempting to locate it, define (or redefine) it, apologize for it, or valorize it—I am replicating the very structures I set out to contest. Certainly we are not required, much less compelled, to lend full credence to the terms created by our own marginalization, terms whose very existence helps sustain that marginalization. Does anyone seriously imagine that if we should once resolve the matter of the correct grounds on which to argue for changes in women's status, all women will rally round, consensus will unfold, and change (as "we" conceive of it) will necessarily occur? Or have we simply created another arena of discourse—an interesting one, to be sure—with the unstated assumption that the right discourse, if once stumbled upon, developed, or argumentatively sustained, will "fix" the problem?

The view from elsewhere can open our eyes.

Notes

1. Myra Jehlen, "Archimedes and the Paradox of Feminist Criticism," *Signs* 6, no. 4 (Summer 1981): 576, 577.

2. Carol Smart writes that since the nineteenth century the basic question for feminist politics has been "whether women should be given special treatment by the state and the law on the basis of their uniquely female capacities and supposed characteristics, or whether justice would be better served by treating women as equal to men, with equal rights and responsibilities." See her *Feminism and the Power of Law* (London: Routledge, 1989), 82. Deborah L. Rhode, in her essay "The 'Woman's Point of View'," *Journal of Legal Education* 38 (1988), notes: "For most of American history, emphasis on women's distinctive perspective has worked against women's distinctive interests." Thus, for example, "the presumed difference in the sexes' capacity for legal work" was used to bar women from entering the legal profession (39). See also Mary Jane Mossman, "Feminism and Legal Method: The Difference It Makes," *Wisconsin Women's Law Journal* 3 (1987); Susan Gluck Mezey, "When Should Differences Make a Difference: A New Approach to the Constitutionality of Gender-Based Laws," *Women & Politics* 10, no. 2 (1990); Martha Minow, *Making All the Difference: Inclusion, Exclusion and American Law* (Ithaca: Cornell University Press, 1990).

3. Smart, in *Feminism and the Power of Law,* cites theorists such as Catharine MacKinnon, M. Thornton, and S. J. Kenney, who have shown that "both of these approaches presume that men are the norm against which women-as-different or women-as-equal are measured. It is women's reproductive capacity that creates a problem for the male norm inherent in law, not for example men's abdication of the caring role. In this respect neither the difference nor the equality approach begin to tackle the problem of the power of law to proclaim its neutrality. Basically these approaches leave law as it is, but seek to find the most successful way of squeezing the interests of women past the legislators and judiciary" (82).

4. The defense of difference has been taken to an extreme by feminists such as Hélène Cixous, with their emphasis on the body—as if there were a necessary relationship between menstrual flow and creative flow. Let me note, as well, that for the sake of the present argument I am disregarding the important issue of difference *among,* and not only *between,* human groups. For an analysis of several contemporary usages of the term *difference,* see Michèle Barrett, "The Concept of Difference," *Feminist Review* 26 (Summer 1987).

5. The very language I am using in this essay is an illustration of the problem I am attempting to address: it is (in terms of the conventional division of reality into stereotypical masculine and feminine modes) an androcentric language rooted in military metaphors of assault and attack, rebellion and struggle. Later in this essay I will cite a passage by Katharine Burdekin that suggests an alternative path—but one in many respects also hedged in by the fact that our very language, if it is to communicate at all, cannot go too far beyond the boundaries of convention at any given moment.

6. For an example in the realm of law, see Regina Graycar, "Equal Rights Versus Fathers' Rights: The Child Custody Debate in Australia," *Child Custody and the Politics of Gender,* ed. Carol Smart and Selma Sevenhuijsen (London: Routledge, 1989). The notion of "equality"—in this case "equal rights for parents," meaning joint custody of children in cases of divorce (183)—as Graycar points out, actually involves a continuation of patriarchal control after divorce. Analyzing the terms of the debate, she notes that they "rely heavily on the ideology of equality at the same time as they ignore the realities of matters such as the day-to-day caretaking practices of divorced mothers and fathers and the

relative economic situations of women and men in Australia" (185). Her point is that the "rhetoric of equality" should not prevent close analysis of the "underlying realities" of custody arrangements. If we are not prepared to undertake such analyses, the "equality" argument, embedded in a traditional patriarchal legal framework, can simply become a means of reasserting that framework. For a comparable discussion of Canadian law, see Anne Marie Delorey, "Joint Legal Custody: A Reversion to Patriarchal Power," *Canadian Journal of Women and the Law* 3, no. 1 (1989).

7. Ann Snitow, "Pages from a Gender Diary," *Dissent* (Spring 1989). Future references to Snitow are to this essay and page numbers will be cited parenthetically in the text.

8. Catharine R. Stimpson, "The New Scholarship about Women: The State of the Art," *Annals of Scholarship* 1, no. 2 (1980).

9. Dean MacCannell, *The Tourist: A New Theory of the Leisure Class* (New York: Schocken Books, 1976), 118.

10. Surplus visibility in my view offers a functional definition of minority status. This concept explains why any "objectionable" action of any member of a "minority" group— blacks, Jews, women, homosexuals—is taken as characteristic of the entire group, thus reinforcing stereotypes, a situation that simply does not exist for the powerful. Members of minority groups are no doubt intuitively aware of this danger; hence their own policing actions, added to those of the powerful, maintain their marginal status. Challenges to the canon or to traditional curricula provide significant examples of the phenomenon of surplus visibility in recent years. This explains the responses of those who, in supporting the status quo, exaggerate the threat from the "left," as if whenever "any of them" get a toe in the door, "all of them" are seen as taking over. See my "Minority Status and the Stigma of 'Surplus Visibility'," *Chronicle of Higher Education*, 30 October 1991, A52.

11. Bronwyn Davies and Rom Harré, "Positioning: The Discursive Production of Selves," *Journal for the Theory of Social Behaviour* 20, no. 1 (1990). Davies and Harré contrast their dynamic and interactionist view of "position" as something produced through discursive interaction with the older concept of "role" that serves to foreground static, formal, and ritualistic aspects. I would add that the notion of "role" also—and paradoxically— implies something that can be sloughed off by merely "changing roles," which effectively disguises the elaborate mechanisms by which a given "reality" is maintained in place. "Position" better allows one to conceive of complex and interwoven social processes. For a related analysis of gender as something that is produced through the workings of everyday interactions, see Candace West and Don H. Zimmerman, "Doing Gender," *Gender & Society* 1, no. 2 (June 1987).

12. I am reverting to the terminology of "sex role" in this instance because "sex-role reversal" has become a standard designation in bibliographies and studies of utopian fiction. The literary technique of sex-role reversal is itself an ancient one, apparent already in Aristophanes' *Parliament of Women*.

13. I want, however, to differentiate between the carefully worked out sex-role reversal in the novels I am going to discuss and the more limited use made of gender defamiliarization in representations of cross-dressing. In cross-dressing, it is not gender power that is reversed but merely personal power, which is either added or stripped away by an effective disguise as the opposite sex. A film such as *Tootsie* offers a good example of the kinds of contradictions that abound in popular (and usually limited) gender switching. While purporting to criticize gender stereotypes, the movie ultimately endorses them. Through the character of Dorothy, the film presents us with an admirable female figure—gutsy, tough, and . . . male. Dorothy, as played by Dustin Hoffman in drag, is a better, in the sense of more admirable, and certainly more effective, woman than the film's actual women. But there is nothing new in the message that a man does it better—whatever "it" happens to be. In *Tootsie*, the scenes in which Dustin Hoffman, as a man, rants and raves to his male roommate about the way he has been (mis)treated as a woman are the only

moments in the film that begin to provide the defamiliarization on which thoroughgoing sex-role reversal utopias thrive. But the main distinction to be drawn between the novels and the film, apart from the problem of the ideological double standard, is that sex-role reversals set an entire society on its head; they do not treat gender oppression as a purely individual problem that can be plumbed by one person cross-dressing in an unchanged society. The viewer can walk away from *Tootsie* marveling at the strangeness of Dustin Hoffman, in women's clothes, being patted on the bottom, and still not think it outrageous to see Jessica Lange receive the same treatment. Or, worse yet, the female attire can so familiarize the behavior it elicits that we may fail to find it strange to see Hoffman's Dorothy character treated in routine sexist ways, and we only experience the sense of indignity the scene is meant to evoke when, once again, we see Hoffman as a man. In such a situation, our emotions may be excessively absorbed by one character, whose fate alone seems to matter, and the political potential of the travesty is nullified. In the film *Tootsie*, such an interpretation is reinforced by the final scene, in which Dustin Hoffman, now in slovenly male attire that would have acutely embarrassed Dorothy, exercises his male magnetism on a hesitatingly receptive and winsomely delicious Jessica Lange.

14. Using such terminology as "either side" once again concedes too much to our prevailing reality and its metaphors of opposition. As Dorothy Sayers points out in a witty reversal, "The Human-Not-Quite-Human," in her *Unpopular Opinions: Twenty-One Essays* (New York: Harcourt, Brace, 1947), it is odd that women are referred to as "the opposite sex." "What," Sayers wonders, "is the 'neighbouring sex'?" (142). The "innocent" question is a very important tool of defamiliarization.

15. Herbert Marcuse, in his essay "Repressive Tolerance," in Robert Paul Wolff, Barrington Moore, Jr., and Herbert Marcuse, *A Critique of Pure Tolerance* (Boston: Beacon Press, 1965), refers to the "institutionalized inequality" of our society: "The antagonistic structure of society rigs the rules of the game. Those who stand against the established system are *a priori* at a disadvantage, which is not removed by the toleration of their ideas, speeches, and newspapers" (92). The "tolerance" accorded these marginalized ideas does not alter their marginal status. That they can be voiced and disregarded contributes to the appearance of free-and-equal competition among ideas and perspectives. Adopting a political, as opposed to an abstractly ethical, perspective allows Marcuse to see the "repressive" functions of such tolerance.

16. Annie Denton Cridge, *Man's Rights, or, How Would You Like It?* (Wellesley, Mass.: Mrs. E. M. F. Denton [1870]). Future page references to this work will be cited parenthetically in the text. For a detailed discussion of this and several other early sex-role reversals, see my essay "When Women Rule: Defamiliarization in the Sex-Role Reversal Utopia," *Extrapolation* 23, no. 1 (Spring 1982).

17. See Snitow, "Pages from a Gender Diary," who quotes Ellen DuBois's words: "My hypothesis is that the significance of the woman suffrage movement rested precisely on the fact that it bypassed women's oppression within the family, or private sphere, and demanded instead her admission to citizenship, and through it admission to the public arena" (214). See also DuBois's essay, "The Radicalism of the Woman Suffrage Movement: Notes toward the Reconstruction of Nineteenth-Century Feminism," in Anne Phillips, ed., *Feminism and Equality* (New York: New York University Press, 1987).

18. In fact, very similar arguments were set forth decades earlier in Ruth Herschberger's witty and incisive book *Adam's Rib* (New York: Pellegrini & Cudahy, 1948; New York: Harper & Row, 1970). See especially chapter 8, "Society Writes Biology." Feminist scholarship has still not gotten past the problem of perpetually losing sight of what should be considered key texts, which seem to need to be resurrected again and again.

19. Gerd Brantenberg, *Egalia's Daughters: A Satire of the Sexes*, trans. Louis Mackay in cooperation with Gerd Brantenberg (Seattle: Seal Press, 1985). Brantenberg has written to

me (letter dated 26 February 1987) that she was alone with her idea for many years and would probably not have taken the trouble to write the book had she been acquainted with other examples of such reversals. The problems of translation, she states, were formidable:

> You have to rethink it in every new language. Since I have spent a lot of my life trying to learn English (as a second language), I co-operated on the translation of the book into this language . . . .
> . . . "Moulding Mothers" of course is a parody of the "Founding Fathers," and they don't exist anywhere but in the U.S. in 1776. But we do have "the Fathers at Eidsvoll" in 1814, which was when we got our independence as a nation (from Denmark), so in Norwegian I've made a parodic version of that—the Mothers at the Demo Mount. . . .
> A lot of words/phrases/ideas get lost in the English translation because there are generally more gender-referring terms in Norwegian than in English. . . . Some words, however, have been gained. Like ladsel. Ladsel in distress. Lordies and gentlewim is a funny phrase which doesn't have any equivalent in the Norwegian text.

Clara Sparks, instead of Karl Marx, was a bit of metonymic inventiveness made possible by Brantenberg's familiarity with England, where a department store chain called Marks and Spencer is colloquially known as Marks and Sparks. In the Norwegian text, the character is called Gulfuria, "just a funny-sounding, made-up name."

20. Brantenberg, letter dated 26 February 1987. *Egalia's Daughters* also depicts the development of a menwim's movement and of a gay movement among the menwim. For the purposes of this paper, however, I am concentrating on the novel's representation of power relations between men and women.

21. Herschberger, in *Adam's Rib*, makes the same point as Brantenberg, but, interestingly, in a radically different context. Discussing the idea that for women "orgasm is a luxury," she draws on Kenneth Walker's *The Physiology of Sex:* "Whereas for the satisfactory discharge of the male function of fertilization an ejaculation, and therefore an orgasm, is indispensable, for the female function of conception an orgasm is unnecessary" (74).

22. A similar and particularly detailed study of what the workplace and household roles might look like if women and not men were the dominant sex while other values of modern society remain intact is offered in Esmé Dodderidge's novel *The New Gulliver, or, The Adventures of Lemuel Gulliver, Jr. in Capovolta* (New York: Taplinger, 1979).

23. Letter dated 9 April 1987. In the same letter Brantenberg also states that she first got the idea for such a book in the early 1960s: "But it takes some experience and maturity to write a book—some knowledge of how society functions, some insights that I didn't have when I first got the idea to write this book when I was about twenty, and started writing it, but never continued. It was very different then." The book was written while Brantenberg was in Copenhagen, active within the Danish women's movement.

24. Thomas Berger, *Regiment of Women* (New York: Simon & Schuster, 1973). The novel culminates in the "righting" of the reversal at least as concerns the protagonists, with the male once again on top (literally). Familiar biological arguments are restored in the novel's last line: "Also, he was the one with the protuberant organ" (349).

25. Snitow, "Pages from a Gender Diary," 209. Here she explicitly disagrees with Linda Alcoff's "Cultural Feminism Versus Post-Structuralism: The Identity Crisis in Feminist Theory," *Signs* 13, no. 1 (Spring 1988).

26. Daphne Patai, "Beyond Defensiveness: Feminist Research Strategies," *Women's Studies International Quarterly* 6, no. 2 (1983).

27. Murray Constantine, *Swastika Night* (London: Gollancz, 1937; reprinted as a Left Book Club selection in 1940). In the mid-1980s I established the real authorship of the novel and it was reprinted under Burdekin's own name in London by Lawrence and Wishart (1985) and in New York by The Feminist Press (1985). See my introduction to the

reprint and my essay "Orwell's Despair, Burdekin's Hope: Gender and Power in Dystopia," *Women's Studies International Forum* 7, no. 2 (1984), as well as my book *The Orwell Mystique: A Study in Male Ideology* (Amherst: University of Massachusetts Press, 1984), chap. 8.

28. Katharine Burdekin, *The End of This Day's Business,* Afterword by Daphne Patai (New York: Feminist Press, 1989). I came across the novel among more than a dozen of Burdekin's unpublished manuscripts, which were made available to me by her literary executor and heirs.

29. Katharine Burdekin, *Quiet Ways* (London: Butterworth, 1930), 239–40.

30. Murray Constantine, *Proud Man* (London: Boriswood, 1934). This novel will be reprinted by The Feminist Press in New York in 1992.

Inappropriate Fertility: Feminism, Poststructuralism, and the Teen Parent

Susan Ritchie, Amy Shuman, Sally Meckling
The Ohio State University

"... and everytime the old folk would say 'gal, ain't you big?'
They would not say that you were pregnant, they'd say aren't
you big, but you would go on denying it."

"TEENAGE pregnancy" is a contemporary, locally situated category, not a biological fact. The woman (a sixty-four-year-old, southern African-American, now living in Columbus, Ohio, interviewed by her granddaughter) quoted above describes a different category than what is known today as "teenage pregnancy." What was important was the girl's physical condition and her social position, not necessarily her age. The current construction of "teenage pregnancy" as the name used for this condition belies a political agenda with specific but rarely articulated messages, and like other constructions of cultural situations as historical or biological necessities, it creates the impression that "teenage pregnancy" is a natural category. Our interest in this essay is with the existence of this category within both governmental institutions and collected personal narratives—in short, where the personal is invented in service of the political. We will pay special attention to the adequacy of structural and poststructural models for understanding these complex interrelations in a manner which we think will be useful for feminist activists.

The poststructural interest in exposing "natural" categories as social constructions will be most helpful to us as we attempt to explain some of the interests behind the emergence of this category of "teenage pregnancy." For it is through the fantasy link established between teenage pregnancy and biology that certain governmental, medical, and personal agencies are able to attribute social danger to the very bodies of women. Yet poststructuralism does pose certain problems for us as feminists. While we agree with the exposure of essentialism, we are still suspicious of whether or not an agenda that is primarily anti-essentialist is

151

adequate to our political interests. We do not plan on rehearsing here the arguments about the difficulties of anti-essentialist feminism or even the argument about whether or not women can assume a poststructural subjectivity, having never known the unproblematic agency that characterized the white, male bourgeois subjectivity of modernity.[1] Rather, we insist that poststructuralist models for socially constructed categories might prove inadequate to feminism in their inability to understand all positions as interested—which is to say motivated by an entire network of discursive and ideological interactions. For while politically interested poststructuralisms such as Foucault's are most valuable for their description of power as a force that exists along all points of the social matrix, they often fail to understand how power—and its hegemonic imperative—might vary or even falter as it manifests itself in different social arenas. It is this blindness that has caused many poststructuralists to assume that resistance is only possible in the form of the emptied-out subject—a subject that refuses to mistake ideology for herself.[2] One of the stranger descriptions of this empty subject was articulated by Foucault in one of his final interviews: "Nothing would change much if I and my books didn't exist," he said. "I find it almost physically pleasurable to think of the causes I'm concerned with just passing through me, of thousands of people and books going in the same direction as me but ultimately flowing way beyond me."[3] The manner in which this subject itself might depend on a Western male privilege has already been explored by various postcolonial critics such as Gayatri Spivak and Mira Kamdar and feminists like Laura Kipnis.[4] We shall make it our task here to enact an alternate way of understanding the political poststructural. For rather than critique once again the ideologically compromised subject, we hope to demonstrate the multiple and often fragile ways in which that subject and the larger social field depend upon each other for their construction. We find it inadequate, then, to simply identify teenage pregnancy as an invented, nonessential category. Instead, our focus here is on the political dynamics that made such a category thinkable—political dynamics which will still remain even after the social construction of "teenage pregnancy" is exposed.[5]

"Teeenage pregnancy" represents first of all an interesting intersection of discourses, persons, and politics. That the category of teenage pregnancy is a construction of these discourses becomes clear when we examine the personal narratives told in different decades by people who became parents as teenagers. The earlier category used widely in the United States was "unwed mothers," and the "teenage pregnancy" category is in part an attempt to spread responsibility to fathers. Including "teenage" in the category added the "too young for sex" message, a message that was conspicuously absent from earlier narratives. For example, the grandmother quoted above explained that she had to work as soon as she had a child because her family considered a parent to be "grown" and automatically obligated by adult responsibilities. A parent was, by definition, an adult. By contrast, current literature prepared by the Ohio Governor's Task Force on Adolescent Sexuality and Pregnancy discusses "too-young mothers" who are "physically ready for sexual involvement at age 13, [but] are not ready emotionally for the interpersonal relationships that accompany this intimacy."[6] We cannot resist pointing out that the "interpersonal relationship" in question is thought to be motherhood even as it implicitly includes the relationship between the teenagers.

Yet merely exposing "teenage pregnancy" as a cultural category, even as a cultural category understood to be the result of the interested, ideological machinations of specific discourses, does little to challenge the idea that hegemonic power can be suddenly and unproblematically invoked by the social critic in need of a handy explanation for a socially existing category. For even when categories are understood to be constructed, they are still thought to bear a resemblance to the "natural" forms that they succeed: they leave intact the idea that individuals and their bodies are necessarily united.

So if the personal narratives told by individuals establish cultural categories, they also construct the individuals who tell them. People relating their experiences do not invent events out of whole cloth but rather integrate their experiences into the existing social categories even as those social categories are integrated and negotiated by their inhabitants.[7] The particular social categories invoked by the teen pregnancy discourse—the humanities, medicine, adolescent studies, parenting, and feminisms—all define teenage pregnancy in such a way as to inscribe not only the category of "teen parent" but also their own rationales. These invented categories are further reinforced through similar social and discursive practices (the assignment of human beings to categories based on their HIV infection, drug use, or "at risk" behaviors has its own effect on the available paradigms for thinking about the "teen parent").[8] "Teen parents" are not the constructions of single persons, powers, or narratives. Rather, the existence of the category indicates the mutual construction of an entire discourse involving many persons, powers, discourses, and bodies.

Yet noting that oppressive categories are the result of discursive networks of various narratives does not suggest that resistance to hegemony might take the form of abandoning narratives altogether. As Meaghan Morris notes in her discussion of Lyotard, his claim that the shift to postmodernism has been marked by the death of master narratives should call attention to the particular failures of emancipation narratives rather than suggesting that resistance to narrative is possible. Morris writes of the death of "all *guiding* narratives, let's say, which can be directly related to knowledge institutions, which are still not so very distant from emancipation fairy-tales (least of all when their failure is lamented), and which do not yet seem to be withering away under the impact of new technologies—despite Lyotard's prognosis that data banks, personal computers and so on will completely externalize the relationship of knower to knowledge."[9] The teenage mothers' narratives and the state's narrative measure themselves against a third, failed fairy tale, in which pregnancy is preceded by courtship and followed by perpetual romance. "Marriage," the missing category in all three narratives, represents the unquestioned, but actually lamented, failed guiding narrative. While it is painfully obvious that the teenage mothers are rewriting a positive scenario for themselves and that the state is specifically not addressing certain topics, it is not then productive to say that what we have are Lyotardian displaced narratives.[10] The problem continues to be the relationship between local narratives and some narrative of a grander scale. The dynamics of construction are particularly problematic when, as is usually the case, the local narrative conceals the failed dimensions of the larger-scale mythic narratives.

Our interest in construction relies to a certain extent on Althusser's concept of interpellation, in which one becomes a subject only at the moment that one hails or recognizes one's oppression:

> I shall then suggest that ideology "acts" or "functions" in such a way that it "recruits" subjects among the individuals (it recruits them all), or "transforms" the individuals into subjects (it transforms them all) by that very precise operation which I have called interpellation, of hailing, and which can be imagined along the line of the most commonplace everyday police (or other) hailing: "Hey you there!"[11]

Instead of a base superstructure model in which one power constitutes one oppression, Althusser presents a model of mutual construction that depends on the individual recognizing herself in the hail and responding accordingly. Although being fully inter-pellated into a system represents the ideological limits of action and identity, the recognition involved in interpellation suggests that when one recognizes one's self in the interpellative hail one sees a moment of possibility—in other words, one imagines the individuality that is constructed through hailing to be a kind of freedom—not, perhaps, as is often thought, the possibility of resisting the hail altogether. For as Althusser's example displays, choice and recognition, often thought to be evidence of free will, are themselves a part of the system.

In this context it is interesting that "choices" are often only presented as possibilities for avoiding negative situations. In the narratives we collected, many of the teen mothers reported that their experiences were exceptions to the familiar scenario in which teenagers have sex, the girl gets pregnant, and the boy deserts her.[12] In this way teenagers themselves buy into the category; however, most of the narratives they tell are counternar-ratives, about how they escaped the trap, and this nonetheless reconfirms, reifies, the trap. What does it mean to be an exception? The whole model somehow relies on our knowing what teenage parenthood is like or bound to be like. This construction escapes the problem of being interpellated once and for all—whatever narrative they construct will carry along trailings of previous ones as well as serve to consolidate the very dominant narrative they purport to transgress. For example, in the narratives we collected, one woman says she has proved all narratives wrong—her boyfriend hasn't left her and she has been married for two months now. An important question in examining the efficacy of these seeming resistances is specifically to ask how their seeming defiance of categories nonetheless keeps those categories intact.

Where categories do not exist, or when an event is not tellable, tellers negotiate new categories. Storytelling is one means for people to assign meaning to their experience and to adjust their perspectives on events to fit or reshape community attitudes. When Kai Erikson was called in to discover the "true story" in a community that had suffered a natural disaster (a flood that wiped out the entire valley), the insurance company was predisposed to imagine a communitywide conspiracy, for everyone seemed to be telling the "same story." Erikson reported that the similarity of the stories did not invalidate their accuracy.[13] Rather, he argued that in a situation of tragedy, it was difficult to figure out how to talk about what had happened. What's important here is that it was not in the interests of the insurance company to believe the people. Carlo Ginzberg provides a similar example in his work on the Inquisition, where the interrogated subject attempts to compose a narrative to fit the expectations of the inquisitors. In the case of the Inquisition, there is obvious coercion and it is clear who are the interested.[14] These types of analyses make the assumption that uncoerced statements *are* true or "natural" or unconstructed.

The assumption that narrative is a matter of individual initiative, or a matter of an individual response to an especially traumatic situation, is problematic because it obscures the determining of larger social forces. Rather, it is more appropriate to understand the existence of these narratives in the context of those social forces—an idea that is not at all strange to hegemonic strategies. Even the State of Ohio, which one would not consider to be a stronghold of poststructuralist thought, clearly perceives the connection between individuals' construction of narratives (and thereby experience) as incidental to larger social structures—in this case the legislative process. As the state literature reads, "Teenage pregnancy . . . will not be remedied by the actions of state government alone. Instead the problem of teenage pregnancy requires a joint effort by local, state and federal governments." In this case, it is important to note that it is not the category of teenage pregnancy that the State of Ohio wishes to "remedy" but rather the persons who might be understood to inhabit that category. But simply noting the constructed nature of the category of teenage pregnancy is not adequate to understanding or interrupting the full range of appropriations and interests that accompany the constitution of the category.

The State of Ohio literature, for example, is able to appropriate feminism as its alibi for maintaining a category that allows for the legislative consignment of entire groups of women to an underclass. The literature notes that: "Teenage pregnancy remains at the hub of the poverty cycle in this country. As reported by *Time* Lucille Dismukes of the Council on Maternal and Infant Care in Atlanta said, '. . . feminization of poverty starts off with teenagers having babies. So many can't rise above it [poverty] to go back to school to get job skills'" (10). The causal patterns suggest that while the feminization of poverty might have a social cause, teenage pregnancy remains a correctable failing on the part of individuals. Here humanism and the naive reinscription of individual free will masks itself as feminism. The fact that the state's authors had to clarify that "rise above it" meant rise above poverty simply indicates the naiveté of suggesting that one can eliminate the feminization of poverty by willpower while the referent, the "it" that condemns one to poverty, is more slippery. The literature thus literalizes the feminization of poverty by attributing it not to sexism but back to women's bodies and moral failings.

The result of this dynamic is the naturalization of class distinctions. The working class, sandwiched between the poverty associated by the state with teenage pregnancy and the upper classes, turns to a bourgeois sexual aesthetic wherein qualities of maturity, romance, and homeownership are thought to be integral to sexual experience.[15] Stephen Greenblatt notes this last distinction in his discussion of the fictions constructed around women's sexuality. He writes:

> A culture that imagines (or, better still, knows as an indisputable biological fact) that women need not experience any pleasure at all to conceive will offer different representational resources than a culture that knows as a widely accepted physical truth that women have occulted, inward penises, which must for the survival of mankind be brought by the heat of erotic friction to the point of ejaculation.[16]

Both of these constructions still reinscribe a bourgeois sexual ethic within which a woman's own Gramscian consent to sexual pleasure is considered a prerequisite to the biological existence of man: hence the myth that women who are raped can't get pregnant unless they want to, an argument frequently exercised by the anti-abortion movement. This is iterated by the character Serena Joy in the film based on Margaret Atwood's *The Handmaid's Tale*. Serena asks Kate, the protagonist, if she wants to get pregnant—believing she won't unless she wants to.

In the narratives that we collected, women repeatedly compared their own sexual experiences with the existing bourgeois narrative. "I would have prepared [for my first sexual experience]. . . . I didn't bleed, and if I would have thought about it I would have put a towel down, but I didn't realize that you were supposed to bleed and then I thought I was abnormal because I didn't." The interviewer then remarked, "You didn't bleed?" To which she responds, "No, was I supposed to?" That the interviewee then goes on to note that she felt that because she didn't bleed she must have been pregnant indicates the extent to which the narrative of the "virgin" experience story is intertwined already with a discourse about appropriate or inappropriate bodily behaviors, the inappropriate always signifying pregnancy. And once again the connection between appropriate sexual behavior and doing well socially in high school is made. As the young women try to assess whether or not bleeding is "normal," they compare the bleeding experiences of cheerleaders with those of noncheerleaders. "I was a cheerleader too and I bled" one woman remarks in order to assert that bleeding is normal.

The category "teenage pregnancy" naturalizes and depends upon humanistic conceptions of the subject that cause people to constantly patrol the boundaries of "normal" or "natural" experience by looking for consistency between their social and biological selves. The invention and negotiation of these borders subsumes the specific considerations of race and class as well as gender. As we have noted, critical models of social construction clearly expose the process by which social categories are naturalized. We would go one step further to point out how agency is not only naturalized, but displaced, often within the arenas of race and class. Race, for instance, apparently increases one's risk of pregnancy. The state literature states that "although three out of every four teenage births are to white adolescents, proportionately, black teens are seven times more likely to become pregnant than white teens" (32). The reasons supplied for this reinforce the racist notion that while white people became pregnant from momentary social lapses or environmental pressures, black people are simply having too much sex. The literature states: "The high incidence of teen pregnancy among minorities is attributed to several factors. One major factor is early sexual activity. The Council of State Policy & Planning Agencies says teenagers living in segregated urban poverty areas are twice as likely to be sexually active at an earlier age than their black non-ghetto urban peers" (32). Note the complete conflation of race and class as "urban teenagers" is used to describe blacks only.

In this way the invention of "teenage pregnancy" becomes an excuse to extend the power and reach of government surveillance and regulation. According to the way these categories have been set up, and this is problematic too, the situations of young persons having babies is a private matter protected from government intervention. For these reasons many people assume that the government's interest in teenage pregnancy is not a matter of social control. Yet teenage parents are constituted as a public concern that merits governmental interference, since teenage pregnancy is thought to be both a public health problem and a fiscal danger (most governmental literature on teenage pregnancy lists the "Costs of Teenage Pregnancy in Real Public Dollars") requiring the full educational and administrative arsenal of government to control. If teenage pregnancy is a health problem, an "epidemic," governmental interference is easily legitimized. Meanwhile, the argument against teen pregnancy spins a web of seemingly causal "social costs," many of which resort to various perversions of cycle-of-abuse narratives, to make interference seem pragmatic. The State of Ohio declares that "child abuse is only one of the many prices children of teenage mothers pay" (18).

Here it would seem that "teenage pregnancy" becomes a category, and the pregnant teen becomes an agent of the state, of education, and of medicine, in contrast to the notion of the personal, willful, humanistic teen, deployed above in the narratives of teen pregnancy and mothering. We would like to suggest, however, that the categories which would make these separate may not be wholly adequate to describe how ideology works with respect to teen pregnancy. It is in this definition of teenage sexuality as an essential category dangerous both to the girls and to the solvency of the state that the government finds its excuse to moralize on a variety of sexual issues, including its predilection for stressing abstinence for young people rather than pursuing initiatives that would make safe and effective birth control readily available to them. One scenario that the educational materials provided by the Ohio Teen Parent Trap suggests should be discussed in classrooms addressed to the "problem" features a young couple who engage in sex against their basic inclinations only because they feel it is expected of them. Sex comes from elsewhere: "Today children are bombarded [by the media] with the message that sex is attractive, exciting" (16).[17]

On one hand, then, the state attempts to understand the "increase" in teenage pregnancy as a result of biological and empirical facts (the increasing gap between the age of puberty and the age of marriage is often cited—marking again the slippage between the state's condemnation of teenage pregnancy and its apparent interest in discouraging premarital sex), while insisting that the "remedy" involves some kind of humanistic reentry into the welfare state, i.e., returning to school, resumption of shopping, and other sanctioned forms of consumerism.[18] Teenage pregnancy is often understood as both the implied result and cause of an academic or social failure in high school. The literature suggests that teen parents can't date as often, go to as many parties, or have as many new clothes as the average teen should (apparently maternity wear doesn't count as new clothes).

So teenage pregnancy prevention programs in Chicago advertise, "What test do teenagers flunk more than any other? THE PREGNANCY TEST," and the State of Ohio literature implies that a low grade point average can lead to pregnancy. The concern for the academic failures of the "trapped" teenage parent is only a symptom of the larger social failure for which these teens are made emblematic—the failure to take the appropriate path to adult initiation. Literature issued directly to teens themselves warns, "Being a teen today is not easy. You'll go through many changes and challenges as you grow up to enter adulthood and its many opportunities. Becoming a teen parent can make this challenge even harder" (4). The inappropriate initiation into adulthood is complicated by the constituted desires of older women in this age of feminist backlash. It is interesting that teenage pregnancy should become such a problem while thirty-something yuppie women are portrayed as consumed with anxiety about trying (or forgetting) to have babies, throwing money at various infertility "problems" often attributed to their career success.

Furthermore, by creating the category of "teens at risk," the government pamphlet conceals the suggestion that supposed medical risks are in fact social problems. Yet the pamphlet constantly uses the metaphor of "cost" to suggest expenditures that are never made. The literature states that the "price" teens "pay" for pregnancy is in sacrificing cars and parties and in earning poor high school grades. Actually, the government does believe that it pays for pregnancy in the form of welfare to poor teen mothers, and in this case this issue becomes not the age of the parent but her economic status. In other public statements, government officials make their concern about welfare payments to teen mothers clear. Why is it, then, that the anxiety about this cost to government is hidden or the connection not made in the teen pregnancy literature? Why are these pamphlets' arguments couched in terms of the best interests of the teens?

We are not suggesting that the situation would be better if either teens wrote their own pamphlets or if the government made its interests clear. Nor is it appropriate to consider teenage pregnancy as an act of resistance to hegemonic power. To do so is to still constitute teenage pregnancy as a "choice" made for or against the dominant narratives of sexual experience, as we suggested in the analysis of the women who insisted that they served as exceptions to the standard narrative. Similarly, a discussion that made the economic concerns of the government clear could not then address the category of "teen pregnancy," because that discussion would be about welfare mothers. The teens writing their own pamphlets or designing their own school programs on teen pregnancy could, at best, only expose their own subjugation, another situation that would not be about the category of "teen pregnancy" but instead would be about sexuality, reproductive rights, or some other topic sanctioned by school "health" classes.

In the case of government representations of pregnant teens, race, class, and gender are concealed categories. Teen pregnancy is ostensibly marked as a kind of pregnancy, but pregnancy itself is unmarked, as is adolescence. There remains an uncritical category of adolescence against which the violators are measured. This is the problem with structural analysis such as that found in Mary Douglas's work *Purity and Danger*.[19] We might credit Douglas with understanding how impurities are not random but are always related to the existing social structure, but, at the same time, categories that make it possible to suppose there are violations are left untheorized. The differences between the structural model and the poststructural is best marked by Althusser's person who hails. To Althusser's credit, interpellation is not a simple matter of choice. Teens do not *choose* pregnancy over shopping, dates, and parties. By setting up the situation as a choice, the government is able to conceal what could be a debate about appropriate fertility. But as we have tried to suggest, even the poststructural adaptation of models such as Althusser's that account for the mutual construction of categories and choices often conceal untheorized categories and agencies whereby the politics behind the construction of teen pregnancy are left unarticulated.

Teen pregnancy is not simply an especially malignant or unfortunate creation of hegemony that must be regretted for its own sake. For, as we have tried to show, the invention of categories such as "teen pregnancy" makes the hegemonic elision of race, class, and gender possible. Indeed, understanding teenage pregnancy as its own homogenous category—whether as the dominant paradigm would have it, as a natural category, or as a simple model of social construction would have it, as a distinct if invented category—is to reinvent hegemony itself. Rather than focus on the products of the ideological apparatus, then, we hope that feminist poststructuralism will increasingly focus on the technologies that are in place for the production of a myriad of social constructions. Only in this way might we hope to interfere not just with the products of the dominant paradigm but with its retooling.

Notes

1. The feminist objection to essentialism is well discussed in "Another Look at Essentialism," a special issue of *differences*. See *differences* 1 (Summer 1989).

2. We prefer Teresa de Lauretis's description of hegemony and feminism. She writes: "It is a movement between the (represented) discursive space of the positions made available by hegemonic discourses and the space-off, the elsewhere, of those discourses: those other spaces both discursive and social that exist, since feminist practices have (re)constructed them, in the margins (or "between the lines," or "against the grain") of hegemonic discourses and in the interstices of institutions, in counterpractices and new forms of community." In "Technologies of Gender," *Technologies of Gender* (Bloomington: Indiana University Press, 1987), 26.

3. Michel Foucault, "Interview," *Impulse: A Journal of Cultural Mechanics* 15, no. 1 (Winter 1989): 55. Foucault's more formal definition of the poststructural subject he calls "the subject position" can be found in Michel Foucault, *Archaeology of Knowledge*, trans. Alan M. Sheridan Smith (1969; reprint, New York: Pantheon, 1972), esp. 52–53.

4. Kipnis writes that "in the recent appearance of the category of the 'decentered subject' lurks the synecdoche of the decline of the great imperial powers of modernity, the traumatic loss of hegemony of the West, which here in the psychic economy of the United States, we have continually reflected back to us in contemporary fantasies [about maleness] like *Rambo, Red Dawn,* and Ronald Reagan." In Laura Kipnis, "Feminism: The Political Conscience of Postmodernism?" *Universal Abandon? The Politics of Postmodernism,* ed. Andrew Ross (Minneapolis: University of Minnesota Press, 1988), 158. Kamdar traces the appearance of the poststructural subject to the beginnings of imperial colonial activity. See Mira Kamdar, "Subjectification and Mimesis: Colonizing History," *The American Journal of Semiotics* 7, no. 3 (1990). Gayatri Spivak criticizes Foucault's understanding of this subject in "Can the Subaltern Speak?" *Marxism and the Interpretation of Culture,* ed. Cary Nelson and Lawrence Grossberg (Urbana: University of Illinois Press, 1988).

5. Michèle Barrett notes the complicity between the reproduction of labor power for capitalism and the reproduction of gender roles. See Michèle Barrett, "Ideology and Cultural Production of Gender," *Feminist Criticism and Social Change,* ed. Judith Newton and Deborah Rosenfelt (New York: Methuen, 1985), 74.

6. All references to "state" or "governmental" literature here refer to a pamphlet, "Teen Parent Trap," issued by the State of Ohio as part of its teenage pregnancy prevention program. See *Teen Parent Trap* (Columbus, Ohio: Ohio Task Force on Teenage Pregnancy, 1986), 34. All subsequent page numbers in the text refer to this document.

7. See Amy Shuman, *Storytelling Rights: The Use of Oral and Written Texts by Urban Adolescents* (Cambridge: Cambridge University Press, 1986), 20–22.

8. As Steven Seidman has written: "Foucault has shown the original intent and political purpose of a discourse on sexuality can be reversed. For example, the scientific-medical discourse of the 'the homosexual' as a perverse or pathological human type promoted new forms of social control." In Steven Seidman, "Transfiguring Sexual Identity: AIDS & the Contemporary Construction," *Social Text* 19/20 (Fall 1988), 202.

9. Meaghan Morris, *The Pirate's Fiancée: Feminism, Reading, Postmodernism* (London: Verso Books, 1988), 223.

10. See Jean François Lyotard, *The Postmodern Condition: A Report on Knowledge,* trans. Geoff Bennington and Brian Massumi (1979; reprint, Minneapolis: University of Minnesota Press, 1989).

11. Louis Althusser, "Ideology and Ideological State Apparatuses," *Lenin and Philosophy,* trans. Ben Brewster (London: New Left Books, 1971), 174.

12. We are grateful to our students in our team-taught course Folklore and Sexual Politics at The Ohio State University, who collected narratives on teen pregnancy and sexuality.

13. Kai Erikson, *Everything in Its Path: Destruction of Community in the Buffalo Creek Flood* (New York: Simon & Schuster, 1976).

14. Carlo Ginzburg, *The Cheese and the Worms: The Cosmos of a Sixteenth-Century Miller,* trans. John and Ann Tedeschi (1976; reprint, New York: Penguin Books, 1987).

15. See Rosaline Coward's discussion of bourgeois sexual relations in *Patriarchal Precedents: Sexuality and Social Relations* (London: Routledge & Kegan Paul, 1983), esp. chap. 5.

16. Stephen Greenblatt, "Fiction and Friction," *Reconstructing Individualism: Autonomy, Individuality, and the Self in Western Thought,* ed. Thomas C. Heller, Morton Sosna, and David F. Wellebery (Stanford: Stanford University Press, 1986), 47.

17. Interestingly enough, compilers of the teenage pregnancy pamphlets consider the fact that they were able to produce anything other than a campaign for sexual abstinence a victory: they were able to appease the more conservative forces by pointing out that nowhere was abortion mentioned.

18. Nancy Fraser argues that the "conjunction of the fiscal crisis of the state and the feminization of poverty suggests that struggles around social welfare will and should become increasingly focal for feminists" and suggests some of the problems feminists might face in the coming "welfare wars." In Nancy Fraser, "Women, Welfare, and the Politics of Need Interpretation," *Unruly Practices: Power, Discourse and Gender in Contemporary Social Theory* (Minneapolis: University of Minnesota Press, 1989), 145.

19. Mary Douglas, *Purity and Danger: An Analysis of the Concepts of Pollution and Taboo* (1966; reprint, Boston: Ark Paperbacks, 1985).

The Philosophical and Political Implications of the Feminist Critique of Aesthetic Autonomy

Mary Devereaux
Bucknell University

INTRODUCTION

On 8 April 1990, the Cincinnati Contemporary Art Center and its director, Dennis Barrie, were indicted on obscenity charges for exhibiting a collection of Robert Mapplethorpe photographs. Months later, Charles Freeman, a record store owner in Florida, was charged and convicted for selling the music of the rap group, 2 Live Crew. Following the Mapplethorpe controversy, artist Karen Finley was one among a group of artists who lost a National Endowment for the Arts grant because the awards panel believed her performance works likely to offend American taxpayers. The National Endowment for the Arts, bowing to pressure from Senator Jesse Helms, began requiring its grant recipients to sign an anti-obscenity pledge.[1] These events testify to a widespread, although not unprecedented, attack on the arts. In America today, as in other times and places, people are demanding that art conform to religious and moral criteria. More important, these criteria are being enforced by government agencies. Artists whose works do not meet these criteria risk legal prosecution, fines, imprisonment, and the loss of state funding. Museum directors, curators, and commercial distributors of art face similar risks.[2]

Forced to defend themselves against government-enforced "standards of decency" and other forms of outside interference, artists and their supporters have traditionally sought refuge in claims of aesthetic autonomy. The concept of autonomy, used widely in these and past debates, covers several apparently heterogeneous, but interlocking, claims. Formulated in a preliminary way, the autonomy defense begins from the assumption that art's

164

primary function is not to serve morality or to support the state but to express the ideas and feelings of the individual artist.

This now widely accepted view of art's function has its roots in a romantic theory of genius which sees artists as specially equipped (not only technically but also spiritually, emotionally, and intellectually) to capture and communicate a domain of experience unavailable to the nonartist. The resulting products of genius have, according to this view, a special value not reducible to their political, moral, or religious value.

Believers in art's irreducible value need not be committed to the implausible thesis that artworks lack political content or value, only to the thesis that the criteria we use to judge art should be nonpartisan. By "nonpartisan" is meant impartial, that is, uncommitted to a particular government, political party, or state-enforced moral or religious agenda. Since governments themselves quite clearly and properly have a political agenda, their involvement in the evaluation of artworks is, in this view, illegitimate.

The romantic picture of art grants artists something like a protected domain: a domain above the political fray and outside the realm of government control. In claiming autonomy, artists reject both the idea that the government has a right to interfere in the production or exhibition of artworks and the idea that political standards are an appropriate or legitimate basis for evaluating art.

Ironically, the widespread reliance on autonomy by art's defenders in the arena of public debate coincides with a growing rejection of autonomy by art theorists. This rejection results primarily, although not exclusively, from the critique of autonomy launched by feminist aestheticians and art historians. Although attacks on autonomy have their roots in Marxist theories of art, it is recent feminist theory that has effectively brought these objections to prominence in mainstream Anglo-American aesthetics.

In aesthetics, as in many other disciplines, feminist theorizing has been responsible for what many thinkers have called a conceptual revolution.[3] Central to that revolution has been a reexamination of autonomous aesthetics. Aesthetic autonomy, feminists have argued, is at best an outmoded remnant of essentialist (i.e., acontextual and ahistorical) thinking. At worst, its critics argue, aesthetic autonomy is part of a patriarchal vocabulary of oppression or simply incoherent.[4]

While, to my mind, these conclusions are too hastily drawn, there is no disputing their enormous effect on contemporary discussions of art. Their influence alone makes feminist critiques of autonomy worthy of study. If, as I have claimed, the principle of aesthetic autonomy also functions as the artworld's preferred line of defense against government interference in the arts,[5] then an analysis of the grounds upon which feminists and others have rejected it may be in order. I choose to focus on feminist varieties of this critique both because they have exercised more influence than their nonfeminist variants and because, as a philosopher and a feminist, I am concerned to explore the political implications of the feminist recommendation that we abandon autonomy for a more politicized conception of art.

One cannot fairly evaluate the critique of aesthetic autonomy without also examining the original theory it is directed against. I therefore propose to reevaluate the theory of aesthetic autonomy as well as its feminist critique. Autonomous aesthetics is now widely regarded as discredited. In deciding to look at it, despite its present disfavor, I have several aims. First, for all its many difficulties, the theory of aesthetic autonomy offers a serious and powerful conception of art. Too often, this conception of art is characterized in terms which make it difficult to understand why anyone ever found it compelling or why it has prevailed for so long. In vulgarizing the theory of autonomy, feminist theorists do an injustice to an important branch of aesthetic theory. They also dismiss a tradition of thinking about art prevalent throughout Europe and North America since the eighteenth century.

Let me make my position clear. My aim in this essay is to criticize certain oversimplifying tendencies within feminist theory. There are sophisticated and compelling feminist objections to aesthetic autonomy. But, for these to gain the attention they deserve, they need to be distinguished from less sophisticated, but historically necessary, arguments. I thus mean to present a criticism of feminism on behalf of feminism. By providing a more accurate account of the theory of aesthetic autonomy, I hope to show that autonomy is a concept worth taking seriously within a feminist framework.

A reexamination of autonomy is worth undertaking for two additional reasons. The feminist conception of art, insofar as we can speak of one, has evolved largely in response to the theory of aesthetic autonomy. Examining the theory of autonomy therefore provides a way of getting clear on the roots of the feminist conception of art. Lastly, and perhaps most importantly, the rejection of aesthetic autonomy raises important political questions. If, as so many feminists have argued, theoretical objections lead us to give up the principle of the autonomy of art, must artists then give up their struggle for independence? And, if they must, then what do we as a society gain or lose?

In raising these political questions, I do not, of course, mean to imply that critiques of autonomy are responsible for the current attack on art. Nor do I mean to imply that individual theorists intend to align themselves with the Helms agenda, although the alliance between some varieties of feminism and conservatives has been widely noted. I am suggesting, however, that the rejection of aesthetic autonomy has important political implications, especially in the context of recent debates over art's function. Despite the success of feminist attacks on autonomy, these political implications have not been thought out.

In order to explore these political implications, I turn now to an examination of the theory of aesthetic autonomy and, then, to feminist criticisms of that theory. This examination prepares the way for recommending an alternative strategy of defending art.

AESTHETIC AUTONOMY

The theory of aesthetic autonomy consists of three central claims, each open to several interpretations: 1) a claim about the independence of artistic institutions from other social institutions; 2) a claim about the universality of artworks; and 3) a claim about the political neutrality of aesthetic criteria. These claims deal in turn with art institutions, artworks, and the criteria we use to evaluate them. At issue in the case of institutions is independence; in the case of artworks, universality; in the case of evaluative criteria, neutrality. These issues appear unrelated; in fact, the theory of aesthetic autonomy connects them in ways I hope to make clear.

Besides using the term *aesthetic autonomy* to describe these three central claims, aestheticians also frequently use it to refer to a specific historical theory, the theory of aesthetic judgment advanced by Immanuel Kant in *The Critique of Judgment*. Although Kant devoted his work primarily to the analysis of aesthetic judgments, and spoke little about art, his philosophy prepares the way for the contemporary discussion of autonomy in three important respects. First, we find in Kant's formalism a basis for the idea of art's universal appeal. Second, prevailing notions of genius have their basis in Kant's theory of genius. Third, the contemporary idea of evaluative neutrality has its roots in Kant's analysis of "purely aesthetic" judgment.

Institutional Independence

In the first instance, institutional autonomy describes the historical separation of artistic institutions, such as museums and galleries, from other institutions, primarily those of church and court. This separation does not occur until the eighteenth century and, then, primarily in Europe.[6]

The emergence of independent artistic institutions reflects changes in prevailing conceptions of artist and artwork. The artist, who throughout the Middle Ages belonged, like shoemakers and butchers, to a craft guild, comes by the eighteenth century to enjoy the elevated status of an individual producer.[7] No longer did the maker of art work in collaboration with others. The resulting product changes from an object of craft to a work of "fine art," thus enjoying a similarly elevated status. Given this new conception, each artwork is original, a unique entity with its source in the imaginative genius of its creator.

The characterization of art as the product of genius derives from Kant. According to Kant's theory of genius, artists are visionaries who have an in-born imaginative talent. This talent enables them to see in ways others cannot. In the tradition following Kant, artistic vision is often described as transcending ordinary experience or as penetrating beneath it to a realm deeper or more primordial than ordinary reality.

Artistic products have social value in that they show us what we might not otherwise see or see clearly. In practice, this view of art's high social value naturally leads to the idea that artists should be granted as much expressive freedom as possible. As in the cases of Gauguin and van Gogh, the demands of art are commonly thought to override normally compelling demands, such as those of family. The modern view that art possesses overriding value leads to treating artists with an indulgence not often granted artists in the past.

Each of these ideas—of art institutions, artist, and artwork—contributes to the idea that art deserves a separate, protected domain: a protected space. By a "protected space," I don't mean the obvious safeguards needed to preserve artworks from vandals and the overly curious. By protected space, I mean instead the principle of granting artists the liberty to exercise control over both their subject matter and means of expression. It is this figurative space, that is, the space in which artists can work without outside interference, which the literal spaces of the museum, gallery and concert hall concretely embody.

Helms's National Endowment for the Arts legislation and public calls for greater artistic "accountability" both deny the right of artists to exercise ultimate control over their works. While advocates of autonomy take this right as fundamental, they do not treat it as absolute. Someone may, for example, choose to have himself or herself shot in the service of art, as Chris Burden did in *Shoot,* but no one may legally have someone else shot, even if arrangements have been made to announce the event as a work of a performance art beforehand. That one may not, not even the strictest adherents of autonomy would regard an infringement of artistic liberty. Other cases are more difficult. Public art, such as Richard Serra's intrusive wall of rusted steel, *Tilted Arc,* confronts the artist's right to autonomy with the competing rights of the public that art is meant to serve. Because it is set outside museum walls, public art poses a different set of questions than artworks which occupy more sharply defined institutional spaces.

The point of advocating autonomy is not to grant artists absolute license but to make clear that where artistic and government interests conflict we should presume in favor of the artist. This presumption is the outcome of the above assumptions about the special capacities of artists and the unique value of the works they produce. It also rests on a view of the government as advancing primarily political rather than aesthetic interests. Since autonomy's defenders grant aesthetic concerns priority in matters of art, their decision in favor of the artist and artistic interests is not difficult to understand.

It is this presumption in favor of the artist which I understand to constitute the core claim of institutional autonomy. Thus, the central issue in debates over autonomy is not the factual question of whether art institutions are independent but the normative question of whether they *should* be. The claim that art institutions are *entitled* to autonomy rests, I am arguing, on the particular conception of artist and artwork outlined above.

The Universality of Artworks

The second autonomy thesis focuses not on the characteristics of artworld institutions but on those of artworks themselves. Artworks are said to be autonomous in the sense that they transcend the conditions in which they are produced to achieve "universality." This claim about the universality of artworks is related to the claim that the *aesthetic criteria we use to evaluate* artworks are universal. The latter claim ascribes universality not to artworks but to the standards by which we judge them. While in both cases the ascription of universality moves the discussion of art out of the historical and sociological realm, I am for the moment concerned exclusively with the universality imputed to artworks.

Advocates of art's universality make two different claims. First, they argue that neither the work's meaning nor its value can be reduced to its social, political, or ideological content. Art transcends its originating influences, speaking not just for its own time and place but for all times and places. Art, in other words, is said to speak not only for its author or its culture but "for all of us" (i.e., for "mankind," for human beings generally). That art speaks for all of us constitutes the claim that it is universal. Second, art speaks *to* all of us. Here the emphasis shifts from art's capacity to transcend the historical conditions in which it was *produced* to those in which it is *received*. The emphasis moves to the artwork's audience. Art, or what has qualified as great art, is held to speak to people in diverse cultures and across time. That art—or at least some art—possesses this diverse, widespread appeal constitutes its presumed timelessness. In transcending immediate social conditions art has the capacity to speak to an audience removed in time or circumstances from its own historical period.

Proponents of this view occasionally talk as though all art achieves this timelessness and occasionally as though only great art does. But in either case, they see the history of art as the working out of a fixed set of invariant problems. This contrasts with the alternative, now prevailing, tendency to see art history as a continually evolving set of varying problems. These problems are held to arise not from the essential nature of art but from historically specific social relations and practices.

Traditionally, art's claim to universality has been justified in two different ways. The first attributes art's universality to its capacity to address certain basic human concerns. So, for example, we say of Shakespeare's *King Lear* that it addresses problems of aging and death that we all must eventually face. Lear speaks to us not only as members of a particular class or nationality but as human beings qua human beings. Although particular works of art may fail to move us to reflect upon such universal concerns, the mark of great art is that it succeeds in doing so. Speaking in a universal voice means more than a call to what we hold in common; its call is to our human essence. As such, this justification of art's universality is compelling to those who believe in a human essence.

The second way of justifying universality appeals not to art's subject matter or content but to its shared formal properties. In this view, artworks have common formal properties, i.e., properties of line, form, shape, etc. It is these properties which explain how works, even works from past ages or distant cultures, may move us "universally."

This formalist line of justification assumes that as human beings we share certain common perceptual and cognitive capacities. Although the actual judgments we make may vary from person to person, our sense organs do not. That we share this "equipment" is merely contingent. That is, there might be beings without vision or with vision differently organized than ours. But, it is the perceptual capacities that we do in fact have that enable us to find art appealing. This appeal does not depend on the work's subject matter or substantive concerns, merely on its formal, "aesthetic" properties. The assumption is that this formal language does not need to be taught. Art is universal then in the sense that its pleasures are presumed to be uniformly available, at least to those with the minimum functional perceptual and cognitive equipment.

Justified on the basis of its subject matter, belief in art's universality extends the hope that art might rise above class and gender interests, political battles, and personal religious commitments to speak to and for general human interests. In claiming to speak universally, art attempts to supersede the prejudices and cultural blindnesses of a particular time and place. In this, art is motivated by a utopian vision. This dream of cultural autonomy underlies the idea that art speaks in a unique and uniquely valuable voice. And it is this voice which in turn underlies the special protections the theory of autonomy claims for art.

Justifying art's universality on the basis of its formal, purely aesthetic, qualities is, as we've seen, a different claim. Nonetheless, it too holds out the promise that art may unite us despite our differences. Here the claim is weaker. It assumes only that we share perceptual and cognitive capacities. However contingent, these common capacities also provide some basis for fellow feeling and the hope of shared experience.

Whether justified in humanistic or formalist terms, universality provides a basis for claiming that artworks are autonomous. Art is autonomous in that it reaches beyond the historical situation of both its production and reception to achieve a timeless appeal.

The Political Neutrality of Aesthetic Criteria

The third and final autonomy thesis is the claim that aesthetic criteria are politically neutral and that these criteria should have priority in evaluating artworks. First, then, what are purely aesthetic criteria and why are they thought politically neutral? The category of the "purely aesthetic" rests on a distinction between an artwork's "internal" and "external" properties which the theory of autonomy takes for granted. It defines internal properties as those formal properties of form, color, shape, etc., discussed above. While not everything one sees on the canvas counts as one of its formal properties (the fly walking across it, the scratch marks left by a careless curator), nothing that one doesn't—or couldn't— see is likely to qualify. So, for example, an author's intentions are regarded as "external" properties, except insofar as they perceptually manifest themselves in the work.

In this view, we can always say with certainty what counts as an internal, or relevant, property of a work and what does not. Moreover, it is claimed, we can make this distinction between internal and external properties without appealing to any particular theory of art. We are meant, in other words, to be able to identify the relevant internal properties of a sarcophagus by Michelangelo or a Barnett Newman painting even without knowing anything about the works or their history.[8] We can make this identification because, in this account, all artworks possess certain shared formal properties. These shared properties make it possible to evaluate all artworks in the same terms. In this sense, aesthetic criteria, like artworks themselves, are deemed "universal." Unlike local criteria, e.g., those bound to a particular time and place or to a particular religious, political, or moral perspective, these universal criteria purportedly allow us to judge art impartially.

The demand for such universal, i.e., "purely aesthetic," criteria arises from the formalist conception of art. Characterizing artworks as entities of irreducibile value leads theorists of autonomy to call for criteria of evaluation which recognize this irreducible value.

Two ways of interpreting this demand are available. On one interpretation, this demand commits us to the claim that *only* aesthetic considerations matter in evaluating artworks, at least insofar as we want to evaluate them *as art*. But one can also interpret this demand as embodying the far weaker claim that aesthetic considerations should have *priority* in evaluating artworks.

In criticizing the idea of neutral aesthetic criteria, feminist theorists often confuse these different claims. The first and stronger claim they easily attack by pointing to cases such as religious or folk art where clearly more than aesthetic considerations matter to art's evaluation. It is, however, the second, more reasonable, claim that we grant aesthetic considerations priority that more accurately describes the evaluative neutrality required by autonomy. This demand is less easily attacked. Autonomy's defenders may consistently acknowledge that authorship, social influence, and ideological content all matter in certain evaluative contexts. The cost of my new Picasso may matter if I am trying to impress you; the misogynist rape fantasies of a new novel may matter if I am selecting fiction for a course in feminist literature. Autonomous aesthetics insists only that if my aim is to evaluate the works in question *as art,* then I must treat these considerations as secondary.

We may have good reasons to evaluate a work morally or ideologically. But, if we want to do art criticism, then the claim is that we must use specifically art-critical standards. And these standards are defined as "purely aesthetic." The idea that artworks deserve evaluation "in their own terms" remains a central tenet of autonomous aesthetics.

FEMINIST CRITIQUES OF AUTONOMY

Feminist critiques of autonomy call for us to revise our thinking about art institutions, artworks, and the criteria we use to evaluate them. In laying out the feminist critique of autonomy, I don't mean to suggest that feminist theorists hold a single, unified account of art or its institutional situation; for, of course, they do not. Feminist theory offers rich theoretical territory, replete with competing perspectives on these and other issues. However, I am assuming it is possible to identify a core set of beliefs which distinguish aesthetic theory broadly defined as feminist. It is this set of beliefs about art institutions, artworks, and evaluative criteria which I propose to examine in this section.

Critiques of Institutional Independence

Feminist theorists challenge art's institutional autonomy on two grounds. First, they deny the factual claim that the artworld *is* an independent domain; second, and more radically, they question the desirability of this independent domain even if it could be achieved. Disputing the factual claim, feminists point to art's many connections with the social and political world. The historical separation of museums and galleries from institutions of church and court is not at issue here. At issue is whether art institutions are more accurately seen as members of complexly interwoven social networks than as the separate units assumed by an autonomous aesthetics.

Along with other critical theorists, feminists argue that no institutions, not even privately funded ones, operate in total isolation from other institutions and social practices. Aside from the restrictions which frequently accompany private patronage, the economic constraints under which museums, art schools, and other art institutions labor constrain their independence. The larger the budget of these institutions becomes, the more dependent they are on outside sources of capital. The more dependent on outside capital, the more involved they must be with people who have control over capital, i.e., politicians, business people, wealthy donors, developers, and socialites.[9] Calling attention to these constraints and the complex allegiances which they entail fosters a less romantic and more realistic understanding of how the artworld operates.

Much recent work in feminist aesthetics therefore sees its task as the investigation of the historical and social factors which enter into art's production and reception. This task replaces the project of searching for some set of essential properties which all artworks purportedly share. For feminist theorists, as for twentieth-century aestheticians generally, art has no such essence. In denying this essence, feminist theorists are on solid ground. Repeated efforts to specify a given set of properties which all artworks share have failed; the project of searching for such essential properties has, since Wittgenstein, been justifiably regarded as misguided.

While not the first to investigate art's social history, feminists, such as Linda Nochlin, have been remarkably successful in deepening our understanding of institutional practices.[10] Feminist art history such as Nochlin's makes clear that even in times less turbulent than our own, art is inextricably linked to, rather than separate from, the larger social world. But, someone might ask, why go to such lengths to defend a thesis that appears a truism of enlightened common sense?

The fact of art's institutional interdependence is worth reiterating because of the widespread tendency to exaggerate art's independence, especially by those working within the framework of an autonomous aesthetic. The claim of institutional autonomy, however, turns not on the factual question of whether museums and galleries *are* independent of other institutions but on whether this is a condition they should ideally aspire to. As I argued earlier, it is this normative thesis that forms the crux of the debate over institutional autonomy. Art's autonomy is meant to function as an ideal; that ideal demands that we grant artists control over their works. This means that they, and the institutions that represent them, must not be under the control of other institutions or authorities.

In questioning the ideal of institutional autonomy, feminist theorists have in mind a different thesis, e.g., that art should be independent from the larger sociopolitical world. Such independence, they argue, fosters a sterile, aestheticized form of art of little consequence to personal or public life. Understood as a demand for an "apolitical" or otherwise disengaged art, institutional autonomy is rejected as undesirable. But, as should be clear, what feminists are rejecting here is not the ideal of institutional autonomy, properly understood. One can acknowledge that an apolitical art is undesirable without insisting that we abandon the principle of artistic control.

Feminist theorists wrongly equate the demand that art should have a separate, protected domain with calls for art to cut itself off from the outside world. But, one might endorse the principle of aesthetic autonomy *because* one thought art had a political function, e.g., because one thought that art's function as an independent, critical voice deserved protection. Granting autonomy does, however, commit us to denying outside institutions the authority to *demand* of art that it function politically or any other way. So, for example, we cannot consistently endorse autonomy and pass legislation requiring that publically funded art promote conservative family values. This is because adherents of aesthetic autonomy regard efforts to take control of art out of the hands of its authors, however pressing the political agenda, as inimical to art's flourishing.

This confusion over what autonomy entails results in an unfortunate alliance between feminists advocating a more political, engaged art and conservatives, like Senator Helms, whose opposition to autonomy rests on quite different grounds. This alliance is unfortunate since many feminists would, I presume, agree with the claim that art should be free from government control. Despite considerations of the harm that art may do—that it may erode family values, encourage various forms of prejudice, etc.— there are, I believe, good feminist reasons to resist the suggestion that government play a role in regulating or suppressing art. Before exploring what these are, however, I want first to complete my examination of the grounds upon which feminists have traditionally rejected aesthetic autonomy.

Critiques of the Universality of Artworks

The second claim of the theory of aesthetic autonomy is that artworks speak in a universal voice. Feminist criticisms of this claim have generally interpreted universality in humanistic rather than formal terms. In rejecting the assertion that art speaks to and for all human beings, feminist theorists have argued that, whatever its intention, art speaks to and for the interests of particular groups. Film theorist Mary Ann Doane, for example, has convincingly shown how Hollywood's "women's pictures" manipulate narrative and stylistic devices to reinforce the structures necessary to a patriarchal society. Such films serve as "recuperative strategies" designed to return the wayward heroine, and the audience member who sympathizes with her, to the patriarchal fold.

Far from describing or appealing to an essential human experience, artworks, in this analysis, address merely what is common to a select group. Contrary to the timeless appeal promised by the theory of aesthetic autonomy, works of art are held to speak only to those who share certain class, gender, or other interests. Even this limited appeal depends on familiarity with certain cultural and artistic conventions.

Feminist theorists therefore claim that most artworks have not succeeded in rising above partisan interests. Partisan in this context means exhibiting allegiance to some person, party, or cause. More distressing than art's partisanship is, in this view, its oppressiveness. Art's oppressiveness follows from the fact that it supports people in power. Those in power, it is invariably stressed, are white male property owners of European descent. So, not only does art not represent universal human interests, the interests it *does* represent function to thwart the interests of disempowered peoples.

Feminist critics and art historians have been enormously successful in uncovering how artworks often support the interests of those in power. The recognition that in speaking of a universal human condition art has not spoken for everyone has radically changed the critical framework in which many critics look at art. The idea that artworks assume particular interests puts the burden of proof on those who would defend art's universality. But, before concluding that such a defense is impossible, there are several questions that need to be answered.

The objection that art's purported universality masks male or other vested interests is most compelling when applied to established works of the canon, such as the novels of D. H. Lawrence or the paintings of Dante Gabriel Rossetti. Not only are these works not exempt from charges of partisanship, they are paradigm examples of works that function to oppress women and other disempowered groups.

Since it is men in power who historically have defined the canon, it isn't surprising that canonical works tend to reflect and serve their interests. But, are there not *some* canonical works of art, such as Virginia Woolf's "Three Guineas" or Sinclair Lewis's *Babbitt*, that also function to question or subvert existing power structures? And, what of noncanonical works? Do anonymous slave narratives, quilts, and the recently discovered works of the seventeenth-century Italian painter Artemisia Gentileschi serve patriarchal interests?

As the above examples illustrate, not all art—not even all canonical art—promotes oppressive, i.e., patriarchal, interests. Nor, I think, need feminists commit themselves to this strong, implausible, thesis. Admittedly, all art is partisan in the very weak sense of speaking for *some* set of particular interests. But, what follows from acknowledging that art is interested in this very weak sense? Might not a feminist theorist consistently concede the possibility that some art, at least exceptional art, like the novels of Toni Morrison, Ralph Ellison, and William Faulkner, can both give voice to particular interests and yet, at least partly, transcend those interests? Even if we grant that most artworks do not transcend particular interests, it does not follow that art lacks the *capacity* for some measure of transcendence.

In focusing on the failure of artworks to realize this capacity, feminist theorists have wrongly assumed that the theory of autonomy is meant to function as a descriptive account of art. This assumption underlies the repeated charge that while claiming to speak to and for all of us, in practice art privileges the interests of particular groups. Here we see the same basic argumentative structure as in feminist criticisms of institutional autonomy. Failing to achieve a stated objective is taken as grounds for rejecting the objective itself.

Autonomy's advocates may easily respond that the importance of maintaining art's universality lies in the normative force of this idea, not in its descriptive accuracy. Seen in this light, a claim of autonomy tells us something about what we believe art should strive for and what constitutes its value when successful.

It is the issue of universality's *desirability* as a goal for art that a more radical line of feminist criticism addresses. Instead of striving for universality, some maintain, art should represent the interests of various groups, "giving voice" to historically under-represented constituencies. This changed conception of what art should try to do rests on the observation that when art aims to speak for universal interests it often works against the interests of disempowered groups. Thus, feminist theorists are suspicious of attempts, however creatively inspired, to "speak for all of us."

There are good reasons for this suspicion. Having seen how women and other disempowered groups have been excluded from "all of us" in the past, feminist theorists are justifiably wary of new efforts in this direction. They quite rightly insist that we need to question who "all" of us are and how we determine who gets to speak for "us." It is this level of reflection which the analysis of gender and other differences between people introduces into the discussion of art.

The feminist emphasis on these differences provides a more textured, more accurate, account of the audience *to* whom, as well as *for* whom, art speaks. Unlike proponents of aesthetic autonomy, feminist theorists do not assume that a given artwork speaks to spectators, even properly attentive spectators, all in the same way.

Critiques of the Political Neutrality of Aesthetic Criteria

Turning lastly to the discussion of evaluative standards, feminist theorists have repeatedly called into question the neutrality of the aesthetic standards used to evaluate art. This discussion, however, often wavers between two different senses of neutrality: political neutrality and a broader concept of value-neutrality generally. Although often confused, these are not equivalent claims. To establish that "purely aesthetic" standards are value-neutral, we must show that they embody no values at all. To establish that aesthetic standards are politically neutral requires far less—only that aesthetic standards embody no *political* values.

The criticism that aesthetic standards are not value-neutral is not unique to feminism, nor is it particularly persuasive. Kant and other proponents of aesthetic autonomy never claimed that the standards in question embodied *no* values, merely that they embodied *purely aesthetic* values. Admittedly, these standards commit us to the values of a specific aesthetic theory (formalism). That all aesthetic standards have a built in set of values needs to be acknowledged, as feminist theorists insist. Often, however, the suggestion is that there is something wrong with an aesthetic standard that advances one set of desirable properties at the expense of others. But, this is what aesthetic standards are meant to do. What would it mean to have an aesthetic standard which embodied no values?

But, what of the claim that what passes for "purely aesthetic" standards are not, despite what Kant and others claim, politically neutral? This, I take it, is the more interesting feminist argument. Although those on both sides of the debate speak as though it is well understood, the concept of "political neutrality" is notoriously difficult to define. Let me assume for the moment that by "politically neutral" we mean something like having no explicit commitment to, or implicit investment in, a given government policy or program or set of social arrangements. Given this definition, a staunch defender of aesthetic autonomy might willingly acknowledge that her theory has value commitments along one dimension (the aesthetic) while nevertheless wanting to deny that her theory has any particular political commitments. This is not an implausible view since few aesthetic theories have *overt allegiances* to a given government or social arrangement. But, what of implicit allegiances?

I suggest that it is these implicit allegiances that feminist theorists have in mind in claiming that even so-called purely aesthetic standards are political. What is wrong with such allegiances? One charge, well documented by recent work in art history, is that these implicit political allegiances have resulted in standards biased against women. While ostensibly distinguishing works solely on grounds of quality, in practice, "purely aesthetic" standards tend to encourage certain kinds of art and discourage, exclude, and ignore others.

Nochlin convincingly argues, for example, that an alleged "purely aesthetic" preference for large-scale historical painting—a type of painting which from the Renaissance through most of the nineteenth century epitomized the highest category of art—effectively excluded women from the ranks of great painters. Women during this period, she points out, were banned from attending life drawing classes. Not surprisingly, then, they were ill-equipped to handle the large-scale human figures needed for history painting in the grand style represented by Delacroix.[11] The aesthetic preference for Delacroix-style history painting over small still lifes and other "domestic" genres is therefore said to reflect and promote an allegiance to the existing gender hierarchy, both in the artworld and the world at large.

This is an important argument. The recognition of past instances of gender bias has led feminists to question the fairness of the evaluative criteria operating throughout the artworld. But, must we assume all past aesthetic judgments have been unfair, or only some? This is an empirical question, the answer to which requires art-historical investigation.

More radical than questions about the unfairness of past and present practices are questions about the very possibility of "objective" standards. Some feminists have argued that the objective standards assumed by the theory of aesthetic autonomy are an impossibility. Implicit political allegiances of one kind or another are, they argue, unavoidable. In this view, all judgments and standards are "ideologically loaded." All judgments are prejudiced in the sense that they reflect a given world view.

This conclusion is thought to follow from the recognition that aesthetic values reflect particular social and historical conditions. As we have seen, artistic institutions and practices, like others, embody often unnoticed values, norms, and interests. These values, norms, and interests admittedly affect not only what art is encouraged and supported but also the standards used to evaluate it and the terms in which it is appreciated. But, to acknowledge that our values are historically and culturally conditioned is not to establish that they have no broader claim. Unless, as feminists, we are willing to relegate our claims for justice to merely "local" claims, we may not want to throw away our stake in objectivity so readily.

PROTECTED SPACE

Where does this analysis leave us? Autonomy's defenders could legitimately claim that the feminist critique misses the point. By focusing on the gap between theoretical claims and actual practices, that critique, as I have said, wrongly assumes the theory of autonomy is meant to function as a descriptive account. This error occurs repeatedly. If I am correct that autonomy's strength rests in its normative force as a conception of what art should be, how its institutions should function, and how art should be evaluated, then autonomous aesthetics is neither as weak, nor feminist criticisms as powerful, as they may have at first appeared.

But, what of the desirability of the ideals advanced in the name of autonomy? In examining the theory of autonomy, my aim has been to clarify more precisely the content of these ideals. Surprisingly, these ideals do not turn out to be wholly incompatible with feminist commitments. The ideal of institutional autonomy calls not for an apolitical, disengaged art but, as I have argued, for artists to exercise control over their works. Feminist commitments tend to support, not oppose, a principle of artistic control and the limits on government interference it supports.

On the issue of art's universal voice, the results of this analysis are mixed. The claim that art should strive to speak for all of us is, I think, rightly rejected as incompatible with a commitment to empower people to speak "for themselves." Admittedly, art provides one means by which people can speak for themselves. But, while feminists may want to endorse the claim that everyone should have some art or other which speaks for them, it does not follow that the same work or works should speak for all of us. The demand that art speak for all of us, in this sense, is at odds with feminist theory.

Art may, however, claim universality in a different sense, striving to speak *to* everyone, not for them. So interpreted, the ideal of universality makes art's wide appeal a standard of its success. As feminist theorists have legitimately complained, the problem with much art is that it does *not* speak to all of us. Thus, the demand that art should do so is one feminists themselves endorse.

Lastly, the theory of aesthetic autonomy insists on the possibility, and desirability, of "purely aesthetic" artistic standards. On this point, feminist theorists and defenders of autonomy do hold incompatible views. As its critics claim, autonomous aesthetics *does* treat artworks as self-contained entities and it *does* separate questions of politics from questions of aesthetics. If we follow its dictates, we must treat Judy Chicago's *Dinner Party* as a ceramic celebration of color and form. This treatment is not by itself problematic. But, it leaves aside the sexual imagery and the political context essential to Chicago's work. Feminist theorists have made it clear that the sharp line we once believed to divide aesthetic from nonaesthetic concerns is remarkably difficult to define or defend. Nor is the line dividing art from politics any clearer.

Even if we could define "purely aesthetic" standards, such standards have great difficulty dealing with political art. To consider Chicago's *Dinner Party* or Goya's war etchings in exclusively aesthetic terms is not to "evaluate the work in its own terms." It is to impose an aesthetic foreign to the works.

Even work not explicitly political is impoverished by the formalist strictures demanded by the theory of aesthetic autonomy. These require that we set aside the work's nonformal subject matter, the social, political, and economic circumstances out of which it arose, and its author's biography. The argument that formalist theory impoverishes our understanding of art does not originate with feminism, but it is, as noted earlier, with feminism that it has gained currency. Significantly, much of the artworld has now stopped asking whether politics has a role to play in the discussion of art and begun to ask *what kind* of role it has. Feminist theorizing has made it impossible, even in mainstream circles, to ignore the cultural and historical context in which artworks are produced and viewed.

Acknowledging the relationship between art and politics need not, however, mean reducing art making to didacticism or its evaluation to *Ideologiekritik*. Part of the task of feminist theories of aesthetics lies in articulating what legitimizes a feminist reading of Hollywood movies but not a Helmsian reading of Mapplethorpe's photographs. If the charge of phallocentrism is not to be dismissed with the charge of obscenity, then we need some account of the difference between them. One might think an obvious difference is that Helms intends to have the government enforce his political agenda. But, as recent events on American college campuses illustrate, some feminists and other members of disempowered groups are now, like their conservative opponents, lobbying hard for government enforcement of their agendas.[12]

Precisely because of these pressures, I want to suggest why feminists have good reasons to defend the protected space for art (and other forms of expression) that the theory of autonomy used to guarantee. For one thing, women have only recently gained access to, and control over, many routes of expression. Although museums, publishing houses, and exhibition spaces devoted to women's works are now a common phenomenon, these institutions for the most part occupy a marginalized position within the larger arts community. Their budgets are smaller, their support more fragile, than larger, more established institutions. They are hence more susceptible to increased government controls on what kinds of work can be funded or shown under public auspices.

Women and other marginalized groups also have fewer "mainstream" channels for communicating and publicizing their views of the world. Preserving institutional autonomy properly understood does not *insure* more room for oppositional forms of expression, but it does *allow* for it. Historically, one of art's functions has been to serve as a locus of resistance. For this, if for no other reason, feminists have an interest in preserving the protected space for art that the theory of autonomy seeks to provide.

Art deserves this protected space not because it is inherently emancipatory (it is not) nor because its good consequences always outweigh its harms (they do not) but because as a practice art can function in an emancipatory way. The tendency among feminists to regard much of art as oppressive follows, ironically, from their focusing on works within the canon. Implicit within feminism itself, however, is a different, broader conception of art. On this broader conception, art is not one thing but many. It is the product not only of high cultural institutions but of schools, public libraries, community arts centers, local access television channels, and institutions not yet formed.

Thought of in these terms, art is not separate from the rest of society but part of it. It is not a unified phenomenon but a set of overlapping practices addressing many audiences.[13] This is not art for art's sake, nor is art making, so understood, the province of a few exceptionally talented individuals. While not denying the exceptional talents of particular individuals, this account characterizes genius as a capacity for creativity developed to varying ways in everyone. It flourishes in widely different forms, i.e., in political cartoons, paintings, rap songs, symphonies, quilts, and poems. It is often as much a collective as an individual enterprise.

While differing in these respects from the romantic conception of art described earlier, the characterization of art I am proposing nevertheless preserves art's capacity to speak in a special voice. Art does not speak in a universal or "politically neutral" voice. Nor is it disinterested. But, art's voice can do more—sometimes far more— than merely express the interests of its creators or "the consensus of the moment." As works like *King Lear* and Toni Morrison's *Beloved* illustrate, art can transform the stuff of everyday life. Often, it transforms us in the process. How it does this has been variously explained.[14] Most plausibly to my mind, this transformation results from filtering the "raw" interests and commitments of everyday life through artistic language and conventions. It is not only that art sometimes shows us things that nothing else can, but that it has developed uniquely powerful means of expression for doing so.

In speaking through art, artists can get us to see what we otherwise might not. Their capacity for uncovering what was earlier masked or hidden underlies one strong claim for art's social value. Art's potential to unmask is closely connected with its *critical* function. Achieving an independent critical vision does not require placing art outside the network of dominant social relations. If it did, we would have no such art. But art does, I am arguing, give expression to ideas that might not otherwise be spoken or, if spoken, might not be heard. Like feminist practices, art opens up the possibility of speaking a language other than the language of private interest or the dominant culture. In providing this alternative language, art functions politically. It may also, however, function in other ways: as entertainment, ritual, or soporific.

In summary, I'm arguing that, as feminists, we have an interest in carving out a protected space for art not despite what it says but precisely because of it. This protected space is not simply a safe haven for formal innovation but for the expression of unhindered thought and feeling. It is form in the service of content as well as form for its own sake that deserves protection. From this point of view, feminists and others can meet Helms's challenge by defending art's right to take part directly or indirectly in the arena of political debate.

Artists as individuals have the same rights to free expression and free speech as the rest of us. If art also gives voice to what we often do not see or dare not say, then it is a uniquely valuable form of expression. Because of that, it is worth even greater protections. Even if no work of art ever functioned as resistance and no group ever won their freedom through art, it would still be worth fighting for the space in which these things are possible.

To protect that space, however, demands more than guaranteeing freedom from censorship. It is not censorship, but something more difficult to name or defeat, that explains why in America so much of art remains the province of a few. In Boston, as in other American cities, for example, only a handful of public schools offer programs in art or music. Not surprisingly, developing the talent and having the resources to use or understand this language remains restricted to a small, highly select group. However, even among those who have had encouragement and some form of training, only a few claim art's language for their own. This, as well as censorship, may constitute a kind of silencing.

Notes

1. Helms's requirement that National Endowment for the Arts grant recipients sign a pledge not to create or show obscene work was ruled unconstitutional by a federal court in January 1991. Although Helms's efforts have not withstood judicial scrutiny on First Amendment grounds, they have succeeded in creating a climate of fear and self-censorship within the artistic community. That climate affects not only what art gets funded but also what kind of art gets made, where and when it is exhibited and how it is reviewed. Thus, despite a subsequent award to Finley and others it originally denounced, the National Endowment for the Arts remains mired in an atmosphere of suspicion and mistrust.

2. No government needs to have federally funded arts programs. But, once such programs are in place, the demand that they put government interests (which we can assume to be political) ahead of artistic purposes is arguably a form of censorship.

3. See my "Oppressive Texts, Resisting Readers, and the Gendered Spectator: The 'New' Aesthetics," *Journal of Aesthetics and Art Criticism* 48, no. 4 (Fall 1990).

4. See Joanne Waugh's helpful discussion of these attitudes in her "Analytic Aesthetics and Feminist Aesthetics: Neither/Nor?" *Journal of Aesthetics and Art Criticism* 48, no. 4 (Fall 1990): 317.

5. One can, as in the case of 2 Live Crew, defend art on traditional, liberal democratic grounds. Here the appeal is to Constitutional protections of free speech.

6. For an analysis of how artistic practice emancipated itself from religious and ritual practice, see Lydia Goehr's *The Imaginary Museum of Musical Works: An Essay in the Philosophy of Music* (forthcoming, Oxford University Press).

7. Harold Osborne, *Aesthetics and Art Theory: An Historical Introduction* (New York: Dutton, 1970), 43–44.

8. For a compelling argument against this view, see Arthur Danto, *The Transfiguration of the Commonplace: A Philosophy of Art* (Cambridge: Harvard University Press, 1981), 102–5.

9. Richard Bolton, "Never Mind the Furthermores, the Plea is Self-Defense!" *Visions* 14, no. 3 (Winter 1991): 37.

10. See, for example, Linda Nochlin, *Women, Art and Power and Other Essays* (New York: Harper & Row, 1988).

11. Ibid., 160.

12. The internal debate over government's role in enforcing a feminist agenda has been heated and difficult. One of the best known and most influential arguments for granting government this control can be found in Catharine MacKinnon's *Feminism Unmodified: Discourses on Life and Law* (Cambridge: Harvard University Press, 1987).

13. Art in this account is a practice which shares many features with feminist practices. See Rita Felski's discussion of a feminist counterpublic sphere in her *Beyond Feminist Aesthetics: Feminist Literature and Social Change* (Cambridge: Harvard University Press, 1989), 170–71.

14. For one account of how art "transforms" its audience, see my "Can Art Save Us: A Meditation on Gadamer," *Philosophy and Literature* 15, no. 1 (April 1991): 32–42.

The Creatively Critical Voice

Diane P. Freedman
Skidmore College

FOR years, writers of doctoral dissertations just don't feel like themselves. They procrastinate, hyperventilate, learn to meditate, turn their chapters in late. They may become dossier dilettantes, Quakerish listmakers, and clean machines. They are known to suffer insomnia, myopia, migraines, back pains, and divorce. They don't feel like themselves because even at the prospectus stage, they aren't writing like themselves. And who can blame them? Stuck between a rock and hard place—the need to cite higher authorities and yet sound authoritative—they are all the time both genuflecting and dissecting, paying homage and nay saying. There is little opportunity to affirm their own voices; poised at the point of making their own way in the profession, they discover they're meant to be part clone.

Prior to such an impasse in my own graduate career, I had worked hard at finding and defending my own voice or voices and developing varied voices in my students. In college, I had thought of myself as a poet before I saw myself as a critic. I applauded the personal-is-the-political practice of the women poets I discovered only in my creative and performing arts dormitory, a creative writing workshop, or among friends—never in the lit-crit classroom. I came to crave the confessional so much I devised a way to read more books on less money: I used the campus store as a lending library, buying the newest releases by Diane Wakoski or Marge Piercy, glutting myself, then returning them to make money for the next in a series. The college library either didn't buy these women's works or they were always loaned out; somehow I had deduced they could be obtained only through extraordinary measures. In part because these and other women's works weren't on our course reading lists, I sensed that my own creative or autobiographical writing wasn't welcome in the classroom. New ideas might be encouraged but not new voices. Without a means, however, I had no message.

While I felt stymied in the classroom, I felt exhilarated by regular Thursday afternoon open-mike sessions at a coffeehouse perhaps oddly known as the Temple of Zeus. Ignoring my adrenalin-rush stomachaches, I'd summon the nerve to read one or two of my new poems each week. Once someone read a poem dedicated to me in response to my efforts, after which he smashed his folk guitar on the podium, also in my honor. It was the early seventies. In comparison, of course, life in the literature classroom continued pretty conservative and formulaic, and I failed to write my new-critical papers with much grace under pressure. I didn't see myself as a capable essayist or critic until my beatnik professor in a course on the beat generation encouraged me to write an essay "as a letter" or "as a series of numbered notes." I was so freed up and ultimately more competent as composer and reader that my professor drew an ear in the margin along with "you have a good ear!" He meant an ear for the rhythms of my own prose as well as for the music in the poetry. I was thrilled. I overcame my writing block. I have a theory about writing blocks. They're subjectivity blocks. Without personality or poetry, writing can be so dry it dries up.

In "Beyond Argument in Feminist Composition," Catherine Lamb worries "after the disruptions, then what?" She asks:

> How can students take these forms and use them in other classes or in the world of work? If we are serious about the feminist project of transforming the curriculum and even affecting the way students think, write, and act once they leave us, we need an approach to teaching composition that is more broadly based and accessible to our students.[1]

My own experience convinces me that students can benefit more from experiments, even with forms they won't necessarily keep using, than from education in strictly conventional structures. As long as we or our students remain tense and too tightly reined in, we will suffer as writers the way I used to suffer as a horseback rider: the more my riding teacher cracked the whip literally and figuratively, the more my legs crept up the sides of the horse and out of the stirrups. Thus contracting my body in fear, I lost stirrups, seat, and balance along with confidence, control, and pleasure in the art or sport. I'm convinced I needed encouragement more than discipline: in order to be better at both riding and writing, I needed to learn rhythms more than rules.

When the time came for me to write a dissertation prospectus, I was clear about my topic: the methods and motives of recent

American feminist poets writing literary criticism in auto-biographical and otherwise mixed-genre modes. But I worried about my own compositional methods as I wrote about those of Adrienne Rich, Alice Walker, Gloria Anzaldúa, Susan Griffin, Marge Piercy, and Audre Lorde; I worried about letting my poetic license lapse for so long it might be revoked. Thus, on the verge of earning the Ph.D. by official decree, I became increasingly nostalgic, playful, willful. I became determined to write a creatively critical dissertation.

It was not only my personal history as a poet that made me want to defy the conventions of dissertation discourse. Deeply influenced by feminist literary-critical and composition theories, I sought a more conversational and cooperative kind of criticism, one "less compulsive, aggressive; lonely, competitive; more communal, caring, and integrated with love and politics," to borrow Carol Ascher, Louise DeSalvo, and Sara Ruddick's description in *Between Women.*[2] I wanted my writing to be in keeping with that of the women I was writing about. I wanted to be, as Jane Tompkins writes in "Me and My Shadow," "released . . . from the duty to say things I'm not interested in, in a language I resist" and "feel free to entertain other people's voices." As Tompkins then notes:

> Quoting them becomes a pleasure of appreciation rather than the obligatory giving of credit, because when I write in a voice that is not struggling to be heard through the screen of forced language, I no longer feel it is not I who am speaking, and so there is more room for what others have said.[3]

I wanted to avoid what I call the search-and-destroy method of inquiry, sizing up and squeezing out a wide range of voices in order to stake a narrow claim. In such a discursive state ("this state ain't big enough for the two of us"), there is finally no room for even one personal voice: not only are the competing critics demolished but so too is the writer herself. The dissertation becomes what my friend Barbara Ryan calls "a massive 200-page academic voiceover, preferably male."[4]

Instead, I wanted to do what Judith Fetterley says she does in *Provisions:*

> exchange the authoritative for the tentative, the impositional for the instrumental, and the antagonist for the lover. . . . If I did what I set out to do right, my words would rapidly become obsolete, overwritten by the dialogue they had started.[5]

Such a subject position or view of the unauthoritative author accommodates expressivist-feminist and postmodernist language claims at once: the self is a construct, yes, but one that can have a say in how it deconstructs.

I began ever more fully to endorse an implicit tenet of the feminist criticism I most admired: the critical is the auto-biographical. I agreed with Sandra Gilbert that "most feminist critics are engaged not just in women's studies but in what we might call Life Studies"[6] and with Maurianne Adams that "our literary insights are perceptions come . . . from our sensitivity to the nuances of our own lives and our observations of other people's lives."[7]

But there were other precedents and parallels to my creative critical endeavors. Poststructuralist or postmodernist Roland Barthes, for example, saw criticism as "ultimately indissociable from autobiography and from reflection on autobiography."[8] According to critic Martha Noel Evans, women's writing also shares other "characteristics with postmodernism as an avant-garde movement, including its defiance of the authoritarian past."[9] The personal, associative, nonhierarchical "feminine" mode has occasionally been employed by males as well as females, by poststructuralists or postmodernists along with feminists.[10] In graduate seminars, I could no longer read whatever was hot off the critical presses (be it feminist, psychoanalytic, poststructuralist, or reader-response) and not be moved to respond in kind, joining and "overwrit[ing] the dialogue they had started." Even if not immediately approved by my doctoral committee, creative and collaborative criticism, I concluded, was swiftly being authorized by "strange bedfellows" from Barthes and Adrienne Rich to Murray Krieger and Geoffrey Hartman; from Jane Gallop and Rachel Blau DuPlessis to Peter Elbow, Patsy Schweickart, and Marianna Torgovnick—in other words, from poststructuralists to feminist poet-critics to composition and reader-response theorists to psychoanalytic and cultural critics.[11] No matter that postmodern critics have declared the "death of the author" and of the unified subject; even such "author functions" as Barthes, Derrida, Julia Kristeva, and Catharine Stimpson, writing under what Stimpson calls that "tent of a word," "postmodernism," paradoxically create prose pulsing with personality—or multiple personalities. (Gilles Deleuze and Felix Guattari, for example, have written: "The two of us wrote *Anti-Oedipus* together. Since each of us was several, there was already quite a crowd.")[12] I wanted that personal voice, that freedom—even if I were to use it to question the notion of a "self" and its capacity to be "expressed." I was spurred on by Derrida's *Spurs* to write my own offshoot. I felt compelled to write two essays, "Wild Apple Associations" and "Wide-Sweeping White Whale," in response to Thoreau's "Wild Apples" and Melville's *Moby-Dick*. (These latter essays soon formed two parts of a five-part "collage essay" I wrote for a course on symbolism in American literature. Intrigued by my experiment, touched not only by contemporary theory but by the spirits of Thoreau and Melville, my professor later agreed to serve as one of the five members of my dissertation committee. Luckily for me, at the University of Washington degree candidates are able to choose their committee members.)[13]

Cheered on further by that model of cooperation and creativity, my writing group, I vowed I would avoid the "adversarial method" Olivia Frey defines in her recent article aptly named "Beyond Literary Darwinism: Women's Voices and Critical Discourse."[14] I vowed that not only would my dissertation be as poetic and personal as I could make it, but as open to other voices as possible, even my own varied voices and genres. (I had at first written that I vowed that my dissertation would be "as poetic and personal as I could *get away with*," which underscores the unfortunate underling and adversarial identity the dissertation had already, by tradition, brought me to. Avoiding the "verbal fisticuffs" Frey so denigrates—and yet ineluctably engages in to some more gentle extent—wasn't going to be easy.) I had the model of my group member Barbara to consider: while I was inspired by her wonderful plan to write a dissertation as a journal in response to other women's journals, I was discouraged by the resistance she received. It seemed she was able to write "Chrysalis: A Thesis-Journal" only because her supervisory committee learned she wasn't planning on becoming a professor after all but a writer of mystery novels or a psychotherapist. And yet her aesthetic was perfectly well justified both by contemporary critical practices and by the statements and structures of the writings she studied, I thought. In the opening pages of her (now defended) dissertation, Barbara writes:

I realized in a visceral way that a thesis is also, inevitably, a story, and that my thesis will be a story of my own involvement with particular kinds of female experience and representation.

The "personal" and "academic" storylines are so mixed that it feels dishonest, even violent, to separate them as I think and write. And so, my thesis becomes a journal, a record of my temporal engagement with readings, experience, theory, life. These elements are always mixed until we choose to separate them; I choose not to separate them here.[15]

Like Barbara, despite (what I thought were) simultaneously reasoned and impassioned justifications for writing my dissertation differently, I received then and later all manners of checks and resistances to what increasingly became my own autobiographical, mixed-genre literary criticism.

My dissertation supervisor—who had also been Barbara's—wanted me to wait until I was tenured. (Only then might I tack on to my career some nonstandard stylistic costume over a body of conventional criticism—and midriff bulge, I supposed.) My adviser added that even if she were to support my alternative dissertation style with its poetic and autobiographical interludes, what would I do when asked by a prospective employer for a writing sample? You can't possibly send out (what turned out to be my first chapter) this piece about your being sexually harassed as an undergraduate by a department chair. She was only thinking of me. I was thinking of continuing my experiment. After all, I had come to Seattle, to the Ph.D. program over law school, so that I might write as I liked. The program brochure offered feminist criticism and theory as a special attraction of the university.

I sensed that if I could assure my dissertation director that my four readers were open at least theoretically to my plan, she would permit me to proceed. I was lucky. I knew one member would approve—he'd liked my creative criticism written for his class. Another was busy flying paper airplanes made out of lecture posters when I'd asked him and he'd been happy to accept. The required outside reader from another department admired the shamanistic poetics of Gloria Anzaldúa, one of the authors my work considered. It was the fifth reader, who'd seen the most dissertations, whom I imagined might have real objections. But she liked Gertrude Stein, was pleased to see I'd made good progress since my Modernism course with her, and enjoyed, I think, my prospectus punning. Though my committee members each preferred the more usual academic prose themselves, the stage was set.

I spoke of my work as prospecting, panning for gold in the west. On a memo I sent them with the completed prospectus, my dissertation director and readers were to check a box next to "go for the gold" if they wanted to signal their confidence in my project, now entitled "An Alchemy of Genres: Cross-Genre Writing by American Women Poet-Critics." Even if they were failures at making gold, alchemists made myth, a poetic aura, a liquidity—those liquid assets of mutability and mobility. As poet-critic Patricia Hampl puts it (in two sentences I ultimately used as an epigraph to my dissertation): "The golden light of metaphor, which is the intelligence of poetry, was implicit in alchemical study. To change, magically, one substance into another, more valuable one is the ancient function of metaphor, as it was of alchemy."[16] The prospectus itself consisted of "formal diffusion," the name I gave to section one, "overview and background." In it, I cited poet-critic Michelene Wandor as someone who shared my mutable metaphors along with my doubts and my penchant for self-assertion. Wandor's textual manifesto (a role my own prospectus played for me) announces:

> I refuse to be bound by any one literary tone, just as I refuse to be bound by any one literary genre. Or I refuse to be bound because I don't feel that one genre does everything I want. And so my voices are wide and wild and sometimes varied. And in the real world this makes it hard for me to be catalogued by publishers, critics, readers. It means I feel the continuous pressure to shout, continual uncertainty that my voice may not be heard, because it does not run smoothly into any single, clear channel.[17]

I subtitled "Chapter One and Beyond" "Playing it Personally" and stated point-blank that "because I was a woman who figured herself a poet before she ever thought herself a critic, I have long been struggling with the problem of integrating my poetic and critical selves, my past and my present, the personal and academic." I wrote that I wanted to "explain, theorize about, and emulate women writers who seem to have struggled with the same writing issues I have."

Next, I supplied "Theoretical Frames" or names drawn from what I perceive to be a confluence of theories (feminist, postmodernist, reader-response, compositionist, etc.) explicating and advocating cross or blurred genres. I had done my homework, or legwork. Then, "refusing to be bounded by a single genre or single identity," I transformed the prospectus into two other (cross)genres, a prose poem and a bookjacket blurb describing my dissertation as though it had alchemized into a book. It was Jerry, another member of my writing group, who had suggested writing a book blurb as an exercise to help me focus on where I was headed.

As it turns out, I successfully defended the dissertation, which afterward earned honorable mention in a dissertation competition in communication, language, and gender. It's true, however, that what has now been seen as the work's virtue has also been considered a weakness or limitation. I don't advise anyone to take on the creative mosaic approach lightly.

For example, when I subsequently submitted my manuscript for publication, I received such mixed-message replies as:

> I've now read your [ms.], a most challenging and innovative revisionary narrative of the literary journeys of the contemporary poet-critics you are writing about. I was especially interested in the way you merged autobiography with criticism. You are obviously working towards a new form of discourse.
>
> I wish we could offer to publish your book, but . . . your work is so broadly based, so multidisciplinary, that it poses too large a marketing problem for us . . . Unfortunately, some of the strengths . . . its hybrid forms and cross genres—work against it when it comes to focusing on a marketing plan. . . . Perhaps we are too mired in the traditional canon that we support to appreciate the possibilities of your book!

After I completed my Ph.D., I did not breeze into a tenure-track position—though I was offered a three-year position, and a year and half later received two more attractive offers. After a brief round of inspection and rejection, my revised dissertation was accepted for publication in part because of its unusual approach.[18] Moreover, I have co-edited, with Olivia Frey and Frances Murphy Zauhar, a collection of autobiographical approaches to literature, *The Intimate Critique: Autobiographical Literary Criticism*.[19] I could not have done what I have without the inspirational examples of scores of contemporary poet-critics, a sympathetic committee, and a writing group in which the members egged each other on—as I hope I have urged and encouraged others toward a creatively critical voice.

Notes

1. Catherine E. Lamb, "Beyond Argument in Feminist Composition," *College Composition and Communication* 42, no. 1 (February 1991): 3.

2. Carol Ascher, Louise DeSalvo, and Sara Ruddick, eds., *Between Women: Biographers, Novelists, Critics, Teachers and Artists Write about Their Work on Women* (Boston: Beacon Press, 1984), xxii.

3. Jane Tompkins, "Me and My Shadow," *New Literary History* 19, no. 1 (Fall 1987): 174.

4. Barbara Ryan, "Chrysalis: A Thesis-Journal" (Ph.D. diss., University of Washington, 1988), 3.

5. Judith Fetterley, *Provisions: A Reader from 19th–Century American Women* (Bloomington: Indiana University Press, 1985), 37.

6. Sandra Gilbert, "Life Studies, or, Speech after Long Silence," *College English* 40, no. 8 (April 1989): 852.

7. Maurianne Adams, "*Jane Eyre:* Woman's Estate," *The Authority of Experience,* ed. Arlyn Diamond and Lee Edwards (Amherst: University of Massachusetts Press, 1977), 141.

8. So writes Candace Lang in "Autobiography in the Aftermath of Romanticism," *Diacritics* 12, no. 4 (1982): 16.

9. Martha Noel Evans, *Masks of Tradition: Women and the Politics of Writing in 20th-Century France* (Ithaca: Cornell University Press, 1987), 223.

10. See Thomas J. Farrell, "The Male and Female Modes of Discourse," *College English* 40 (1979):922–27 and Diane P. Freedman, *An Alchemy of Genres: Cross-Genre Writing by American Women Poet-Critics* (Charlottesville: The University Press of Virginia, 1992).

11. Jane Gallop calls Roland Barthes and Adrienne Rich "strange bedfellows" who paved "the passage between theory and life story" for her. See *Thinking through the Body* (New York: Columbia University Press, 1988), esp. 4ff. For a further discussion of "analogs, precedents, and parallels to cross-genre writing by American women-poet critics," see Diane P. Freedman (n.10 above).

12. Gilles Deleuze and Felix Guattari, *Anti-Oedipus: Capitalism and Schizophrenia,* trans. Robert Hurley et al. (New York: Viking Press, 1977), 3. Foucault speaks of the "author function" in "What Is an Author?" in Josue V. Harari, ed., *Textual Strategies* (Ithaca: Cornell University Press, 1979), 141–60, while Stimpson refers to postmodernism as a "tent of a word" in *Where the Meanings Are: Feminism and Cultural Spaces* (New York: Methuen, 1988), xix.

13. For a pedagogical discussion of the role of such "interactive" writing in the literature classroom, see Diane P. Freedman, "Case Studies and Trade Secrets: Allaying Student Fears in the 'LitComp' Classroom," *College Literature* 19, no. 1 (February 1991):77–83.

14. Olivia Frey, "Beyond Literary Darwinism: Women's Voices and Critical Discourse," *College English* 52, no. 5 (September 1990):507–26, esp. 511.

15. Ryan, "Chrysalis," 5.

16. Patricia Hampl, *A Romantic Education* (Boston: Houghton Mifflin, 1981), 219.

17. Michelene Wandor, "Voices Are Wild," *Women's Writing: A Challenge to Theory,* ed. Moira Monteith (New York: St. Martin's Press, 1986), 86.

18. See n.10 above.

19. Diane P. Freedman, Olivia Frey, and Frances Zauhar, eds., *The Intimate Critique: Autobiographical Literary Criticism* (Durham: Duke University Press, forthcoming).